SPYMASTER

OTHER INTELLIGENCE-RELATED TITLES FROM
POTOMAC BOOKS, INC.

Operation Overflight: A Memoir of the U-2 Incident
by Francis Gary Powers with Curt Gentry

*Sacred Secrets: How Soviet Intelligence Operations Changed American
History* by Jerrold Schecter and Leona Schecter

Silent Warfare: Understanding the World of Intelligence, Third Edition by
Abram N. Shulsky and Gary J. Schmitt

*Soldiers, Spies, and the Rat Line: America's Undeclared War Against
the Soviets* by James V. Milano and Patrick Brogan

*Stealing Secrets, Telling Lies: How Spies and Codebreakers Helped
Shape the Twentieth Century* by James Gannon

Why Secret Intelligence Fails
by Michael A. Turner

SPYMASTER

My Life in the CIA

TED SHACKLEY

WITH
RICHARD A. FINNEY

POTOMAC BOOKS, INC.
DULLES, VIRGINIA

Library of Congress Cataloging-in-Publication Data

Shackley, Theodore.
  Spymaster : my life in the CIA / Ted Shackley with Richard A. Finney.—1st ed.
    p. cm.
  Includes bibliographical references and index.
  ISBN 1-57488-915-X (alk. paper)
  1. Shackley, Theodore. 2. United States. Central Intelligence Agency—Biography. 3. Intelligence officers—United States—Biography. 4. Spies—United States—Biography. I. Finney, Richard A. II. Title.
JK468.I6S26 2004
327.1273'0092--dc22

                                                    2004013453

Printed in Canada on acid-free paper that
meets the American National Standards Institute Z39-48 Standard.

Potomac Books, Inc.
22841 Quicksilver Drive
Dulles, Virginia 20166

First Edition

10 9 8 7 6 5 4 3 2 1

CONTENTS

ACKNOWLEDGMENTS

TED Shackley died December 9, 2002, soon after he and I completed the manuscript of this book. His regular practice upon completing a chapter of his manuscript was to ask one of his former colleagues to check it for accuracy and, perhaps, remind him of some forgotten facts. Three whose contributions I know Ted would have wished to acknowledge are Samuel Halpern, Warren Frank, and Jim Lilley. I am also aware of the support and assistance Ted received throughout the writing process from his wife, Hazel T. Shackley, and know that he would have wanted to recognize it here.

For advice on preparing the manuscript for publication, I have leaned on my son, Richard Finney, and my daughter, Martha Finney, both professional writers. And without my agent, Nina Graybill, the book might not have seen the light of day.

The CIA's Publication Review Board has reviewed the manuscript for this book to assist the author in eliminating classified information and poses no security objection to its publication. This review, however, should not be construed as an official release of information, confirmation of its accuracy, or an endorsement of the author's views.

— Richard A. Finney

FOREWORD

THE late Ted Shackley's life as a "spymaster" in the CIA could make a great novel. But he was much too serious about life to have written one. Life to him meant work. During the three decades of his career in the Central Intelligence Agency, he stands out as one of a comparatively small group of men who have had a significant impact on the agency's clandestine operations.

The title of this book, especially his use of the word "my," suggests that he was writing an autobiography or perhaps a memoir in the classical vein. Not so; this book offers very little insight into his own background. Instead, it is an effort to distill from Shackley's own experience in the intelligence business the kernel of knowledge that he deemed essential. Wearing his instructor's hat, and with no preliminaries, he launches the reader into a systematic examination of what the old master Allen W. Dulles called the "craft of intelligence."

Drawing largely on his own experience in Berlin, targeted at East Germany and the Soviet bloc and using real life illustrations, he addresses the full range of the operational disciplines falling under the intelligence rubric—i.e., collection; covert action, including political operations, propaganda, and paramilitary operations; and counterintelligence. We are told that Shackley found the training that he had received in the agency less than dynamic. He is evidently trying here to compensate for that weakness and has therefore given us a veritable handbook for spies. As many who knew him will recall, he had a didactic streak and was always ready to mentor a subordinate. He looked to his old boss, Bill Harvey, as a guide to getting the job done and getting ahead careerwise.

Shackley reveals that as he rose to more senior positions in the mid-sixties, his supervisory responsibilities began to cost him cherished friendships. This problem, if one should call it that, arose more than once as the years passed. Coauthor Richard Finney, who also died before publication, writes that in Latin America and Vietnam, Shackley's pressure on his case officers to produce more intelligence reports earned him "derision and another crop of ill-wishers." That he was a hard-driving and hard-boiled leader is true, but he knew what he was doing, and he was generally right in the way he went about it. Even though some of his people felt that he pressed them too hard, he often succeeded in getting underachievers off the dime and into productive work. His critics claim that he was driven by ambition. But then, who wasn't?

I found Shackley's discussion of aggressive counterintelligence operations in Berlin, East Europe, and the Soviet bloc particularly interesting and well written, the most concise writing on the subject that I have encountered. Interestingly, he shows a more balanced understanding of the controversial James Angleton, former chief of the agency's counterintelligence staff, than could be said for most of his peers. His analysis of deception operations is impressive. Shackley is very good on covert action, drawing heavily on his experience in the free and easy environment of occupied Germany, where almost everything was permissible and there were few restrictions. I think he should have stressed more sharply the post-1967 restrictions on covert action by the Katzenbach guidelines and by subsequent congressional action, which made it much more difficult than ever before to undertake covert action operations.

Regime change, focus on Cuba, was Shackley's assigned objective in Miami in early 1962. As we all know, the hoped for removal of Castro was eventually subsumed in the Cuban missile crisis. Public attention then and subsequent postmortems have been largely devoted to the U-2 photography and the showdown with the Soviets. Little attention was ever given to the excellent collection of intelligence on the ground in Cuba, which showed the tactical build up of the Soviet military presence and pinpointed the location of the missiles against which the eventual U-2 flights were targeted. His Miami team probably deserves far more credit for its performance than it has ever received.

Ted's three and a half years in Florida were followed by another interlude in Germany. He was particularly irked, and said so bluntly, about being asked to transfer from the front burner operation that he had led in Miami to the Berlin outpost, a stagnant spot which head-quarters wanted to resurrect. But as a good trooper, he went to Berlin. His cogent observations on the important subject of defectors are sourced largely to that period. Unexpectedly, in 1966, his personal horizons were widened abruptly when he was asked to go to Laos. It was a surprise to him and to everyone else. Among all his assign-ments, his job as chief in Vientiane was the one he enjoyed most. His tour of duty there later led to some severe criticism, derived largely from an otherwise good book about the war in Laos—*Backfire*, by Roger Warner (later published again as *Shooting at the Moon*, Steerforth Press, 1996). Certain agency officers who had worked un-der him in Laos argued that when Shackley took over he pushed the Hmong people in northern Laos from the guerrilla warfare level, at which they excelled, into a conventional posture of large battalions in the line, facing tough North Vietnamese forces beyond their capabili-ties. As a consequence, Hmong manhood was decimated and the im-pact on the civilian population was disastrous. There is truth in this contention. But it was not Shackley's fault. By 1966, U.S. ground forces were fully committed to the war in Vietnam; the war had ex-panded enormously. The American presence in Laos entailed two fundamental goals—preserve the Royal Lao Government against the North Vietnamese invasion, and do whatever possible to back up the U.S. effort in South Vietnam. There was sustained pressure from Washington to intensify the Laos-based effort, and Shackley re-sponded. For an assessment of what was accomplished in this con-text and in the agency's effort as a whole, the reader's attention is called to Richard Helms's posthumous book, *A Look Over My Shoulder* (Random House, New York, 2003), and specifically Chapter 25 on Laos, entitled "The War We Won."

Another vein of criticism focused on the battle of Nam Bac, where Shackley is blamed for a huge buildup of Lao government forces at a distant northern location, which invited a heavy North Vietnamese assault and led to the destruction of the Lao forces. In fact, he had no direct involvement in the Lao build up. The only commitment of his irregular forces in this action was a limited sup-porting role undertaken at the behest of the embassy. In some quar-ters, Shackley is also blamed for the loss of Phou Pha Thi, where the

U.S. Air Force had built a sensitive communications installation on a seemingly impregnable mountaintop in northeast Laos to support bombers en route to North Vietnam. Manned by USAF personnel, it relied on the irregulars to defend it as best they could. Shackley had warned the mission and Washington about the growing threat from the NVA, and urged withdrawal, but his warning was ignored. The irregulars were overpowered as the NVA overran the position and all the USAF defenders were either killed or captured.

Notwithstanding such criticism, Shackley's tour of duty in Laos was very successful. The build up of the Laotian irregular forces, which he had initiated, had extended to the central and south military regions of Savannakhet and Pakse, and continued under his successor. When I replaced the latter in 1970 the irregulars had increased in number, firepower, and tactical competence, and were in turn strengthened appreciably by Thai volunteers, without which they might have succumbed to the intensified NVA incursions in that climactic phase of the war.

Unlike his account of his immersion in the Laos scene, which he spells out in great detail, when recounting his transfer from Laos to Vietnam as he took over operations in Saigon, Shackley does not address the larger picture of the U.S. posture in Vietnam. He writes in detail on various facets of the Vietnam scene on which he had strong views—the Phoenix program (where his views were probably at odds with those of William Colby); John Paul Vann (whom he saw much as Neil Sheehan did in *A Bright Shining Lie*); the Chuyen case highlighted by the suggestion of "termination with extreme prejudice"; and the complicated case of Tran Ngoc Chau. He says little or nothing about the Tet offensive, but of course it had occurred long before he took over the station. But his coauthor suggests that he saw Tet as a shocking and inexcusable intelligence failure.

After dealing at length with the Chuyen and Tran Ngoc Chau cases and their implications, Shackley changes the subject rather abruptly, and we find him back again at Headquarters, in charge of the Latin American Division. I would have welcomed his thoughts on Vietnam itself, and on the issues currently dominating discussion of that subject. His focus turns instead to Chile and the suspicion in some quarters that he had a hand in the death of Allende. He tells of an interesting exchange with Charles Meyer, assistant secretary of state for Latin America, bearing on Allende's election victory in September of 1970. Meyer told him that in White House and other Washington circles Allende's victory was regarded as a major policy failure directly attributable to the CIA. I found Meyer's statement hard to reconcile with my own recollection of a policy meeting I attended in July of 1970, during which Undersecretary of State U. Alexis Johnson responded to a complaint by Henry Kissinger, asking why nothing was being done to assure an acceptable outcome in the election. Johnson attributed the situation to "opposition in the State Department"—i.e., Assistant Secretary Charles Meyer. Perhaps Meyer, two years later, had seen fit to revise his stance by blaming the CIA. Be that as it may, Shackley was duly edified and devoted himself to a careful review of the march of events leading to Allende's death, whether by suicide or assassination. There are many questions still extant about those events, but in my opinion Ted disposes effectively of such baseless allegations.

In 1973, in the aftermath of Chile and Allende, Shackley went on to head the East Asia Division. He has no comment on those years, and he proceeds at once to his final chapter, called "A New Structure." There we find him in a more reflective mood—no more case studies, no operational postmortems. Instead, Ted Shackley offers his philosophy of intelligence, addressed to the new and changing pattern of national requirements in the years to come. Intelligence must be freed of its current "muscle-bound" condition, and enabled to see and respond to change as it occurs. He offers an approach to identification of the major elements of missions and functions likely to remain valid over the next ten years. They encompass all the threats that we face in today's world, from nuclear proliferation to terrorism and everything in between. The establishment of collection requirements and priorities necessitate greater precision, backed up by greater authority than we have experienced to date. He believes this can only be brought about through the appointment of a cabinet-level director of national intelligence. Much of what Shackley has to say along these lines was undoubtedly affected by the latter years of his own experiences as associate deputy director of operations in the agency. Unfortunately, he offers no commentary on that very trying period in the organization's history.

Drastic as some of Shackley's suggestions may be, one must admire his prescience in light of the calls for reorganization echoing in

Washington today. He goes so far as to call for an end to the CIA, and its replacement by a "Foreign Intelligence Service." Another change he visualizes is a virtual end to the use of diplomatic cover in favor of commercial cover. Finally, he urges a streamlining of congressional oversight, which, more than most of his suggestions, might seem like pie in the sky.

As his health deteriorated, even those who knew Ted Shackley well were surprised at his calm, even systematic, preparation for the end. I called on him just two days before he died and I was impressed with his sharpness, clarity of mind, and good humor. I remarked, "Ted, you don't look as sick as people say you are." He laughed, and said that he had an appointment that afternoon with the funeral director. To him, it was obviously a matter of looking "downstream," as he often phrased his approach to an operational problem, and then dealing with it. His aplomb in facing the inevitable surely drew strength from a side of Ted Shackley that few of us were acquainted with—his Catholic faith, which had undergone a recrudescence in recent years, and had become a significant part of his life. If, as he acknowledges, his supervisory style had lost him some "cherished friendships" over the years, there was no sign of this in the attendance at his funeral Mass in Bethesda, and in Florida where he was finally laid to rest. In both instances, his former case officers and old troopers came in impressive numbers to say goodbye to their old boss.

—B. Hugh Tovar

B. Hugh Tovar served in the Office of Strategic Services in the China Burma India theater during World War II. He joined the Central Intelligence Agency in 1948 and served for thirty years in the Operations Directorate. His overseas assignments included senior positions in the Philippines, Malaysia, Indonesia, Laos, and Thailand. At CIA Headquarters he headed the Covert Action and Counterintelligence staffs.

PREFACE

WHEN the Central Intelligence Agency (CIA) was new, its clandestine elements were housed in a chain of four wooden, two-story structures near the Lincoln Memorial. Known as Temporaries I through L, they had been thrown up during World War I and were still in reasonably good shape, although hard to cool in the summer. Visitors were admitted through a door in Temporary L and directed by an armed guard to a reception area. It was there early one morning in September 1951 that I noticed an Army officer, conspicuous for being in full uniform in a strictly civilian environment. Young, blond, and bewildered, was my first impression. There was more to him than that, I would learn eventually, because in time he would become my boss and ultimately my friend.

But bewildered might have been an understatement. Just twenty-four hours earlier, Second Lieutenant Theodore Shackley had been on a field in West Virginia, putting a platoon of young military policemen through their morning calisthenics. Now, here he was complying with a top-secret order transferring him to some anonymous government body. Everybody was staring at him, and he didn't know where he was.

At some level, though, he may have guessed. While serving in 1947 with the U.S. Army's Counterintelligence Corps, Ted had been given rudimentary training in covert operations. Later, when a CIA recruiting officer had dropped in at the University of Maryland, Ted had filled out papers expressing interest but had heard nothing more. Then, with the cold war heating up, the CIA had levied a requirement on the military for personnel with fluency in one or more of the languages spoken in the Soviet satellite countries; an IBM punch card had dropped; and Ted had found himself seconded to the CIA.

It was his fluency in Polish, of course, that had brought him here; Ted's immigrant grandparents were to thank for that. The awards he had received in college for scholarship in history and political science most likely had gone unnoticed.

Ted was assigned, naturally enough, to the Polish unit of the Office of Special Operations (OSO) and was sent immediately to basic training. Hardly anybody in those early days, except for veterans of the Office of Strategic Services (OSS), had any useful field experience to share, and this applied especially to his instructors. Dissatisfied with the relevance of the training he was receiving, Ted began a lifelong program of self-education in intelligence, reading all the open-source literature he could find in English, German, and Polish and seizing every opportunity to "consult the cranial files," as he put it, of anybody with a background in the clandestine arts.

In West Germany he came under the tutelage of Bill Harvey, the legendary chief of base, Berlin. Harvey was a former special agent of the Federal Bureau of Investigation (FBI) credited with good work against Nazi agents during World War II and renowned for carrying a concealed weapon, a practice that later caused consternation in the Secret Service when he was found to have been armed during a meeting with President Kennedy. Harvey's reading in the German philosophers had exposed him to a theory that potential leaders have to be forced into a cone from which only the best will emerge. Having put Ted through a "testing cone" of demanding assignments, he now began promoting him through a series of increasingly responsible managerial positions. And it was Harvey who eventually put Ted into his first senior posting and introduced him to the paramilitary operations that were to absorb the remainder of his career.

Ted would always regard Harvey as a friend and a mentor.

It is a curious fact, and a significant one too, I think, that for every time the words "agent" or "spy" occur in the chapters that follow, the word "friend" or its variants occurs five times. Ted treasured his own friendships. In West Palm Beach, Florida, he had formed a close bond with a fellow member of the high school football team, and the two had agreed to attend the same university so that they might continue to play together. Ted was offered a scholarship to Princeton, whereas the best his friend could aspire to was the University of Maryland, so it was to Maryland that they both went. There are some who believe that the lack of an Ivy League degree disqualified Ted from the agency's top job of director of central intelligence, in other words, that his attachment to a friendship cost him his profession's best prize. However that may be, I think his dedication to his profession also cost him many a friendship. He has written tellingly of a relationship that managed to remain intact despite Ted's rise to a position of authority over his friend. "[Joe Lazarsky's] solution to the problem of how to relate to a person junior to him in years but senior in rank," Ted wrote, "was to call me by the Polish word for 'old one.'"

My own friendship with Ted Shackley matured slowly. After working under him in Miami, Berlin, and Saigon, and even in the more relaxed atmosphere of the company that he founded in retirement, I was in awe of him, and it took many acts of kindness on his part before it sank in that he wanted to be friends.

Along with his friends, he had his ill-wishers. While I never heard anyone refer to him as "the blond ghost," I can easily believe that there were those who did use that epithet and worse, for in his drive to carry out the policy directives laid on him by Washington, he sometimes left hard feelings in his wake.

Hard feelings piled up in the Latin American Division shortly after Ted reported there in 1972 and learned that a renegade case officer, Philip Agee, had gone to Havana and was cooperating with Cuban intelligence. Every operation that Agee might conceivably have known about and every case officer with whom he had ever been associated was deemed compromised. Ted ordered the wound to be "cauterized." This meant that productive operations had to be discontinued, favorite agents terminated, and case officers uprooted from their comfortable billets in Latin America and reassigned to often less congenial places. The resentments that this caused have probably never died.

It was customary in those days to divide clandestine activities into three categories—foreign intelligence (FI), counterintelligence (CI), and covert action (CA). Although Ted was clearly at home in CI and CA, I think his heart was in FI, it being the field in which he won his spurs along the East German and Czechoslovak borders. The mission assigned him in 1962 vis-à-vis Cuba was to unseat Fidel Castro, a CA task; but the first thing he did upon reaching Miami was to strengthen the station's intelligence-collection capability. His reaction to the building of the Berlin Wall was that our inability to anticipate it was an intelligence failure; upon taking over as chief of base in 1965, he took steps to reestablish contact with agents lost behind the Iron Curtain and to recruit new ones.

Ted reacted similarly to the Vietcong's so-called Tet Offensive of 1968: With so many CIA case officers on the ground in Vietnam, why did it come as a shock? To guard against further unwelcome surprises, he ordered that the station disseminate more intelligence reports. The theory, of course, was sound. An officer with the primary duty of serving as adviser to a South Vietnamese district chief, once attuned to the importance of positive intelligence, might be less likely to overlook a priceless nugget of information. But the theory disregarded fundamental differences between Berlin in 1965 and Saigon in 1970. Most CIA personnel in Vietnam at that time were ungrounded in the country's history or politics, were unable to speak the local language, and were draftees serving a curtailed eighteen-month tour and marking off the days on a FIGMO[1] chart. Ted's attempt to increase the flow of positive intelligence out of Vietnam earned him little more than derision and another crop of ill-wishers.

Ted liked to say that an ideal espionage operation should resemble a surgical laser beam, for the beam leaves no trace to show that the target has been penetrated. So, perhaps it is appropriate that while his public recognition consists of three separate awards of the Distinguished Intelligence Medal for his skillful management of three separate, spectacular paramilitary operations, his achievement of quietly extracting from Cuba the intelligence information leading to the discovery of the Soviet intermediate-range ballistic missiles remains largely unnoticed.

—Richard A. Finney

1

ESPIONAGE

I make no secret of the fact that I am a strong believer in HUMINT, collection of intelligence by a human source, in other words, by a spy. I don't dispute the usefulness of photographic intelligence or signals intelligence, both of which are actually superior to HUMINT when it comes to such things as counting missile launchers or assessing a potential enemy's progress in telemetry. These collection systems can tell us much of what we need to know about another country's capabilities. But this isn't enough. If we deployed our armed forces to counter every threat of which every other country is thought to be capable, we would be stretching them pretty thin. In addition to its capabilities, we need to know that country's intentions, and neither the eye in the sky nor the big ear can tell us much about that. For intentions intelligence we have to rely on a methodically selected and trained human being.

If I stress the word "methodically," it's because twenty-eight years of work with human sources has imprinted the word on my mind. Winging it or playing it by ear simply won't do.

Method begins with the listing of all the questions that the government wants answers to, eliminating from the list those questions that can be answered by PHOTINT or SIGINT, and analyzing the remainder based on where the desired information is located. Only then can human-source collection function as it should, that is to say, with the precision of a scalpel. Or, to bring the metaphor up to date, with the precision of a surgical laser beam, for the beam leaves no traces to show that the target has been penetrated, and neither should an ideal HUMINT collection operation.

When I arrived in Nürnberg in 1953, human-source collection was being conducted with the precision of a vacuum cleaner. This remark, I hasten to add, is not meant to be quite as critical as it may sound, for in many respects a vacuum cleaner was just what was wanted in those days, only five years after the Berlin Blockade, four years after the Soviet Union exploded its first nuclear bomb, and three years after the outbreak of the Korean War. It seemed prudent to assume that the Soviet Union would try to seize all of Germany, so the intentions question was more or less moot. The burning questions that remained were when, where, and with what. Early warning was the order of the day, and physical reconnaissance behind the Iron Curtain was the means chosen for achieving it.

Reconnaissance was conducted in much the same way, and often by the same people, as in World War II. During the war, agents were recruited from the prisoner-of-war camps, removed to "Joe houses," given rudimentary training in observation and reporting, assigned a mission, and pushed across the front line. Sometimes they returned.

If you substitute refugee camps for POW camps, safe houses for Joe houses, and international borders for front lines, you will get a fairly accurate picture of the black border-crossing operations that were being run from Nürnberg in 1953 and 1954, the main difference being that the agents we were dispatching to Poland had to cross two borders. Some would go from West Germany into Czechoslovakia, from Czechoslovakia into Poland, and—if they were lucky—back again. Others got to Poland by crossing first into East Germany. Either way, the dangers were not negligible. First of all, crossings in the early days were usually accomplished with the aid of smugglers, sheepherders, game wardens, and loggers who knew all the secret pathways and kept themselves up to date on the routes and schedules followed by the border patrols. Of course, it did not take the security forces (StB in Czechoslovakia, Stasi in East Germany, and UB in Poland) long to catch on to this and to recruit informants from the same circles in which we were operating. As the odds in this equation shifted significantly in favor of the communist security forces, our agents had to start going it alone against increasingly formidable obstacles, including barbed-wire fences, watch towers, plowed strips, trip wires, and mine fields. Simply put, these operations were very risky.

Looked at coldly and in the context of a near-war situation, these operations' costs in terms of human loss might have been acceptable if the intelligence product had not been so marginal. Typical of our quality problem was the reality that we had very little chance to check on the product's reliability. An agent might come back and say, "Well, I visited my cousin and he has talked recently with his uncle, and the uncle said there is an infantry division at *x* and *y* coordinates." Interesting though the remarks attributed to the uncle may be, how can you evaluate such a report? And then, for this report to be truly meaningful, you want to be able to observe this infantry division over a certain period in order to know its state of readiness, whether it is being reinforced, and so on. Illegal border-crossing operations, unfortunately, very rarely give you this continuity of coverage. I kept thinking to myself that there had to be a better way.

One of my principal agents at that time was an Austrian named Hans Freisinger. Now, the relationship between a junior case officer and a principal agent is comparable to that between a second lieutenant and a master sergeant. The shavetail has the rank, but the noncom has the experience, and if the shavetail is wise, he'll keep his ears open when the noncom is speaking.

Freisinger was worth listening to. Before 1939 he had worked in Poland for the Dunlop Tire Company, and toward the end of World War II he had been in German intelligence as a Polish interpreter. One day in conversation with him I casually mentioned my dissatisfaction with the state of our Polish operations. "What we should be looking for," he said, "are commercial people. German business is only now beginning to get back into Eastern Europe, particularly Poland, because this is their natural market. We need to find ways of getting into Siemens, AEG, and Telefunken."

Another principal agent whom I remember now only by his alias of Erwin Bellermann was a Polish-born German from Pabjanice who had been in the textile business before the war. Fluent in Polish and German and nearly fluent in Russian, he was working in the early 1950s at a uranium project outside Dresden as a translator for the Russian colonel in command, and he might well have stayed there had he not been falsely suspected of being a spy. A fellow case officer from Frankfurt who knew I was looking for Polish speakers referred him to me. I assessed him, found him to be a man of good quality, and gave him a job.

In due course I asked Bellermann how he thought we could get better information out of Poland. "Recruit East German assembly technicians," he said. From his own experience, he explained, he knew that companies in East Germany were shipping heavy equipment to Poland, Czechoslovakia, and the Soviet Union and that East German technicians, or "monteurs," were being sent to these countries to install the machines. A good idea, I thought, but that raises the question of how to recruit these people in large enough numbers to assure us of a steady flow of information.

Still, a third principal agent, whose name, unfortunately, I have completely forgotten, gave me another idea. He had been an officer in Polish military intelligence (O-2) before 1939, had served during World War II as a colonel in General Anders's Polish Corps, and in 1954 was helping me interview Polish refugees at Camp Valka.

Reminiscing one evening about prewar Polish intelligence operations, this gentleman told me that one technique used by O-2 officers was to ride the trains between Berlin and Warsaw, seeking out and cultivating German businessmen and engineers who were en route to the Soviet Union. As friendships blossomed, the Polish officers would invite their new acquaintances to stop off for a day or two of sightseeing in Warsaw. There, if all went well, the prospects would be recruited to observe important details of the factories and plants their firms were building in the Soviet Union and, upon their return, to spend a week in Warsaw being debriefed. O-2 had a stable of such agents according to the colonel, and the product from this effort was regarded as first-class. This was my first programmatic exposure to what we were eventually to call legal-travel operations.

In June 1954 I was transferred to Berlin to manage Polish operations. For me, steeped as I was in Polish history, Berlin was haunted ground, for it was here, just twenty years before, that a Polish cavalry officer named Jerzy Sosnowski and two high-born German ladies were arrested by the Gestapo and charged with obtaining secret information from the German War Ministry and transmitting it to Poland. Sosnowski was eventually traded back to the Poles for three German agents, but the two women who had been arrested with him, Benita von Falkenhayn and Renata von Natzmer, were beheaded. According to one version of the execution scene, Falkenhayn had carried a portrait of Sosnowski with her to the block so that his face would be the last thing she would see in life.

Whether true or not, the story creates an image both horrible and romantic that sticks in the memory.

There was a Polish embassy in Berlin—in East Berlin, to be precise, although in those days before the Berlin Wall went up, the distinction was not as important as it became later. Sosnowski was believed to have used the embassy as a support base for his espionage operations between 1927 and 1934, and there was every good reason to suppose that his successors were doing the same thing. Berlin Base, therefore, was keeping a close watch on the embassy and its affiliated consulate, as well as on the Polish military mission in West Berlin. With the authority that we enjoyed as an occupying power, we were able to put taps on the military mission's telephones and coverage on its mail. We had concealed cameras to record the comings and goings of visitors, any one of whom could be a latter-day Sosnowski, and we had surveillance teams for tailing and identifying the more interesting of our suspects.

Another important function of Berlin Base was the interrogation of refugees. There was a constant stream of them in the days before the Wall, and they could generally be counted on for tidbits of positive intelligence that might occasionally confirm or amplify what our border-crossers were telling us. Some of them, indeed, could be recruited for cross-border operations. And, in rare instances, a refugee might be able to tell us something about our operational environment that could be put to immediate use.

One day one of our interrogators was told that much of the freight that was moving from East Germany to Poland was going by barge down an inland waterway system that began in East Berlin and ended in what was once the German harbor of Swinemünde but had been renamed Swinoujscie when the Poles took it over after World War II. Part of Swinoujscie was being used by the Polish Navy, so here was a military target that, for the first time, was accessible to us through the kind of legal-travel channel to Poland that my principal agent back in Nürnberg had suggested to me. Only barges made in the river cities of Finow or Breslau, however, would do, as these were the ones most frequently employed in the Swinoujscie traffic.

We now alerted our interrogators to look for refugees who had recently worked on the canals and knew captains of "Finow Mass" or "Breslauer Mass" barges. Many of these people could be persuaded to return to East Berlin long enough to recruit their acquaintances as observation agents, and before long we were getting a regular flow of information about the goings-on in Swinoujscie.

Becoming more ambitious, we had one of these barge captains recruit a woman employee of the Swinoujscie port captain's office, and now we were getting documentary intelligence in the form of ships' manifests. As these things had to be hidden from the prying eyes of Polish and East German customs inspectors, we began to invent and install concealment devices in the barges. This was made the more necessary because bargees were notorious smugglers, a fact well known to the communist authorities, and random searches were a fact of life on the canals. We tried to pay our captains enough that they wouldn't be tempted to smuggle, but there was no way we could guard against the possibility that one of their crewmen might try to make a deutsche mark or two with a bit of contraband. So, we had some losses, but there was never a time when we were in danger of running out of barges.

There was a very junior ensign in naval intelligence in Berlin in those days who was also interested in the barge traffic and was developing more leads than he could handle. Furthermore, he was beginning to realize that he was "crossing wires" with us, that is to say, he was talking to some of the same people we were talking to. This is always an undesirable situation as it implies a breakdown of compartmentation and a consequent decrease in security for both of the agencies involved. A system called the Interagency Source Register (ISR) had been put in place to guard against wire crossing. Whenever a member agency decided to recruit somebody, it first had to submit the name to the ISR, and if told that another agency had a prior interest, it would have to back away.

It was through this mechanism that Ensign John Barron became aware that he was fishing in waters where the Central Intelligence Agency (CIA) was also present. Through an intermediary he approached our base chief, Bill Harvey, and Harvey told me to "go over and meet this guy." John discussed barge operations with me and turned over some of his surplus leads. Our dialog was thus of immediate benefit to Berlin Base, but for me personally the contact had a lifetime payoff as it was the beginning of a friendship that has lasted to this day.

In July 1955 I became chief of satellite operations and, thus, responsible for Czech and Hungarian as well as Polish operations. My deputy in this new organization was Herb N., a man who had a master's degree in German studies from the University of Wisconsin. His excellent command of the language was due partly to this circumstance and partly to the accuracy of a German anti-aircraft gunner, although I don't think Herb ever saw the years that he had spent in a German POW camp in quite that light.

The U-2 photoreconnaissance aircraft had begun its flights over the Soviet Union by this time. The excellence and timeliness of its product and the fact that continuous coverage of a target was possible at last made our cross-border operations largely obsolete. With the funds and manpower that were released by the termination of old programs, I was now able to test out the theories of my Nürnberg principal agents. I assigned Herb the responsibility for day-to-day management of our legal-traveler program.

Our ability as an occupying power to monitor and censor mail gave us our start. First, we made a study of all mail coming to West Berlin from Poland and Czechoslovakia, noting which West Berlin firms were getting official correspondence. With a target list in hand, we then tapped these firms' telephones and opened their mail, looking for two things—the projects that they were working on, especially in Poland, and the names and addresses of the monteurs who were installing the equipment. For each firm, each project, and each monteur, a file was opened.

Now we subjected the project files to a winnowing process to eliminate those without strategic interest. As many of the projects had to do with power plants, we had to ask in each case how the plant was related to the power grid and whether it was intended to supply some new industry that might be under development or whether it was to be tied to a military installation.

With this work done, we were able to concentrate on the individual monteurs. From methodical analysis of their mail, we learned that they would be sent out to work for periods of between six months and one year and would then be recalled and replaced by others. We learned which of them were on deck for early assignment to Poland, and through our liaison with the Berlin police, we were able to eliminate those whose antecedents, we felt, might make them unsuitable agent material.

All that remained was to meet our prospects, either by way of carefully planned social cultivation or by simply knocking on their doors. We would offer them the opportunity to supplement their income by doing nothing more onerous than memorizing a short observation brief we would give them, and then allocating to us a few days of their time upon their return so that we could benefit from their work-related experiences and observations. For most of them, the money was the big inducement, but some also welcomed the opportunity to strike back at the communist system. A spirit of adventure motivated some of them, and for a very few there was the worry that, if they refused to cooperate, something would be done to cancel their assignment, which was both financially and professionally important to them in terms of their status with their firm.

For us, the reward for all this work was a flood of economic information—plans for reconstruction of preexisting industries or the development of new sectors and, in some cases, the relation of new construction to Poland's military potential. But we did not get very much out of it in terms of military plans or intentions; nor did we get much political information. The rub was that the political situation in Poland was very tense in 1955, and Germans were still not really welcome there, so the opportunities for these monteurs to learn much of political interest from seemingly casual conversation with their Polish contacts were quite limited.

This was new ground we were plowing, but we had no monopoly on it, for Jack Gieslin and Dave Murphy in the section responsible for the Soviet Union were prompt to pick up the idea and expand on it. Instead of asking their recruits to do nothing more than observe and report economic intelligence as we had been doing, they urged their agents to collect political intelligence and carry out such operational tasks as emptying and loading dead drops and—riskiest of all—recruitment of Soviet citizens. Their more aggressive approach to legal-travel operations had some successes, and our boss, Bill Harvey, encouraged us to try the same thing.

With time and experience, I came to see legal-travel operations as just one aspect of what we called third-country operations, which is to say, operations against country x, in which the chosen agent was neither an American nor a citizen of country x, but a citizen of some other country y.

Legal travelers could include Communist Party types, businessmen-technicians, and religious figures. Another form of third-country national who turned out to be very useful was the foreign diplomat, a Finn, let's say, under assignment to Hanoi or Beijing. Still another kind was the one who was already a resident of a target country, doctors perhaps who went to those countries and got fascinated by the society and stayed there.

One way of looking at third-country operations is that they are an espionage application of what military theorist Basil H. Lidell Hart called the strategy of indirect approach. In both types of endeavor, clandestine as well as military operations, the roundabout way is often the quickest and least costly road to the objective.

Another example of the indirect approach in espionage is "false-flag" recruitment in which the recruiter poses as a national of a country not his own. This is not as easy to do as it may seem at first, even where the recruiter has native fluency in the language of his pretended country, for there are many other clues to nationality, such as the cut of one's clothing or the way one cuts his hair. Thought has to be given to pocket litter; if the recruiter presents himself as a London-based member of a Polish émigré group, as I once did, it will not be helpful if he is seen to carry a matchbook from a Washington, D.C., restaurant.

Travel arrangements tend to become sticky when one is operating under false flag. If a recruiter wants to seem to have come to country y directly from country x, he must take care to make his appearance on a day when an airline has a scheduled arrival from country x. Often it will be simpler for him actually to come via country x, but if he wants to be taken for a citizen of country x, he will have to enter country y on a false country x passport, taking a chance that the document may not pass muster under examination by immigration authorities. Weighing up all the odds, the recruiter may decide it is safer to enter country y in his own clothes and with his own passport, then lie low for a day or two while shifting identities.

Why go to all this extra expense and trouble? There are really only two sets of circumstances in which false-flag recruitment is justifiable. One is when the target can't be reached in any other way. This was the case, for instance, when I posed as an émigré Pole in an attempt to recruit a Polish official who was thought to be anti-American but perhaps not unsympathetic to the greater Polish cause. It also explains why Israeli intelligence officers sometimes portray themselves as Britons when attempting recruitments in

Libya or Egypt. On one occasion that we became aware of, the German intelligence service (BND) successfully used American cover in recruiting a target of opportunity who had shown himself favorably disposed toward the CIA.

The other reason for attempting recruitments under false flag is to minimize political damage or even deflect it onto a worthy scapegoat in the event that the attempt fails and turns into a scandal. This was why we used Cuban and East German cover in our approaches to Latin American Communist Party types. Once we even had the recruiter pose as a Soviet working on behalf of the Soviet intelligence service (KGB).

While we in Berlin were learning and applying these lessons, policy makers in Washington had become increasingly concerned with the possibility that hot war might break out at any time. What they wanted and were not getting, they said, was information relating to the imminence of hostilities. So, in a way, the wheel had come full circle. There was now a sufficiency of capabilities intelligence, and we were to concentrate on intentions. Of course, nobody at the policy-making level used the words "a spy in the heart of the enemy camp," but down at our working level there was no doubt that this was what was required.

Although still absorbed in legal-travel operations, I had not lost interest in the embassies, consulates, trade and military missions, and news agencies of Poland, Hungary, and Czechoslovakia. Wire taps and mail covers were still working, and our surveillance teams were still tracking the movements of suspect officials. It occurred to me one day that perhaps our emphasis on these installations had been misplaced. Instead of counterintelligence (CI) information, perhaps we should be seeking positive intelligence. Perhaps the road to the inner sanctum of communist decision making led through these outposts.

The installation-penetration program that I began at Berlin Base and continued in the later stages of my career turned out to be the most painstaking work I had yet undertaken. As we told ourselves, it was harder than selling refrigerators to Eskimos. It was selling treason, which is the toughest sales job in the world. Fortunately, not all of our prospects saw it that way. Some were already disaffected and looking for a chance to change sides. Others, as it turned out, nurtured a passionate hatred for their communist regimes because of some injustice done to them or their families and wanted revenge. We were glad to offer them the opportunity.

For some, there were other considerations more important than the loyalty they were thought to owe their governments. Most of our recruits were motivated by material gain. The individual wanted something that he couldn't get within his system.

When I had the Czech account in Washington, a Czech diplomat walked into the American embassy in Vienna and said he was in trouble. He had misappropriated funds and was in dire need of money. Jack Whitten, the case officer who was put in touch with him, was able to come up with the funds very quickly and keep a dialog open with him. This led to a recruitment that not only gave us the political and economic information available from the Czech embassy in Vienna but enabled us to train the agent so that when he returned to Prague he could serve as a penetration of the Foreign Ministry.

Some of our recruits were bored with the monotony of their lives and gladly seized the chance to take a risk if only for the sheer excitement of it. Others found that their new acquaintances could help them with their professional advancement, writing research papers, for example, or advising them on how to enroll as part-time students in the local university.

Some of our prospects, during the long warm-up period that was often required before recruitment could be attempted, formed legitimate friendships with the persons doing the cultivating, found that they had interests in common, and acquired a readiness to agree with their new acquaintances' points of view. In one case involving a Chinese operation, the common interest was Western music. Membership in a small musical group led to discussions about the prospect's long-term future and, ultimately, to a recruitment that was all the more welcome because the Chinese target is always hard to attack.

Some people have an unsatisfied need for appreciation. Recognition of this need can transform what the agent might privately regard as a temporary working arrangement into a permanent allegiance. During the directorship of Stansfield Turner, when I was associate deputy director for operations, we had a very good in-place agent in a certain diplomatic installation. He was doing excellent work, and his field handlers sensed that a pat on the back was in order. At their suggestion, and with Turner's concurrence, we prepared a message for Turner's signature, complimenting the agent on a job well done. The message was duly transmitted to the field, and the agent at his next regularly scheduled meeting was shown the correspondence. After a long pause, he said, "You know, this is the first time one of my superiors has recognized my good performance."

We once brought a Soviet diplomat to an advanced stage of development and put a third-country national in touch with him. In time we learned that this man's great interest in life was stamps. The third-country national and the American case officer were able to evaluate his collection, and they realized that he was only four stamps short of having an exhibition-type collection.

We made one of these four stamps available to him at bargain-basement prices, and he now became fully aware that only three stamps separated him from his goal. Making a calculated guess as to how much money he had, we fed him a second stamp at a price that wiped him out. Now, at last, we were able to offer him the prospect of obtaining his third and fourth stamps in return for cooperating with the third-country national and the latter's American "friend."

As a rule of thumb, for every hundred people we looked at, we came to the conclusion that only ten were really worth pursuing, and as we zeroed in on the ten, we invariably came to the point where we could afford to concentrate on only three. Of the three, we could usually expect to recruit one.

It was difficult sometimes to get an inexperienced field station to take the crucial step of thinning out its prospect list. As chief of the Latin American Division, I once ordered a balky station to review its file one more time and then pick some Soviet, any Soviet, to zero in on, if only for the experience.

So, the station made its selection, put its selectee under surveillance, and soon noticed that he was behaving in a singularly clandestine fashion. Further surveillance showed that he was having an affair with a woman.

We now did an appropriate background investigation of the woman and found her to be an outstanding businessperson with an excellent reputation and no apparent interest in politics. So, we finally had a station asset approach her with the line that she and we had a shared interest in preventing the relationship from causing problems for either party and that we ought to cooperate to this end.

My hat goes off to the individual who carried out this intrusive task with what must have been a model of delicacy and tact. The lady explained that she had had an unfortunate marriage, that after her husband left her, she had worked hard and built up a good business and had finally decided to find someone to share at least part of her life with. She had made a survey of all the men in her environment and had decided that the one who was most charming and interesting was this Soviet citizen. In effect, she had done what we had been trying to do and had been the first to succeed. But we, at least, came in second. After I had left the Latin American Division, the lady helped the station recruit her lover.

If I use the word "we" in discussing cases in which I had no direct involvement, it is because installation penetration, more than any other type of intelligence operation, requires teamwork—between the surveillance team manager, the telephone tap coordinator, the tape transcriber, and the access agent. In the latter category, I liked to have the target in touch with a local from the country where he was assigned, be it a businessman or a diplomat from the Foreign Ministry. Then, for the different view that this gave, I tried to have a third-country national in touch with him. Third, I always liked to have an American who knew him, who could develop him slowly over a long period of time, in place as the least aggressive of the three. The idea was to weave a cocoon around the target, to dominate his time.

Then, finally there were the recruiter and the agent handler, not always two different people, but frequently so. It often happened that in the preliminaries leading up to recruitment, the new agent got to know a lot about the recruiter. In such cases it might be considered prudent to let the recruiter fade out of the picture and be replaced by a man or woman who could maintain a clandestine relationship with the agent.

To complete the matrix, the agent handler needed the support of specialists at headquarters if the limited time he had available for meetings with his agent was to be made as profitable as possible. The agent, if his absences from his usual haunts were not to be noticed by his colleagues, might be able to spend only thirty minutes with his handler. Some of this time had to be spent in social chit-chat and some in talk about the agent's problems. (Most of them did have problems.) This might leave as little as ten minutes for the agent handler to ask his agent questions and obtain vital answers, the end product of all the work that had gone before. It was and is headquarters' responsibility to ensure that the right questions are asked so that this time will not be wasted.

What are the results of all the time and effort that this human matrix expends on its scrutiny of diplomatic and trade installations? First, it enables you to recruit people. Over the years, we've been successful in recruiting people in every category we wanted. Second, even where recruitments are not possible, you usually do get a technical penetration; in most such cases, a careful screening of recorded conversations gives a positive product. Third, collecting all this information gives you the opportunity to run a surreptitious entry and, in so doing, to open the enemy's safes and photograph their contents without letting him know he has been had. Fourth, it gives you defectors, helps you to establish their bona fides quickly and decide what to do with them in a relatively short time. Fifth, it gives you counterintelligence information and allows you to know who the intelligence officers are and what targets they are working on.

Ordinarily the big bonus from installation penetration activity is that it enables you to handle walk-ins. By doing all this work, when you're blessed with an opening, you can handle it professionally, quickly, and expeditiously.

One day in Berlin I happened to be alone in the office around lunchtime, finishing some paperwork. One of the things I was signing off on was a report we had just completed on the Hungarian embassy in East Berlin. It was a very detailed, comprehensive report on how the installation was organized and who the personalities were, and I reread it carefully.

The telephone rang. With no secretaries present, I picked it up. It was the Marine guard over in the Consular Section on Clay Allee. He said he was calling in compliance with the procedure that had been set up for walk-ins. He had called a couple of other numbers and nobody had responded. The switchboard in our office complex had given him my number, and he thought I ought to come over right away.

There, in a private office where the Marine had put him, was a very nervous man. From his general appearance it was clear he was no Berliner but a Central European of some sort. He told me he had come to pass on some information about the status of Jews in Hungary. He very much wanted the Americans to have this information, but once he had imparted it, he wanted to get away, and fast.

I tried to draw him into general conversation, wanting to slow him down so that I could get a better assessment of him, but he would have none of it. Finally, I said, "I've come to the conclusion that you are a Hungarian official in the embassy in East Berlin. There are a lot of things we could talk about that would be interesting to us both."

"No, no," he said, "I can't do that. If anybody sees me here or learns I have been here, it will be my head."

"It isn't as bad as that," I said. "We can protect and help you."

"How could you possibly do anything?"

"As an example," I assured him, "we know all about the AVH *rezidentura* in East Berlin." This was the local station for the Hungarian intelligence service.

"Impossible, impossible."

"I'll tell you what I'll do," I said. "I'm going to write down on this piece of paper the name of the head of the AVH *rezidentura* in your installation, and I'm going to fold it right here and I'll pass it over to you. If I'm right, you should feel comforted by this and continue to meet with me."

Salesmen will recognize this ploy. Instead of making my visitor a passive recipient of this information by simply speaking the name aloud, I made him take a step toward obtaining it. He opened the paper, looked at it and said, "Well, yes, you're right. Amazing!"

We talked a little longer and agreed to stay in touch. After a few more meetings under more clandestine circumstances, I recruited the man. It turned out that he was plugged into a network of small entrepreneurs and operators in Berlin who could be counted on to supply wanted merchandise at attractive prices, and this connection made him a person of consequence whenever important visitors would arrive from Hungary. From them, he was able to provide us with very good information on the political developments that were to lead to Imre Nagy's coming to power in 1956.

In the ensuing upheavals, one of the other officials of the

Hungarian embassy defected. We were afraid that this would trigger an investigation of the entire embassy staff, and to deflect it we decided to give the AVH something else to occupy its time.

We prepared phonograph records that began with a few words in the recognizable voice of the defector, then in another voice continued to lay out much of the information that our source had given us, trying to create the impression that the defector had already been an agent in place. We put East German labels on the records, packaged them in several sets together with legitimate dance-music disks, and had them delivered to several embassy people.

It happened that one of the recipients was throwing a little party one night in his home and thought this would be a nice time to find out what the records were like that somebody had sent him. Consternation followed. There was so much there about the AVH, the rezident, and the deputy rezident that the AVH shut down all their Berlin operations for about a year.

No harm came to our agent. He stayed in place for a few years more, and eventually came out and became a successful businessman in Germany.

2

COUNTERINTELLIGENCE

NEWTON Miler, a former chief of operations of the CIA's counterintelligence staff, used to say that explaining counterintelligence is a lot like trying to explain how to understand art. Despite this warning, I do try on occasion to explain counterintelligence, but only in terms of the objectives that a case officer can realistically aim for when in contact with a hostile intelligence service.

There are four such objectives in my scheme of things, and I rank them in order of probable net gain. The one to which I have assigned the lowest priority is deception of the enemy. I suspect that manipulation of an enemy service, which we sometimes see put forward as one of the minimum functions of counterintelligence, reflects a certain fascination with the so-called double-cross system, the World War II operation that enabled the British to manipulate the entire German espionage apparatus in their country. Whether it is realistic for a democratic country's intelligence service to aspire nowadays to manipulations of this magnitude is questionable. The double-cross system owed its success in large part to a circumstance that is unlikely to be duplicated soon, at least not in peacetime, namely that information in Britain was tightly restricted. There were few sources of information other than the reporting of their own agents to tell the Germans what was going on in the island, so when these very agents were caught, doubled, and brought under British control, the Germans were unaware of it. Then, as the British played these cases, they profited in time from the added advantage accruing to them from Enigma, the code-breaking operation that enabled them to read the Germans' internal high-grade traffic, from which they could discover how the Germans were reacting to the deception being fed to them. All of the advantages in the Double-Cross Operation belonged to the British. German intelligence never had a chance of success against this uniquely stacked deck.

I believe that a case officer should engage in deception and disinformation operations only when he and Washington are sure the deception material he feeds in will be picked up by the other side and reach its inner reporting mechanism. It is only then that we can be reasonably certain that a deception operation has a chance of success. And I must add that the case officer should be careful how he defines success. In one case I am familiar with, the CIA used deception material to provoke Fidel Castro into firing one of several valuable subordinates. In a limited sense this was indeed a success because it caused some disruption and discord in the enemy's bureaucracy. But, since revolutions notoriously devour their young, disruption and discord are common occurrences, so the downfall of this one apparatchik was hardly a major event. It contributed little if anything to national goals and gained the agency little more than experience, plus the satisfaction of poking Fidel in the eye.

Another legitimate objective of a counterintelligence operation, one to which I assign third priority, is to absorb the time and resources of an opposition case officer so completely that he is rendered ineffective. As every polygraph operator knows, however, it takes more energy to lie than to tell the truth. In every double agent operation, it is the counterintelligence officer who has to do the most lying because he not only has to feed his opposite number with deception material, or *Spielmaterial,* but he has to pretend to believe the lies that his opposite number is feeding him. Consequently, there is some risk that more than one counterintelligence officer will be required to neutralize the efforts of a single positive intelligence operator on the other side.

In short, the neutralization of an opposition case officer and the befuddlement of his political masters are both acceptable objectives of a counterintelligence operation, but they are not the first things that should come to mind when an opportunity presents itself. The first two objectives on my list are the following: (1) protection of the security of our own personnel, operations, and installations, and (2) getting to know the enemy by identifying his intelligence officers, discovering the missions they have been given, learning their modus operandi in pursuit of these goals, and recruiting some of them as double agents.

Others may disagree. My list is a personal one based on certain defining experiences that happened to me in my early days as a case officer. The first of these involved the so-called WIN case. While being briefed for my first foreign assignment by the Polish specialists of both the Office of Special Operations (OSO) and the Office of Policy Coordination (OPC), units responsible for intelligence collection and covert operations, respectively, in the agency's early days, I couldn't help noticing the pulling and tugging that accompanied the merger that was then in progress and realizing that more was at stake than the question of who was to be the chief of the new combination. The bitterest acrimony, it seemed to me, was caused by arguments over the future management of the Freedom and Independence Movement, or, to use its Polish acronym, WIN.

WIN was an underground Polish army that was expected to put up a fierce resistance to the anticipated Red Army advance into Western Europe. Its representatives in the emigration claimed for it an active membership of five hundred, a partially active membership of twenty thousand, and the promise of one hundred thousand more who would flock to the colors in the event of war. Despite the lack of any real confirmation of these claims, OPC had been secretly air-dropping money, arms, ammunition, and radios to WIN cells inside Poland.

While the turf battles raged around me, I read up on the WIN organization to the extent that I could, and it struck me even then that nobody really understood what this organization was, how it functioned, who its people were, and so forth. The one point that did shine forth with icy clarity was that there was very little compartmentation in the operation. My own readings in intelligence history had not yet reached the point where I might have wondered whether OPC and OSO were fighting over a poisoned chalice, but officers senior to me might, it seems to me now, have detected certain similarities between WIN and the Trust, a largely fictitious, promonarchist organization with which Soviet intelligence kept Russian émigré groups and Western intelligence services in check for six years.

As it turned out, WIN lasted only a little over five years, from mid-1947 when Polish security forces succeeded in taking it over, until December 1952 when Polish radio revealed the extent of the fiasco. Of all the cuts that our Polish unit had to endure, the unkindest was the report that the Poles had taken the money that the CIA had sent to WIN and used it to fund the Communist Party of Italy. The sight of my colleagues wrestling with the realization that five years of strategic planning and many millions of dollars had just gone down the drain convinced me that more attention had to be paid to the protection of our own personnel, operations, and installations.

The fates must have decided that I needed another lesson and a sharper one. It was not long in coming. During the period from 1952 to 1954 when I was running border-crossing operations out of Nürnberg, one of the places that I frequented was just east of Kassel where the twin towns of Bad Sooden and Allendorf sat near a wooded area through which ran a lightly defended and poorly demarcated border with East Germany. It was a good place for slipping agents over, and when the wind was right, it was a good place for them to return to, for the smell that wafted from the sulfur baths at Bad Sooden was as good as any homing beacon.

On the day in question, my principal agent and I were preparing to dispatch an agent team into East Germany with the aid of one of the numerous border guides we were employing in those days. There had been some hitch in the delivery of the false documents and concealment devices which the agents were to carry with them, so I had had to stay behind in Nürnberg to await the completion of these essential items, while my principal agent went ahead to make last-minute arrangements with the guide.

About an hour behind schedule I arrived in Allendorf where I received an urgent message from my principal agent. On his own arrival in town an hour before, he had been intercepted by the border guide's girlfriend who told him that the guide had been arrested and doubled by the VoPo (the East German *Volkspolizei* or People's Police) and that an ambush had been laid for us.

The fact that the guide had been arrested and interrogated was not in itself surprising, for mishaps like that did happen from time to time to the shepherds, rangers, loggers, and smugglers we were employing, and I had become accustomed to thinking of these tragedies as part of the cost of doing business. No, what came as a shock to me was the realization that I myself had come within an inch of being shot or kidnapped. Suddenly the abstract principle of protecting personnel, operations, and installations from hostile penetration acquired tangible reality.

In the never-ending search for agent material, I and the other case officers who were running border-crossing operations were constantly screening refugees from Poland, East Germany, and Czechoslovakia, and increasingly we found that many of the people who appeared to have the qualities and contacts we were looking for had already been recruited and dispatched by the other side in the hope of penetrating our networks and neutralizing our operations. Sometimes the individuals themselves would volunteer the information to us. In other cases, some aspects of their stories would arouse our suspicions, and with the aid of the polygraph we would obtain confessions. Gradually we understood that it was no longer just the enemy, but we ourselves, who needed to see to our defenses. No longer content with trying to detect and double our agents, the enemy was now aggressively seeking to plant his own people on us. This ploy illustrates the second of my two counterintelligence objectives, the acquisition of information about one's opponent's missions, personnel, and modus operandi. Two can play at this game, though, and before long it was our turn.

It was May 1959, and the Czech intelligence service, popularly referred to in the media as the StB, was doing its best to penetrate and neutralize Radio Free Europe (RFE). Having just become head of the Czech unit, I therefore encouraged the officers working on Czech operations in Munich to dangle one or more RFE employees in areas where StB agents were known to be lurking in the hope that they would take the bait and recruit one of our offerings.

One of RFE's Czech staffers was selected as the dangle. We briefed him to be outspoken in his dissatisfaction with his working conditions and in his desire to return home at some point in the future. Then, we sent him on holiday to Salzburg, Austria, a city within easy range of RFE's Munich headquarters and one of the StB's happy hunting grounds. He had not been there long when, in one of the *Weinschenken,* he met a congenial soul who in time introduced him to a new circle of drinking buddies, one of whom turned out to be Jaroslav Nemec, an StB officer stationed in Salzburg under diplomatic cover. Nemec offered our man a chance to earn his passage home. Our man agreed with a show of reluctance, and we had our double agent.

The Czechs first assigned him the easy task of reporting low-level information on the personalities and politics within RFE, and we were able to go along with this. Then, however, they gave him an assignment that we could not tolerate.

Exactly what the StB thought they could achieve by it is hard to fathom. If there was any rational purpose behind it at all, it may have been to portray RFE as a disease-ridden place to work, but more likely it was simply bloody-mindedness. In his book about his career in the StB,[1] Ladislav Bittman has said the Czechs were just amusing themselves. As things turned out, it was we who had the last laugh.

At one of his Salzburg meetings with our double agent, Nemec gave him a saltshaker that the agent had previously taken from the RFE cafeteria at Nemec's request. Nemec told the agent to take the saltshaker back into the RFE cafeteria. When the agent showed his CIA case officer the shaker, it had a white substance in it that looked like salt. We had the substance analyzed and were told it was atropine. A derivative of belladonna, atropine has legitimate medical uses. Ophthalmologists use it to dilate the pupil of the eye, but when taken internally in a large dose, it is a poison. In the concentration in which the Czechs had prepared it, it was not a deadly poison, only a strong laxative, but it was certainly enough to make people sick.

Our double agent operation had partially served its purpose by giving us some insight into the StB's way of doing business, but it was now obviously at an end. To milk a little more profit from it, we had our agent give the story to the press. As we were to learn later from Bittman's memoirs, pinning the label of "poisoners" on the Czech intelligence service damaged the prestige of the entire regime. At the personal level, Jaroslav Nemec was recalled to Prague with what I would expect to have been reduced career prospects.

While working in West Berlin from 1954 to 1958, I had occasion to observe an example of what I have listed as my third counterintelligence objective—rendering an opposition case officer ineffective by absorbing his time and resources.

The flow of refugees coming through Berlin was much like what I had been seeing in Camp Valka, except that the volume was greater. Whereas down in the Nürnberg area one might in the course of a week talk to five or six good potential leads, in Berlin if one really spent his time at it, he could talk to ten in a day. And, of course, we had about the same percentage of hostile agents to contend with, which implied a much larger absolute number.

Official West German government figures compiled between 1951 and 1961 show that the BfV, the equivalent of the FBI, knew the identities of twenty-three thousand satellite or Soviet agents who had either been dispatched or prepared for dispatch into the federal republic during the period. This worked out to roughly six per day.

Many of these people simply volunteered the information that they had been recruited as agents. They were perfectly safe in doing so because they were protected by the federal republic's amnesty law, which was designed to encourage confessions. The law may have been counterproductive, however. According to information coming to us from the East German Ministry for State Security (MfS) defectors, the East Germans were regularly sending people over to the West under orders to confess, the theory being that we would be so tied up in interrogating them that we would have little time and attention left over for detecting the really dangerous infiltrators.

These were coming at us from all directions. East Berlin, besides being a funnel for Czech, Polish, Hungarian, and East German agents, was the site of the Karlshorst Compound, the largest Soviet *rezidentura* anywhere in the world. Even if we had been disposed to forget this fact for a moment, which we were not, we were constantly reminded of it by the reports we received from our French, British, and German liaison partners.

One of the Polish refugees who fled to the West by way of Berlin in the early 1950s was a certain Gustav Gorecki. Case officers from the Frankfurt operations base interviewed him, liked what they saw, and recruited him for cross-border operations back into Poland. Gorecki became a star performer. He made a number of operational trips to Poland, each time bringing out observation reports that were always a cut better than anything anybody else was producing. Unlike the run-of-the-mill border crosser, he would bring back names and descriptions of possibly recruitable people he had talked to back home. He enjoyed unusual luck in evading traps and border controls, and everybody thought very highly of him.

While I was running my own cross-border operations from Nürnberg and Frankfurt, I often heard my colleagues talking about the exploits of this paragon. Their tales at first stuck in my craw because my agents certainly weren't enjoying that kind of success. Then, as my experience with this type of operation grew, the greater became the divergence between the pictures that Gorecki was painting for his case officers and my own perception of the border realities.

I suggested that it was time that a counterintelligence review be done on Gorecki's operations. Some neutral person, I said, somebody like myself, ought to be brought in to talk to him. Except for Will Burke, Frankfurt station's coordinator for satellite operations of all the German bases, who agreed with me, the suggestion was not well received. "You've got your operations and we've got ours," I was told. Somehow we never got around to it.

A year or so later in Berlin Base, Jack Reiser brought me a sheet of paper and said, "Hey, there's a bunch of Polish citizens on this list. You ought to look at it."

The list in question was something that we received routinely from the Berlin police, a daily rundown on the foreigners registered in the local hotels and boarding houses. Scanning the list as it came in was somebody else's job, but this time I agreed to do it. I picked up the sheet, let my eye run down the column, and the name Gustav Gorecki jumped out at me. This was a red flag. Gorecki had no reason to be in Berlin. Frankfurt Base would have let us know if he was to be there on an operation.

One of Reiser's responsibilities was to manage a number of surveillance teams. I called him back and said, "Put surveillance on this guy. There's something wrong here."

Within twenty-four or forty-eight hours, the surveillance team followed Gorecki onto an S-Bahn, or elevated train, and saw him get off at an East Berlin station. Lacking proper documentation for being in East Berlin, the team was unable to follow. We put another team on Gorecki, and in a day or two they followed him into East Berlin and all the way to a meeting that was obviously being held under clandestine conditions.

At this point we notified Frankfurt and headquarters of the situation and were told in reply that Gorecki was "sort of on ice," by which they meant he hadn't actually been taken off of active operations, but that he wasn't working at the moment either. It was agreed that Gorecki's presence in Berlin was most peculiar, and we were to consider ourselves at liberty to pursue the matter if we so desired.

Using some members of the surveillance team to finger Gorecki to the Berlin police, I had him arrested and taken to a safe house where we began to interrogate him. He denied everything at first, but as we started peeling back the onion, he admitted that yes, he had met some people in East Berlin, but we were putting the wrong interpretation on it. As he was unable to sustain this story for long, he retreated to his next cover story and agreed that yes, he had had some "problems" on his last mission to Poland, and in order to get free he had had to agree to cooperate, but that everything before that had been fine.

At this point it was clear to us that a much longer interrogation would be required, so we moved him to a center in West Germany where the full story eventually came out. He was a legitimate refugee when he first came through East Berlin. He was being straight with us when he was recruited, trained, and sent on his first mission. But then he was apprehended, so from that point forward, everything he did had been under the direction of the other side.

After Gorecki had been fully debriefed, we made a damage assessment of all personnel, installations, and other assets that had to be deemed compromised, and for our future guidance we studied the ways in which he had deceived us. His technique had been to take the ordinary observation reports that he submitted and pad them with information allegedly obtained from persons he encountered in bars, the idea being to tempt his American handlers into sending him back with a brief to recruit these "promising contacts," set up channels of communication, and create organizations around them. Maybe there had been some minor recruitment, but in general things never went that far.

With interrogation complete, Gorecki was turned over to the Germans, but they were not interested in prosecuting him. They merely deposited him in one of the refugee camps, and he soon dropped out of sight. Years later I heard that a CIA officer, while visiting the Baltic resort city of Sopot, Poland, had found Gorecki managing a luxury hotel. Evidently this job was his bonus for his past espionage activities. Later, Gorecki applied for employment with the American embassy in Warsaw. Was this chutzpah? Or was Polish intelligence testing Washington's institutional memory? In any event, the coordination process between the CIA and the embassy was such that Gorecki did not get the job.

As a counterintelligence coup in which successive roles were played at several CIA installations, I remember the Goleniewski case. My own meager contribution to the recruitment of this Polish intelligence agent began in Berlin in the late 1950s when our mail-intercept program turned up a letter signed by somebody calling himself "Heckenschuss" and written in an impenetrable form of double talk. Several of us had a go at it, but could make nothing of it. The name Heckenschuss itself looked as though it ought to be conveying something of deep significance. With its literal meaning of "stern shot," it seemed to imply either that the author was fighting a rearguard action or was covering his rear, reinsuring himself perhaps. Hoping that some day we would hear from Mr. Heckenschuss again, I had the letter safely filed away.

A few weeks later we had a visit from Howard Roman, an old OSS hand, gifted German linguist, and sensitive, people-oriented operations officer. Formerly chief of the Polish unit, Howard was then working out of headquarters as a senior case officer specializing in the running of exceptionally valuable in-place agents.

Howard said he was on the track of something that might admittedly be a provocation, but that on the surface appeared to be an effort by somebody to use the mails and newspaper advertisements as a channel for open-code intelligence communications. Had we perchance, he asked, run across any strange messages in our mail-intercept operations?

As a matter of fact, I replied, we had recently had one oddball letter from a certain "Heckenschuss." Howard became visibly excited at the news, and his joy when I handed him the letter made it clear that it was just what he was looking for. Being the professional that he was, he gave me no insight into what the letter meant.

Years later, Howard confided to me that the Heckenschuss letter was one of the opening gambits in a complicated game that finally led in 1960 to the defection of Michel Goleniewski, a Polish intelligence officer who had been recruited by the KGB to report on the activities of his own service. In his postdefection life he turned out to be something of a problem child for the CIA because he had come to believe he was the last of the Romanovs. However, the information he provided led in time to the exposure of important long-time KGB agents, including Sergeant Robert Lee Johnson, Heinz Felfe, Gordon Lonsdale, and George Blake.

I still grit my teeth when I think of George Blake. As many know now, he was one of the KGB's most successful penetrations of the British intelligence service (MI6). Unmasked, arrested, and imprisoned, he escaped and now resides in Moscow. Although his four-year tour in Berlin more or less coincided with my own, I don't remember ever meeting him, although colleagues of mine who also served in Berlin at that time say that our paths must have crossed at some party or other.

As the Berlin Base's chief of satellite operations, I was deeply involved during much of this period in an operation against the Polish Military Mission, a curious leftover from World War II in which Poland had functioned as an ally in the war against Germany and consequently qualified for participation in the Allied Control Authority. It had always been clear to us that penetrating the Polish Military Mission would be complicated because the installation was located in the British sector of Berlin. The British would certainly be contemplating, or perhaps already doing, something against this target, so temptingly close to hand, and if we were to barge in on our own account, we would run the grave risk of stumbling over and exposing their operation. Or vice versa.

The occasion for coordination arose late in the 1950s when the Poles appointed Wladyslaw Tykocinski, an experienced Foreign Service officer, to be head of the mission. Tykocinski was a fluent German speaker and a German-affairs specialist obviously overqualified for the position of minister in what had until then been an unimportant facility somewhat on the margin of affairs. The logical conclusion was that the Polish Military Mission had been upgraded and given a new assignment. Having become more important to Poland, it was now more important to us as well.

Our sources soon reported to us that the mission staff was diligently shopping for a residence for its new minister. Evidently none of the existing properties was prestigious enough, a fact that soon got us thinking in terms of an audio penetration.

The state of the art of audio surveillance in the late 1950s, although primitive when compared with what can be done today, was nevertheless far advanced from the days when the most that could be done along these lines was to clamp a microphone to the underside of a table and run the wire down the table leg, under the carpet and out to a listening post no further away, perhaps, than a basement storage room. For full advantage to be taken of the more sophisticated hardware that was available to us, however, we needed a degree of control of the surrounding area, and this dictated that the minister's new home be in the American sector. Our first task, therefore, was to use whatever influence we could exert over Berlin real estate agents and brokers to ensure that the only truly representational property shown to the Poles, immediately available and free of all encumbrances, would be a villa in Wilmersdorf or Charlottenburg.

Success crowned our efforts, and we then proceeded to bug the chosen place from top to bottom. Some of our miniaturized microphones were connected to wires that ran down through the footings of the basement, out through pipes that we had put in with pipe pushers, and down the street or across the block into the houses containing our banks of tape recorders. Other microphones were linked to equally tiny, battery-powered radio transmitters, all of which could be switched on or off by radio-controlled servomotors.

When Tykocinski moved in, the product that we started getting exceeded our fondest hopes. He began receiving visits from West German and West Berlin politicians who wanted to discuss long-term settlement of matters of interest to both Poland and Germany, including the question of the Oder–Neisse border line. Poles who came to East Berlin on business with the Polish embassy crossed over to the West for an evening of fine food and wine at the minister's residence. All of them talked, and Tykocinski himself talked the most, making a point of briefing his staff on developments at home and the substance of the cable traffic that was coming in from Warsaw. It was a gold mine.

Then, our microphones picked up a conversation we would rather not have heard—the voices of a counteraudio sweep team going about their business of looking for hidden microphones. At first we hoped this was a routine precautionary measure, and we were confident that our installations would resist discovery by all but the most determined search. To be on the safe side, we switched off those microphones that were broadcasting to us, using the hardwire mikes to tell us where the sweep team was working and what techniques it was using.

There were arguments between the team members, some of them complaining they were getting nowhere and urging that they pack it in. Unfortunately, the voice that we identified as that of the team leader kept saying in effect, "This is really a tough job, but we know these things are here."

In the end, slow and steady paid off; all our microphones were found and our operation went up in smoke. This was bad enough, but even worse was the realization that the sweep team had been brought in because of a reliable report that the minister's residence had been bugged. Somewhere on our side there had been a leak, and we conducted an extensive counterintelligence review, beginning with the principal agents who had handled our negotiations with the real estate brokers and ending with all British and American staffers who had been involved in any way with the operation. We found no evidence of indiscretion anywhere, and finally had to categorize this debacle as just one of those inexplicable things that happen now and again in the intelligence business.

And there matters rested until 1961 when George Blake was arrested and confessed that it was he who had closed our gold mine. Apparently he had overheard two MI6 staffers chatting about it in their Berlin headquarters and had picked up just enough of their conversation to enable him to tell his Soviet handler that an operation was in progress against an unidentified Polish installation in West Berlin. The Soviets passed the report on to the Poles, the Poles zeroed in on their newly acquired property, and that was that.

The intensity and persistence of effort shown by the Poles in the Berlin counteraudio sweep is a hallmark of successful defensive counterintelligence operations. Experience shows that when a valid counterintelligence lead appears, it must be pursued with a mixture of imagination, vigor, and perseverance. All of these traits, however, must be wrapped in a blanket of sound judgment. When they are not, bad things happen. That is particularly true when an intelligence service has to confront the daunting possibility that treason by one of its own staff officers has allowed a hostile service to penetrate it. Unfortunately, no major Western intelligence service has been immune from hostile penetration in the post-1945 period. For example the West German intelligence service (BND) had to acknowledge in 1961 that one of its senior officers, Heinz Felfe, was a Soviet agent. The CIA has suffered renegades like Philip Agee,

Edward L. Howard, William Kampiles, Larry Wu-tai Chin, and Aldrich H. Ames. Britain's MI6 has known numerous traitors, none worse than the KGB agent Harold "Kim" Philby.

A virtual cottage industry has developed in the world of intelligence literature about Philby. Not wishing to invite an argument on this matter, I will say only that Bill Harvey asserted more than once in my presence that he had identified Philby as a probable KGB penetration of MI6 as early as 1951. The British obviously took the American charges into consideration, conducted their own investigation, and cleared Philby in 1955.

One of Philby's defenders in those days was Nicholas Elliott, an MI6 officer who, in a long career, had gotten to know many of the movers and shakers of Africa. After I had retired, I was introduced to Elliott by a mutual London friend. Later, as we participated in foreign policy conferences in London, Washington, and Vienna, we found opportunities for quiet chats. On one such occasion, when I was his guest at White's Club in London, our talk turned casually to the topic of Philby. The tone of the conversation then took a subtle shift. In a matter of minutes, the jovial Elliott had become pensive and proceeded to make a couple of fascinating revelations of the kind that one listens to and remembers but feels under no compulsion to confirm.

Elliott admitted that he had been taken in by Philby and believed in his innocence until late 1962. In that year Dick White, head of MI6, showed Elliott a report that made an ironclad case against Philby. Angered by the realization that he had been duped, Elliott said he had persuaded White to let him go to Beirut where Philby was then working as a journalist, confront him, and try to get a confession.

As Elliott told the story, he and Philby had a dramatic encounter in Beirut in early January 1963, the culmination of which was that Philby admitted to being a KGB agent. Interrupting his narrative, Elliott then said to me, "Ted, your old boss Bill Harvey was right in his original suspicions. Philby was a traitor."

Regaining his composure, Elliott glossed over the details of what happened next in his handling of Philby's revelations. He did say, however, that he had obtained a signed confession from Philby in return for a guarantee of immunity from prosecution. The next step, apparently, was that Elliott agreed with Philby on a plan for future meetings, an arrangement that permitted Philby to stay in

Beirut while Elliott flew to London to report the state of play and work out with Dick White a plan for getting a full debriefing from Philby. While this was in progress, perseverance apparently took a holiday. For reasons that Elliott chose not to explain, he reported to White and then started off on a trip to Africa, he being then either the MI6 controller or acting controller for Africa. London, for its part, moved slowly to replace Elliott in the Philby loop, and Philby seized the opportunity to flee Lebanon for sanctuary in Moscow.

When I probed ever so gently into MI6's reasons for not acting more aggressively, either by detaining Philby through an appropriate legal mechanism or by remaining in constant contact with him, a laconic Elliott replied, "We misread his state of mind." I sensed that this was not the first time that Elliott had heard this question. From his subsequent remarks I inferred that he harbored mixed feelings on the subject of Kim Philby, deriving great satisfaction from having obtained Philby's confession, while simultaneously knowing that there were those who blamed him for giving Philby an opportunity to escape. This knowledge must have been a heavy burden to bear, but to his credit Elliott carried it with dignity.

A lack of continuity of effort in pursuit of a counterintelligence investigation was the single most important factor causing the CIA to plait its own crown of thorns, the Aldrich Ames case. This turncoat inflicted more damage upon America's worldwide clandestine intelligence interests than any other traitor since the passage of the National Security Act of 1947. Yet, after he made contact with the KGB in 1985 and American agents began to disappear in Russia for unexplained reasons, there was a lackluster search for the reason. When suspicion eventually fell on Ames, there was no dynamic investigation of him until shortly before his arrest on February 21, 1994. On the contrary, a story circulating among CIA retirees in mid-1994 indicated that at one point in the investigation, Washington asked the CIA people in Bogotá, Colombia, to check on Ames's wife because Ames, in an attempt to explain away his KGB-funded economic well-being, had let it be known that his Colombian-born spouse had inherited a sizeable estate upon her father's death. According to the story, Bogotá replied that it had no time for such trivia, and Washington meekly accepted the rebuff. All I can say is that if the story is true in any degree, heads should have rolled, although to date none have.

You can't talk about counterintelligence during the period that I'm concerned with here and not address the issue of James Jesus Angleton, chief of the counterintelligence staff. I had my first meeting with him in the mid-1950s when he was still shrouded in a lot of secrecy. I was a junior officer having just come back from my initial Berlin assignment, and before going back out, I went to give Angleton a letter that Bill Harvey asked me to deliver. What should have been at the most a ten-minute courtesy call ended up being a two-hour soliloquy. Doodling on his pad all the time, he explained the world communist conspiracy, including the whole Trust case. I went away from the meeting trying to figure out why the guy spent so much time talking to me. Later, I understood that if you struck some kind of responsive chord with him, he wanted to contribute to your education.

I really got to know him when I was the chief of the headquarters Czech unit, as we were running some sensitive operations that required his coordination. The problem was that a lot of these things were time sensitive. I could never just leave anything at Angleton's office for him to get around to eventually. I had to see him personally, and sometimes it was late in the afternoon or early evening before I could do so, but then he was always helpful and supportive.

The volume of traffic eventually got so heavy on many of these cases that I said to him, "Look, I don't think it's right for me to be coming in to see you all the time. It will raise questions of what kind of operations we are coordinating on. Can't somebody else on your staff work with me on some of these cases?" So he made arrangements for Jim Hunt, who was his deputy, to work with me on some of the cases. That simplified my life tremendously because Jim Hunt was a very decent kind of a guy who kept regular hours, and if he said, "Come down and see me at two o'clock," you could expect him to be there at two o'clock, something you could never be sure of with Angleton.

When I was station chief in Miami and would come up to Washington on coordination meetings, he was one of the people I would touch base with. I remember when I was back from Laos on a coordination trip, I went around to all the appropriate staffs. His words to me were, "Ted, I never worry about counterintelligence in those places where you are the station chief."

It was on one of my periodic visits to Washington from

Vientiane, at one of Angleton's infamous two-martini luncheons, that I regaled him with a couple of modern-day counterintelligence war stories. The first involved the Polish delegation to the International Control Commission (ICC). I said I had been surprised at the ease with which the Polish speakers at the Vientiane Station, myself included, could develop and maintain contacts with the members of the Polish representation. These included weekly volleyball games at different places, including my residence, postgame drinks, and a steady stream of socializing at luncheons and diplomatic receptions. This honeymoon lasted about fourteen months, during which we targeted two Poles for possible recruitment.

We were moving forward on these twin opportunities when the Iron Curtain came crashing dramatically down. The Poles had been scheduled to play volleyball at my residence and then have a buffet lunch with ice-cold beer and a free flow of conversation. All of the Americans who were scheduled to play—from the U.S. Agency for International Development (USAID), the attachés' offices, the embassy, and the CIA—showed up. But no Poles showed up. More importantly, they made no attempt to send any word of apology by telephone, messenger, or note.

Looking back on the incident over the next two days, we were able to draw a correlation between the arrival from Warsaw via Bangkok of a diplomatic pouch for the Polish ICC delegation and their abrupt breaking of social relations with the American embassy. Our postmortem conclusion was that the Polish delegation had asked Warsaw for name traces on the three or four American Polish speakers they had met in Laos, that the pouch had contained a reply identifying one or more of us as confirmed or suspected intelligence officers or operatives, and that the Poles had then decided to reduce their exposure to the "forces of imperialism."

In the weeks that followed, one of the American military attachés asked a Polish contact why the volleyball games had come to an end. "The games with the Americans," the Pole replied, "had turned out not to be what they seemed, so it was better to get our exercise at matches within our own compound."

After that the Poles limited their social exposure to American Polish speakers in Vientiane to cool exchanges of greetings at diplomatic receptions and invitations to attend Polish National Day celebrations.

I used this story as a launching pad from which to chide Angleton good-naturedly about the slowness with which headquarters was answering our requests for name traces on Poles, Czechs, Chinese, and Russians. Angleton deftly deflected this administrative jab, saying in essence that such detail was beneath his notice.

On the Russian front, I recall telling Angleton that while we had the Soviet embassy covered with telephone taps, surveillance, and low-level informants, there appeared to be limited prospects for opening a solid recruitment dialog with any of the Russians in Vientiane, their being a primitive bunch.

To underscore my point, I told Angleton about our encounter with the Soviet military attaché Lieutenant Colonel Vassily A. Federov. At a New Year's Eve black-tie ball in Vientiane hosted by Prime Minister Souvanna Phouma, the Lao traditional dance, the *lamvong,* was being performed. In the course of the dance's evolutions, my wife Hazel became separated from her original dancing partner and found herself facing Federov. The latter, always a hard drinker and now having coordination problems between feet and hands, told Hazel in a stage whisper, "I know who you are."

Looking at his dress uniform, Hazel replied, "You are the Russian military attaché."

"No," said Federov, "I know who you and your husband really are." With that, the lines moved forward and Hazel was able to walk off the dance floor with her original dancing partner, the Australian military attaché Lieutenant Colonel Robin Hone.

As we regrouped, Hazel pulled me aside to tell me of her encounter with Federov. Seeing no profit to be gained from staying in touch with Federov, I told Hazel to ignore him. If, however, Federov insisted on playing his little game, she should tell him, "We know who you really are."

Sure enough, later in the evening as people moved around the dance floor, Federov said to Hazel, "I really know who you are."

She responded, "We know who you really are."

After hearing about Hazel's second encounter with Federov, I decided to intervene indirectly. Arrangements were made for General Oudone Sananikone and another Lao military officer to engage Federov in a chat. As the Lao were talking with him, I walked up to speak to the Lao, totally ignoring Federov. After a lapse of about a minute, Oudone Sananikone asked if I knew Federov. I replied that we had not met formally, and we were introduced, Federov as the Russian military attaché and I as the first secretary of the American embassy. Looking Federov in the eye, I said it was a pleasure to meet him for I had recently finished reading his most interesting dossier and was hoping we could have a talk. Federov paled noticeably, became flustered, and quickly excused himself to rejoin his Russian colleagues.

My two Lao friends, who knew of my CIA role, asked me what the byplay was all about. I told them that Ambassador William Sullivan had a good relationship with the Soviet ambassador, Boris Kirnassovsky, and that I therefore saw no need to open a channel to Federov. However, the latter seemed to want me to know he was a man of importance in the Soviet embassy. As far as I could see, his interests were in American airfields in northeastern Thailand and the level of American assistance to the Force Armée Royale (FAR). These were topics best left to others to deal with, so I had let Federov know that my interest in him did not include having an exchange of casual views. My message to him had been that I was interested in him only as a spy who would work on the CIA's behalf. That got his attention and he disengaged, which was precisely what I wanted.

Angleton agreed with me that Federov had been acting like a loose cannon. While always very supportive on all my counterintelligence cases involving Czechs, Poles, Hungarians, Vietnamese, and Cubans, on Soviet cases he was biased. In his view, it was impossible to run a Soviet case because no Soviet case is clean. I never agreed with him on this, which made for some lively—and, on occasion, heated—exchanges. Needless to say, one never came away from such a session feeling that any dent had been made in Angleton's basic theory on Soviet operations.

In retrospect, Angleton was clearly wrong "big time" on the Golitsyn case. Anatoly Golitsyn was a KGB officer who defected in 1961. The information he provided convinced Angleton of a high-level penetration of the CIA. This launched a destructive hunt within the CIA. No penetration was found, but the lives and careers of a number of CIA officers were ruined.

There is no sound rationale to justify Angleton's sending case officers' personnel files out to Golitsyn to help him identify the mole. In September 1993 I discussed that point with Ray Rocca, Angleton's longtime deputy. Rocca subsequently told me at a chance encounter that giving the personnel files to Golitsyn was not Angleton's finest hour. Rocca also said he had to take some of the blame for that breach of procedure.

The Sino-Soviet split was another situation that Angleton misread. He thought it was a hoax. On the contrary, events proved it was a real split between the communist giants.

When Colby told Angleton he should retire and a new team was brought in to modernize the counterintelligence staff, a number of promising counterintelligence leads that should have been pursued earlier came to light. Once these cases obtained the attention that they warranted, the gains to Western security were significant. One such case was the recruitment by Soviet military intelligence (GRU) of Brigadier Jean-Louis Jeanmaire, a Swiss general staff officer who had been the head of Switzerland's air defenses. When the Swiss acted on this lead, they made a case, and Jeanmaire was prosecuted and sent to prison. There were similar cases in Indonesia and France.

This is not to say that everything Angleton did was bad. Actually, he did a lot of good. He developed excellent liaison links that produced top-notch intelligence on the Soviet Union in a cost-effective manner for years. As an example, he obtained the text of Khrushchev's speech to the Twentieth Congress of the Communist Party of the Soviet Union (CPSU) and was one of the first to see that it was properly appreciated and exploited. Angleton favored a selective approach to surfacing the speech so that it would have the maximum negative impact on communist parties around the world. Dr. Ray Cline, then the deputy director for intelligence, advocated publishing the document in toto in order to reveal the true state of turmoil within the CPSU to the world at large. The Cline view eventually carried the day. Allen Dulles took the speech to the Department of State, and shortly thereafter the full text appeared in the *New York Times*. The rest is history.

When all is said and done, the bottom line is that Angleton was allowed to stay in the counterintelligence job too long. The burden of that error in judgment has to be shared by a string of directors of central intelligence, starting with Dulles and running through John McCone, William Raborn, Richard Helms, and James Schlesinger. A rational explanation of why these men, each in his own way, contributed to this situation has never been offered to me by anyone in a position to know the truth.

3

KNAVISH TRICKS

COVERT action has always held a special fascination for me. I attribute this to the fact that, according to the oral history relayed to me by my grandmother, one of my paternal ancestors was our country's first practitioner of the craft. His name was Silas Deane, and in 1776 the Committee on Secret Correspondence sent him to France under commercial cover to try to organize a clandestine supply of weapons for the Continental Army.

While Deane was hatching his schemes, the British were learning to sing their new national anthem, "God Save the King." Its second verse calls upon the Almighty to "Scatter [the king's] enemies and make them fall, confound their politics, frustrate their knavish tricks."

"Knavish tricks" equates pretty well with covert action. Politics can, perhaps best, be confounded covertly; witness the way secretaries of state or foreign ministers avoid saying clearly what their intentions are. Enemies can be scattered covertly; although this is not easy to do, it's worth trying, and many generals have tried. You can save yourself a lot of casualties if only you can get the other fellow to throw down his weapons and run away.

There is nothing new or uniquely American about covert action. In successor states and former satellites of the Soviet Union, these activities are called active measures. And other societies appear to have no distinctive label for them at all, possibly because influencing an adversary's behavior and keeping one's plans and projects to oneself are inseparable aspects of statecraft and generalship.

For this reason, covert action is not a weapon that intelligence services can wield at will. Spymasters may be called upon to help kings and field marshals with their intrigues, but the latter call the shots. And a corollary to this is that no covert-action operation mounted by an intelligence service has much chance of success if it is not solidly supported at the highest levels of government and coordinated with the leadership's other means of persuasion— diplomatic, military, and propagandistic. As an example, take the poisoned saltshaker case that I wrote about in chapter 2. It seems to have been undertaken by Czech intelligence more as a lark than as an underpinning of state policy, and when it failed, it caused the Czech government some embarrassment.

Turning to examples close to home, compare two CIA-sponsored invasions, first of Guatemala and then of Cuba at the Bay of Pigs. The important things to remember in this context are that (1) the U.S. government heartily endorsed and supported the Guatemalan operation, whereas the Cuban operation enjoyed only a grudging acquiescence by the administration that inherited it; (2) the American press was friendly in the first instance and hostile in the second; and (3) we succeeded in the first and failed in the second.

Covert action operations can be as deceptively peaceful as a letter-writing campaign or as flagrantly violent as a guerrilla uprising. In every case, though, the instigating government must make at least a token effort to hide its hand. The flood of letters inveighing against the neutron bomb during the Carter administration and apparently sent by simple, peace-loving citizens would have been ineffective had they been signed by the KGB's Yuri V. Andropov. Here the need for tight cover by the Soviet sponsors of the letter campaign was imperative.

For simplicity's sake, we classify covert-action tactics under the general headings of psychological warfare, political action, and paramilitary, but in doing this we risk muddling strategic thought because the lines between these pigeonholes are not always sharply defined. For example, influencing public opinion clearly falls under the heading of psychological warfare, but how about influencing a government? Changing a government through elections is undeniably a form of political action, but what about changing it through terrorism? And how clearly drawn is the line between terrorism and guerrilla warfare? In what follows, I will use these three "P" words many times, but the reader should be warned that not all of my examples will fall neatly into one category or the other.

The acknowledged masters of the art of exercising hidden influence over a target country's public opinion were the Soviets. While we have won victories in this theater of war, nothing we have done has matched Soviet strategic gains achieved through the use of covert action. The reasons for this should be obvious, the principal one being that opinion-forming media and pressure groups in the West are open and vulnerable to anyone with the time and money to devote to them, whereas in totalitarian countries this is most emphatically not the case. On balance, on this battlefield the United States and its allies have been, and probably will remain, on the defensive. We must therefore be fully aware of what has been done, and what still can be done, against us.

The Soviet agent for exploiting Western media was the KGB. Instead of trying to recruit owners, publishers, or editors as might be expected, they found that they could get their line into print more easily by working directly with reporters. In spotting and screening their candidates, they gave priority to writers who were known experts on political, military, or economic matters.

Whittaker Chambers, who as a former Soviet agent was in a good position to know, wrote in 1952 that there was probably no important magazine or newspaper in the United States that was not communist-penetrated to some degree.[1] And when we consider how few Soviet propaganda assets have been exposed in the intervening forty-odd years, we can appreciate what a safe occupation this is. If an asset keeps his head down and if his case officer makes no mistakes, he is virtually assured of being allowed to live out his days in freedom.

In Berlin, while I was head of satellite operations, someone in the base introduced Jim Kelly to a certain third world freelance reporter. After their first couple of meetings, Kelly and I discussed where we should take things. Having a byline in a number of publications, the man showed promise as a good covert-action asset if we could recruit him. And this is how we began.

It quickly became evident that everything was moving in the right direction. The reporter proved to be an aggressive, imaginative fellow, so we steered him in the direction of satellite officials. Soon he was coming back from his talks with Poles, Czechs, and

Hungarians with interesting intelligence, information that in some cases was so amazing that we had to ask ourselves why it was being shared with him.

As time moved on he started dealing with Russians and ended up in touch with Yevgeniy Petrovich Pitovranov, head of the KGB in East Berlin. So, a case that had started out with the acquisition of a possible covert-action agent had developed into an intelligence-collection mechanism and now was taking on overtones of counter-intelligence.

We began to run all of the necessary checks to determine if our agent was telling us the truth. We were told in advance the route that he intended to take from West Berlin to East Berlin, and we had him surveilled. When he said he was going into the Soviet embassy, we saw him going in. On a couple of occasions we even had people inside the Soviet installation who saw him arrive and be ushered from the reception room to some private office. Everything that we could possibly do to authenticate the man was done.

It became a terribly complicated case. Finally, Kelly and I took him down to West Germany and spent a week debriefing him in isolated quarters and basically came to the conclusion that what he was reporting was correct. The case was still in full bloom when I left Berlin.

An innocent reporter or editor can sometimes be duped into writing a sensational story if he can be shown supporting documentation. To forge whatever might be required in this line, there was a special unit of the KGB (Service A of the First Chief Directorate) standing by. To cite only one example of their work, the Bombay daily newspaper *Free Press Journal* in February 1968 received a forged letter purportedly written to the editor by Gordon Goldstein of the U.S. Office of Naval Research offering assurances that the United States meant no harm by stockpiling bacteriological warfare weapons in Vietnam and Thailand. The letter, when published by the *Free Press Journal* and replayed by the *Times* of London, seemed to provide proof that the United States was admitting to having done something that in fact it had not done at all. With this evidence in hand, Radio Moscow was then able to beam broadcasts to Asia charging the United States with having caused an epidemic of contagious diseases in Vietnam.

The CIA, of course, has run its own psychological-warfare

operations. Perhaps the oldest of these, and certainly the best known, are Radio Free Europe and Radio Liberty, which began broadcasting news and propaganda into Eastern Europe in 1950 and 1951, respectively. Their thin cover of private financing and operation broke down before long, but they continue to exist because they have been so well received by their audiences.

In Laos we had the Union of Lao Races (ULR) radio station, which was started in July 1964 by Vint Lawrence as a two-hundred-fifty-watt station broadcasting out of the royal capital of Luang Prabang. By 1965 it was blessed with a one-kilowatt station operating out of Long Tieng. During my stewardship of the Vientiane station, we were able to increase the power of the transmitter at Long Tieng to five kilowatts. This permitted us to broadcast 8 hours a day for a schedule of 248 hours per month. In linguistic terms we found our best audience response was obtained when we broadcast 108 hours per month in Lao, 93 hours in Hmong, and 47 hours in Lao Tung. We continually adjusted the thematic content of the radio's programming so as to encourage an ever-expanding audience. In time we learned that our most effective themes were the king as father of the Lao nation and the unity of Laos. The programming that garnered our largest audiences included local and international news, medical advice, child guidance, music, and views of life in the Pathet Lao (PL)–held regions of the country. Another technique by which we sought to enlarge our listenership was to get regional leaders like General Vang Pao to give small villages a transistor radio tuned only to ULR's frequencies.

Our testing of audience response included participation in lotteries and requests that listeners send written comments to a postal address. Surprisingly, we found on average that the ULR radio received about one thousand letters per month. The debriefing of refugees from PL areas revealed that people in enemy-held areas listened to the ULR radio for objective news and information. Captured PL soldiers stated that they were forbidden to listen to ULR but did so whenever they could because the ULR broadcasts were simply better than what they could get from any other station.

The radio at its peak had ninety-nine indigenous employees and one case officer devoted to it on a full-time basis. Its operations built indigenous troop morale, enhanced Vang Pao's stature as a Lao political figure, and contributed to the task of nation building.

Newspapers have been another favorite medium for the CIA, just as they have been for the KGB. In the early days we tended to go whole hog, acquiring entire newspapers by funding them at the top, but gradually we learned—just as the KGB did—that it was usually more effective to have a relationship with an individual and to get our messages into print through the stringer, the staff writer, or the editor. An apparent violation of this rule was our funding of the Chilean newspaper *El Mercurio,* but our purpose in that case was to keep the paper alive as a symbol of resistance as well as a vehicle through which to surface anti-Allende material.

When I was first in Berlin, the base had a very good working relationship with a local newspaper. Later, when I was chief of the East Asia Division, we had a wide choice of newspapers to work with, from the most prominent to the most obscure, low-circulation weeklies in the various national capitals. Our selection would depend on whether we just wanted to get our message to a given newspaper's readership or whether we hoped to reach a wider audience. In the latter case, the important consideration would be the newspaper's credibility because we would take clips of our selected outlet's story and mail them to other newspapers, any or all of which might then be willing to replay the story once they had a source to which they could attribute it.

As one very good attributable source, Berlin Base had its own news service that mailed news stories, commentary, jokes, and cartoons to newspapers in free-world countries other than the United States. The CIA had created this proprietary as a mechanism for calling the world's attention to the injustices and human tragedies created by the Berlin Wall, but by the time I had returned to Berlin as chief of base, it was also being used to drum up support for U.S. intervention in Vietnam. Recipients were not charged for the material. They were asked only to send clips of anything they used. We would then bundle this up and ship it to headquarters for the covert-action staff to replay in other outlets.

To get its messages out to book-reading audiences, the CIA has inspired the writing of some books and assisted in the distribution of others. When in 1954 the Yugoslav communist cadre Milovan Djilas broke with the party and subsequently wrote a book in which he denounced the corruption and privilege of Yugoslavia's new rulers, the CIA saw to it that his effort reached the widest possible readership.

We have also written some books ourselves. The Russian agent Oleg Penkovsky used to speak at length in his debriefing sessions about the injustices of the Soviet system and his wish that the Russian people might some day enjoy the many freedoms taken for granted in the West. When he was arrested and executed in 1963, there was no longer any reason to keep his views from the public. The CIA therefore arranged for a careful culling and editing of his operational file and had the book published under the title *The Penkovsky Papers.*

In 1959, when I assumed responsibility for Czech matters at headquarters, I had my first opportunity to put together a major psychological-warfare operation of my own. As it was clear to me that intellectuals in Czechoslovakia were feeling restless under the restrictions of the communist regime and that this feeling was likely to intensify, I asked myself whether there was a rallying point to which they could turn. Finding none, I then considered whether I could create one.

The model I chose to follow was a magazine that one of the East European units had been running for a number of years as a covert-action asset. From its editorial offices in the West and under the able leadership of its founder and editor-in-chief, it carried literary criticism and political commentary to intellectuals inside the target country, much of it written by people living there and bylined, with their permission, in true name. It was typical, I thought, that they would be willing to take this risk. In case of any confrontation by authorities, they were evidently prepared to say that yes, they had written the pieces in question, but no, they had never intended for the magazine to publish them; somebody must have smuggled them out without their knowledge. It was an article of faith among these writers that national literature had to continue to flower and be recognized in the West if they were to survive as a people.

I brainstormed the idea with Milan Halla, a native-born Czech who was our mainstay on matters having to do with Czechoslovak history and culture. Milan liked it. He'd been thinking along much the same lines already, he said, but hadn't had any support. Previous branch chiefs, he said, were old OSO types for the most part and had wanted to concentrate on the collection of intelligence. They had shown little interest in covert action.

I felt there was no reason why we couldn't have some of both. With any luck our magazine would attract high-level dissidents, people who in time might feel free to talk about matters of intelligence interest.

Milan said that he had good contacts in the Czech émigré community and that he thought he could find someone to edit and publish a magazine. "Please do so," I said.

In a gratifyingly short period of time, Milan produced two candidates—an exiled Czech writer and a young Slovak who had lived in Austria and was now working on a Ph.D. in the United States. I agreed to open an office for them in Paris and to cover the production costs of a magazine.

We distributed their product in three ways. First, we had a list of Czech intellectuals who were already receiving mail from abroad and who we thought would be sympathetic to this kind of stimulus. We would mail the magazine directly to them in the hope that some of those copies would get through. To our surprise, many of them did.

Second, we watched for Czech delegations to conference centers like Paris and Vienna and arranged for copies of the magazine to be delivered to their rooms or left for them with the concierges of their hotels. Although we couldn't be sure that the recipients would take the magazines home with them, it seemed likely that some at least would be curious enough to read an article or two.

Third, we gave the magazine to Westerners who traveled legally to Czechoslovakia and who were willing to take one or two copies with them as gifts for their friends.

It eventually became obvious that the operation was having the desired effect. Czech intellectuals arranged with trusted friends to smuggle their articles to Paris, and the magazine was able to trumpet the fact that its material was coming from writers behind the Iron Curtain.

By the mid-1960s the magazine was even receiving and publishing classified documents from the Prague headquarters of the Czechoslovak Communist Party. This upset Antonín Novotný, first secretary of the party, and he ordered the StB to do something about it. In August 1966 the StB arrested the writer Jan Beneš and the film director Karel Zaměčník on charges of contributing to the magazine. In the ensuing trial Beneš got five years and Zaměčník was acquitted. The sentencing court also gave our editor fourteen years in absentia.

As I mentioned earlier, there is a gray area where psychological warfare and political action overlap. The covert action resulting in the 1937 purge of the Soviet Red Army is a case in point. According to one version of the story, documents seeming to prove treasonable plotting by Marshal Mikhail N. Tukhachevsky, vice commissar of defense and commander-in-chief of the Red Army, were forged by the German *Sicherheitsdienst* and sold to a Berlin agent of the KGB's forerunner, the NKVD. This agent then passed the documents to Moscow as genuine. If this version is the true one, the operation has elements of psychological warfare and political action, its probable targets being both the morale of the Red Army and the composition of the Soviet government. In an odd way it also resembled a paramilitary operation, given the casualties it inflicted on the Red Army's leadership: 3 of its 5 marshals, 14 of its 16 Army commanders, 60 of its 67 corps commanders, and 136 of its 199 division commanders were purged.

Another version of this story, though, holds that the incriminating documents were forged by the NKVD itself and delivered to a double agent whom they had planted in a Paris-based anticommunist exile group. The double agent then turned them over to the *Sicherheitsdienst,* which in turn planted them on President Eduard Beneš of Czechoslovakia. Beneš, having just signed a mutual-aid treaty with the Soviet Union, passed them along to Stalin. The latter had many reasons to wish to be rid of Tukhachevsky and acted accordingly. If this version is the true one, the operation was political action and nothing else. The rule known as *Occam's razor* says that a simple explanation is to be preferred to a complicated one, but this does not apply to covert action, where complications are essential if tracks are to be concealed and cover preserved. If forced to choose between the two versions of the Tukhachevsky forgeries, I would take the second one, partly because it is so complicated and partly because forgery had been a standard Soviet tactic since the first days of the Bolshevik revolution and they were so good at it. In any case, it is clear that both Hitler and Stalin had reasons to want to be rid of Tukhachevsky and that, in one way or another, both the German and the Soviet services had their fingers in this pie—as such, it was a classic example of forgery in covert action.

I tried my own hand at this technique when I was chief of the Czech unit. After looking at the entire leadership of the Czech government and party, Warren Frank and I chose as our target a senior communist official. He attracted our attention for two reasons. First, he was a hard-liner and, from our point of view, could easily be sacrificed. Second, there was vulnerability in his past: He had been arrested and imprisoned in 1941 by the Gestapo.

Warren therefore oversaw the fabrication of two documents: One was a carbon of a letter from the Gestapo chief in Brno to the *Reichssicherheitshauptamt* in Berlin, reporting that our man had volunteered to serve the Gestapo as an informer in the Slovakian underground and recommending that he be released from prison; the other was a reply to the effect that the *Reichssicherheitshauptamt* had no objection. The two letters were put in final form by the Technical Services Division (TSD) of the CIA, using papers and inks of the period and employing all the cachets, formats, and bureaucratic language with which we had all become familiar from prolonged study at the Berlin Documents Center.

These forged documents were then packaged together with an accompanying letter addressed to the editor of the Vienna newspaper *Wochenpresse* and purportedly smuggled out of Czechoslovakia by a legal traveler. Its author presented himself as a Slovakian patriot who had discovered the file when he entered Brno after World War II with the Soviet Army. This, he wrote, was his first opportunity to unmask the rascal, and he was taking advantage of it.

The editor bit hard on the bait and reproduced both of our creations in his issue of May 5, 1962. I don't believe that this operation was the sole cause of our victim's eventual fall from grace, but I do think it was one more dab of grease that helped set the skids for him.

The Czechs, meanwhile, had been busy planting agents throughout the West German political structure. Czech defector Ladislav Bittman has said that all German political parties were penetrated at both the federal and state levels, and I see no reason to disbelieve him. These agents served mostly as collectors of confidential information, but in some cases they were used to exert direct personal influence on policy makers.

Specialists in this latter type of persuasion are called agents of influence. Although the KGB and its satellite services are all known to have employed them, few confirmed examples have come to light. If, as it would seem, agents of influence lead an even safer life than propagandists, the main reason for this could be that they are rarely obliged to leave a paper trail. A word in the ear of the right person and perhaps nothing more than a nod, a wink, or a shrug at a crucial moment can suffice to get their job done.

For reaching target audiences larger than are available to the agent of influence, there are the mass organizations. One type of such organizations that we liked to work with was the student movement. Students can be energetic and noisy, qualities that are useful in the more boisterous forms of covert action. As spokesmen for the younger generation, they can often command more media attention than perhaps they deserve, something the KGB has known for a long time.

How the KGB and its satellite services manipulated students in our own country can be illustrated by pointing to Students for a Democratic Society (SDS). Leftist from its inception in 1962 but perhaps not yet Soviet-controlled, it began its move in that direction in 1965 when it removed from its constitution a clause barring members of the Communist Party. The party then promptly began sending its youthful militants into the organization.[2] The next step was taken in 1969 when the more violence-prone SDS members succeeded in fashioning an urban guerrilla organization, the Weathermen, later the Weather Underground. In preparation, Cuban and North Vietnamese surrogates of the KGB had been recruiting American students to go to Cuba as part of the Venceremos Brigade, ostensibly to help with the sugar harvest but actually to receive training in advanced guerrilla-warfare techniques.

The Soviets wrote the book on the student movement in 1946, however, when they created the International Union of Students (IUS). Working from its headquarters in Prague, the IUS had immediately set to work infiltrating and controlling student bodies in other countries. Reacting slowly to this threat, the CIA waited until the 1950s before offering financial support to the IUS's American counterpart, the anticommunist National Student Association (NSA), and the umbrella organization to which it belonged, the International Student Conference. Though belated, this subvention of about $200,000 per year was successful in blocking IUS penetration of the free world's student organizations.

This covert action began unraveling in February 1967 when

Ramparts magazine published a series of three articles revealing the connection between the NSA and the CIA. Had this happened only a few years earlier, the impact might not have been so severe. But the agency's image had been so tarnished by a massive propaganda bombardment beginning right after the failed Bay of Pigs landing that the public was ready to believe that the CIA was using the NSA to infiltrate the student anti–Vietnam War movement.

The resulting heat was so intense that the CIA passed a self-denying ordinance prohibiting the recruitment of students of any nationality for any purpose whatever, an absurdity that was carried to its logical conclusion when headquarters ordered the termination of a productive agent who had thoughtlessly enrolled in a night course.

Before this, I had had my own experience with a student organization, a bunch of young anti-Castro activists working out of Miami during my tenure there as chief of station. They did good work for us in getting their views of Cuba aired at international student conferences. However, being volatile as students tend to be, they were hard to control. Finally, on their own initiative and without telling any of us what they were up to, they took a small boat into Havana harbor and sprayed machine-gun fire over the Malecón, the once elegant waterfront boulevard. This was too much, and we parted company.

4

REGIME CHANGE

THE CIA had toppled foreign regimes before: in Iran in 1953, in Guatemala in 1954. And it had tried again and failed disastrously in Cuba in 1961. Now, in 1962, Bill Harvey was telling me that the agency was being ordered to try once more. But with this difference: Whereas in the three previous cases our interventions had been motivated by considerations of cold war advantage, the driving force now was personal vendetta. President Kennedy and his brother Robert, smarting from the humiliation of their failure at the Bay of Pigs, wanted to remove Fidel Castro from the picture, no matter whether by palace revolt, military coup, popular uprising, or assassination.

An interdepartmental group—the Special Group (Augmented)—comprising Ed Lansdale,[1] Richard Helms, Bobby Kennedy, and others was to supervise the effort, with the actual work to be performed by the CIA's Deputy Directorate for Plans. Helms, the new deputy director of plans (DDP), had delegated the task to Harvey's Task Force W, and much of Task Force W's responsibility would fall to the Miami Station, known cryptically as JMWAVE. It was years before I learned that the name "Task Force W" was an invention of Harvey's. The "W" stood for William Walker, an American adventurer who was executed by firing squad in Honduras in October 1860 after an attempt to conquer Central America. I still wonder whether a premonition of what was in store for him led Harvey to use this ill-omened letter.

Harvey wanted me to go to Miami as JMWAVE's chief of operations, with every prospect of succeeding to the top job in what was to become the CIA's largest station. "Ted, this is a chance to grab the brass ring," he told me. "Take it."

Of course, I wanted the brass ring. Harvey had been prodding me toward senior management ever since 1954 when I had started with him in Berlin as a junior case officer. I had balked because I really liked the warmth of the one-on-one human relationships that came with handling agents on the street, and the increasingly responsible supervisory jobs into which he had been placing me had begun to cost me some cherished friendships with my colleagues.

However, my professional development was not Harvey's only interest. He also saw himself as having obligations to the agency. "Ted," he had told me bluntly in Berlin, "at this point in the agency's development, if a man is a case officer who can manage, you exploit him to the utmost for his management skills." And this was still his credo in the spring of 1962. Whatever reservations I had (and by now they were few), I swallowed and agreed to go.

My reception at the Miami Station was correct but cold. Station Chief Al Cox was on leave, according to what his secretary told me. It was agreed then that his deputy, Bob Moore, would handle the day-to-day traffic of the station, while I, in the capacity of chief of operations, would organize and prepare for the future. What followed were four and a half intensive days of breakfast, lunch, and dinner meetings, lots of quick chats over a *café cubano* with contract agents and Cuban personalities, and conferences with station officers, particularly Dave Morales and Tony Sforza, who were fluent Spanish speakers and had seen service in Havana. Morales, who was chief of paramilitary, was frequently accompanied by his assistant, Tom Clines. I learned to look forward to my contacts with these three outgoing street men.

As far as I know, none of the field stations in 1962 was even taking a defensive posture against the narcotics traffic. The issue was never touched on in the various briefings I received at headquarters, and I did not learn from our liaison with the FBI, Coast Guard, and Border Patrol that these agencies were concerned about the increase in the smuggling of drugs into the United States from the Caribbean and Mexico until after I entered on my new duties.

Tony Sforza and Dave Morales then alerted me to the threat posed by the Mafiosi, who had been pushed out of Cuba and needed a new base of operations for their narcotics business.

Especially worrisome, I was told, was the possibility that the notorious Santos Trafficante would settle in Miami.

I had never met Trafficante or had communications with him in any manner, shape, or form; nor to the best of my knowledge had anyone else in the station. I intended to keep it that way. If it had turned out that we had to share the southeast coast of Florida with Trafficante, I would have been prepared to issue the strictest orders against any kind of contact, direct or indirect, with him. As things turned out, I didn't have to. The Cuban refugee community picked up vibrations indicating that Trafficante had set himself up in the area of Tampa, a part of Florida where we set foot only on the few occasions when we had to berth a ship there. In due course, law enforcement officials confirmed the welcome news of Trafficante's relocation to Tampa.

However, the same sources told us that crime bosses had made Miami an open city. It was the exclusive territory of none of them, and any of them could engage there freely in fun and games in the sand without fear of being hit by rivals concerned with turf, influence, or revenge.

Although the CIA was not yet ready to become part of the solution, I at least wanted to be sure the Miami Station would not be part of the problem. Our paramilitary teams and boat operators were in and out of Cuban waters all the time and had the opportunity to meet with Cuban fishing trawlers at places like the island of Cay Sal. I did not want the teams and operators moving illicit drugs out of Cuba.

In order to protect against that, we set up an elaborate system of security checks. Our primary emphasis was on equipment and body searches of teams returning from missions to Cuba. Each team would be met on its return by its case officer and in most cases by a security officer as well. The men would be taken to a safe house and debriefed, and all items in their possession would be inventoried. This gave us a chance to search their clothing and equipment, all of which was then retained under our control. With the inventory completed, the men were given their civilian clothes, which had been in our custody during the mission.

We also performed spot checks of training sites, safe houses, and boats to make certain that no criminal activity was going on. Additionally, routine polygraph examinations of all personnel would touch on the question of drug trafficking or use.

We knew the nightspots in Miami's Little Havana where our people hung out, and we seeded them with informants. We could be confident the system was working because from time to time it produced strong evidence that some of our men were lax on operational security. This made the lack of any information about drug trafficking all the more gratifying.

With the wisdom gained from experience, I know now that there were numerous ways in which a determined trafficker could circumvent our defensive measures, but at least they put pressure on our people to stay clean. It may be as much a tribute to the quality of our personnel as to the efficacy of our security system that, in my stewardship of the Miami Station in the period 1962–1965, not one staffer or operational asset was found by us or by law enforcement agencies to be involved in narcotics trafficking.

Dave Morales was the first person to educate me in the Cuban use of "war names," by which resistance fighters were frequently better known than by their family names. Years earlier in Havana, Cuban agents had dubbed him "El Gordo," or "The Fat One." Now in mid-1962, Morales let me know that the Cubans working with the Miami Station had given me the war name "Tequila." Morales explained that the Cubans equated my blondness and what they saw as my gentlemanly demeanor and no-nonsense style of business with the characteristics of tequila—something pale that goes down easily but is not to be fooled with because it packs a wallop.

From the intelligence we were receiving from our agents inside Cuba and the refugees being interviewed in Opa Locka, I could soon see that the cherished options for regime change were all non-starters. The old-line Soviet-controlled Cuban Communist Party was not going to make any attempt to replace Fidel. The military had disgruntled elements in it but not enough of them to mount a coup. Nor did the prospects of a popular uprising look much better, but this was the will o' the wisp in Bobby Kennedy's strategic thinking. In his mind, economic sabotage was the key. What he wanted were "boom-and-bang" paramilitary operations mounted by the Miami Station against major industrial targets like the Matahambre copper mine. It sounded to us in Miami as though Bobby wanted sabotage operations to be a substitute for strategic bomber sorties, targeting and destroying an enemy's industrial base. Unfortunately, Bobby's mind was focused on fighting a World War II–type battle against Cuba with unconventional warfare techniques. Where he got this idea or how he developed it into a strategy, no one could ever explain to me. In any event, it was the wrong approach.

The simple fact is that the destruction of Matahambre, Casilda, and similar facilities would not have brought the Cuban economy to its knees. Our paramilitary operations, therefore, should have had the hallmarks of a guerrilla-warfare campaign that would have taken the war to the central government by pinprick attacks, hopefully countrywide, causing government forces to be spread thinly in responding to multiple incidents. With a series of minor successes, we would have tried to give the Cuban body politic the sense that resistance was widespread or even islandwide, motivating islanders to participate more in the resistance. Acts of arson in the sugar fields could have increased. The world at large would probably have concluded that there was more to the resistance in Cuba beyond a handful of *gusanos* (a Spanish word meaning "worms," Castro's favorite epithet for opponents of his revolution). Would that have slowed the pace of Castro's consolidation of power? Who knows? It certainly would have followed Castro's own example, which proved that projecting an illusion of strength in the early days of a guerrilla struggle is as important as having a real armed capability to fight the central government.

Because Bobby Kennedy and Task Force W were never able to read from the same sheet of music on the boom-and-bang issue, constant tension and pressure to do more came from the Bobby part of the orchestra. The "more" motif forced us to stretch our resources in an attempt to be responsive. We were also being asked to provide such a level of detail on each sabotage operation that something as simple as blowing up an electrical transformer or highway drainage culvert required a forty- to fifty-page operational plan, to be second-guessed in its turn by the wise men of the Special Group (Augmented).

In an attempt to keep this mind-boggling second-guessing at a minimum, Jack Corris, chief of support, and Rudy Enders, a maritime case officer and graduate of the Kings Point Merchant Marine Academy, put together a procedure designed to review each sabotage operation at least twenty-one days before it was scheduled to be launched. They called this review procedure a murder board, a term otherwise used by the Washington bureaucracy for its informal in-house rehearsal of an anticipated grilling by a congressional or other investigative body, and they sold it to me. So, in late January or early February 1962, we scheduled our first murder board to review the March operational schedule.

This exercise was something I felt Harvey should observe and participate in. He was persuaded to come to Miami for the day to be a player in the event.

On the designated date, I picked Harvey up at Miami International Airport. Seeing me as his only greeter, he grumpily asked, "Where is Cox?" Startled somewhat by the question, I told Bill that Cox was probably at home, as he had not been in the office in the last two days.

"What is the problem with this guy?" asked Bill. I said he might have been trying to cope with a major medical issue. Cox's secretary, I added, was very devoted to him and spent a lot of her working time caring for him at his residence.

Bill said, "Let's go to his house right now and sort this out." I objected that the murder board was set to roll in about an hour, and that was where I needed to be. On reflection, Harvey said, "You're right."

After arriving at the station, Harvey parted company with me, went to the security office, and disappeared. I pressed on with the murder board dry-run exercise, which turned out to be a great success as an operational-review technique.

About three hours later, Harvey returned to my office. He said he had found Cox at home in bed and had relieved him on the spot as chief of station. Harvey said he had already sent a cable to Helms outlining this development and telling Helms that, as of that time, I was the acting chief of station. That "acting" label lasted until May 1962 when I was officially confirmed as chief of station, JMWAVE.

Once the murder-board procedure was in place, it was decided to review what sabotage operations were being considered for implementation. This revealed that the team of Rip Robertson, Grayston Lynch, and Mickey Kappes had been working for months planning an operation against the Matahambre copper mine complex in Pinar del Río Province, an important export earner and therefore valuable to Castro.

Rip had a good bunch of Cubans in training for this mission. The two team leaders were surviving veterans of the previous year's landing at the Bay of Pigs. The plan for the raid was ambitious, but as it was against a high-impact target, we decided to try to carry it off.

We completed the planning for the operation, got policy approval from the Special Group (Augmented), and launched it. The team got into the Matahambre complex as planned, placed the explosives on the key conveyer belt equipment, and successfully exfiltrated Cuba. Unfortunately, there was no boom at the time the explosives were set to go off. What happened? Who could say?

We learned later that Cuban authorities had found the explosives, disarmed them, and were grateful the operation had not been a success.

In our own postmortem we concluded that the operation had failed due to human error. One of our Cuban infiltrators apparently had improperly set the timer despite hours of premission training on this relatively simple task.

Needless to say, our Matahambre failure was not well received by Bobby Kennedy. His caustic tongue worked at full speed to let all and sundry know we were the new Keystone Kops.

On October 20 the team was back at Matahambre. This time they were detected by Cuban security forces. A short firefight followed. Of the eight men on the team, six were captured. Castro broadcast his triumph over Havana radio. Heartburn was suffered in Washington, and of course the displeasure was conveyed to us in Miami with a string of biting and unflattering remarks.

Meanwhile, as I have come to learn in retrospect, our higher echelon, Task Force W, was pursuing the assassination option. In August 1975, the Senate Select Committee to Study Governmental Operations with Respect to Intelligence Activities asked me whether I had known that Harvey had been meeting in Miami with Mafia figure John Roselli. I replied that I knew Harvey was having periodic meetings with someone in Miami because he would go off for lunches or dinners by himself while on an inspection trip, but that he never told me whom he was seeing. This was standard Harvey procedure. Back in Berlin it had taken me nearly two years to learn about the tunnel that engineers under Harvey's direction had driven into the Soviet sector. If I didn't need to know about something, I wasn't told.

Of necessity, Harvey had had to lower the veil a bit in April 1962 when he required me to transfer $5,000 worth of gear, including guns, from JMWAVE's account to Task Force W's and have the stuff loaded into a U-Haul truck and left in a parking lot. My interrogators on the committee staff said they had heard that the matériel had been intended for the Cuban exile leader Tony Varona. Whether or not I was told that at the time, I now think it highly likely that this episode was part of an operation described by Helms as an approach to the Mafia begun in 1960 by the CIA's Office of Security for the sake of arranging Castro's removal.[2] Helms also wrote that when he learned about it, he ordered Harvey to close it down. However that may be, I never experienced anything more like this after the spring of 1962.

Were the words "arranging Castro's removal" a euphemism for assassination? Probably so, because my interrogators said they had evidence that the CIA had been talking to the Mafia in October 1960 about projects such as poison pills, exploding sea shells that Castro might pick up while scuba diving, and the gift of a wet suit contaminated with bacteria injurious to his health. I have seen nothing in station records to indicate that matters like this were ever presented to JMWAVE prior to my tour of duty there, and I can flatly state that nothing of the sort was ever proposed to me.

However, on one occasion that I can remember, we in Miami were ordered to canvas our agent assets for suggestions. Suggestions were a dime a dozen. It was impossible at that time to sit in any of the coffeehouses of Miami's Little Havana without hearing a scheme for disposing of the "maximum leader." They were all unrealistic. Cuban males are not suicidal. They love life, particularly the good life of women, food, and alcohol. As a result, if they ever were to attempt an assassination operation, one of their main objectives would have been to survive the event that was to make them a national hero. Thus, while brave and dedicated to the cause of defeating Castro, Cubans did not see themselves as being prepared to pay the ultimate price—their own lives—in order to kill Castro. Built into all their assassination outlines was action at a distance, an element that inevitably reduced any prospects of success.

So, we complied in a pro forma sort of way, but I never had occasion to discuss any assassination proposal with anybody in my chain of command: director of central intelligence (DCI) McCone, DDP Helms, or Task Force W Chief Harvey.

5

CUBAN MISSILE CRISIS

WITH the arrival of new manpower in 1962, JMWAVE's intelligence-collection activity shifted into high gear. New agents were sought among the legal travelers—businessmen, technicians, diplomatic couriers, diplomats—who were arriving weekly in Miami on the regular air links from Havana and were expected to return. We also fished in the refugee pool, looking for people who had not so thoroughly burned their bridges that they could not plausibly return home. Those people willing to cooperate with us— and in those heady, optimistic days, there were many—would be instructed in the kinds of information to look for, trained in secret writing (SW), and sent back to Havana.

The SW techniques we used had progressed far beyond the days when the only available secret inks were things like lemon juice, milk, or urine, substances that could easily be made visible by scorching. We had even abandoned the use of more sophisticated chemical inks because the very act of applying liquid to paper with the sharp nib of a pen disarranges the fibers of the paper, leaving tracks that can be detected under ultraviolet light. Mostly we used a sheet of bond paper that had been impregnated with a chemical and could be placed under the paper on which the agent would print his secret message, thus transferring a deposit of the invisible chemical onto the paper on which the cover letter would then be written. We could be relatively confident that this system of SW would pass scrutiny by a censor provided that nothing on the envelope or in the text of the cover letter aroused suspicion.

One of our new case officers, a man whom I will call Juan, was unusually successful in the recruitment of turnarounds. I had asked for him by name because I had been a friend of his back in the 1950s when we were both serving in Berlin, and I knew him to be imaginative, aggressive, and a Spanish speaker. As I was to discover, he had other talents that became apparent when SW messages from his new agents started arriving at JMWAVE. One after the other of these contained not the hoped-for intelligence, but declarations of love.

It was only when Juan began employing these talents among our own staff that I was obliged to take notice, and that was only because I had received an official complaint from a young lady's mother. Juan manfully admitted his transgressions and promised to behave. But our own relationship had changed, and some years later Juan was to be the source of some personal trouble for me.

While recruiting new agents, we worked to improve the ongoing operations. One such operation had had its origin in 1961 when three young Cuban males arrived in Miami in hopes of joining some anti-Castro organization. The CIA had picked them up, trained them in SW, and hustled them back to Havana. In the aftermath of the Bay of Pigs landings, one of them was shot by firing squad in the courtyard of La Cabaña prison, and another took political asylum in the Venezuelan embassy.

The third, a man who used the war name "Julio," kept his nerve and maintained his normal social and business contacts. Among the latter were former associates who had accommodated themselves to the revolution and wanted to persuade Julio to do likewise. In the flow of SW correspondence passing between Havana and Miami, we encouraged Julio to cultivate these people.

One of Julio's regular contacts was a former associate who had risen to a high bureaucratic position and enjoyed periodic meetings with high government officials. One day in the late summer of 1962 this individual told Julio, "NATO is a belt of bases surrounding the Soviet Union, and Cuba is the buckle that is going to open that belt."

Then, in September 1962 Julio was told by a commercial pilot that he had been drinking one night with Fidel Castro's personal pilot and that the latter had told him approximately as follows: "Cuba doesn't need to fear the U.S. anymore because it has long-range missiles. We will fight to the last man, and perhaps even win, because we have all we need, including nuclear warheads."

A new player had entered the Cuban ballgame and changed it overnight—the Soviets with their buildup in Cuba of men and equipment. We had detected this through other on-island human sources as early as July 1962 when the Soviets started to put into Cuba what turned out to be coastal defense cruise missiles and Frog rockets. Initial human-source reporting described the weapons as being the size of small palm trees. Moved at night and wrapped in canvas, they were not vulnerable to detailed description by our agents who saw them. Analysts in the Deputy Directorate for Intelligence (DDI) pooh-poohed our reports at first, arguing that the Soviets would not want to escalate the tension over Cuba by deploying missiles there. That flabby rationale changed later to a thesis that the weapons deployment was a defensive move aimed at helping Cuba defend its coast from Miami raiders or an American-inspired invasion.

One school of thought has long hypothesized that the Kremlin detected our buildup in Cuban operational capability in South Florida in early 1962, and both in reaction to that and in order to checkmate an American pretext invasion of Cuba, the Soviets decided to beef up Cuban defensive capabilities. In other words, the advocates of this theory suggest that Washington, by its actions, provoked a Russian response that led to the Cuban missile crisis. This theory never made sense to me. A more likely explanation can be found in the assumption that Soviet premier Nikita Khrushchev, a man with a riverboat gambler streak, had concluded, based on his assessment of Kennedy's lack of resolve over the Bay of Pigs and weak performance at the Vienna conference of June 4, 1961, that Cuba offered an opportunity to change the nuclear balance of power. It was a bold play, and by making it, Khrushchev brought the world to the edge of a nuclear war.

So, an unexpected vectoring of events that had started in July 1962 was really playing itself out. Washington was assessing what could be done against Cuba. This was an intelligence-collection exercise. Moscow was trying to change the correlation of nuclear forces, with Cuba being the central playing field. The divergent goals crossed by accident, allowing Washington to detect the missile buildup and catch Moscow with its hand in the cookie jar. Thus, while the CIA with all of its collection resources had not provided a clear, unambiguous strategic warning to policy makers that

Khrushchev intended to place offensive nuclear weapons in Cuba, the Miami Station detected the buildup at a tactical level before the weapons became operational. This permitted the president to take actions that in time defused the threat of nuclear war.

The tactical intelligence that produced the warning of a Soviet buildup was a patchwork of collection techniques, luck, and diligent background research. By July 1962 we were receiving fragmented agent reports of Soviet agricultural specialists arriving in Cuba by air. Subsequent agent reporting on these new arrivals persuaded us they were military men. We were obviously keen to find out how many of them were now in Cuba and what their mission was. A newly recruited agent turned out to be uniquely well placed to help us with the numbers.

The new agent was employed in a Cuban communications facility. Having learned about him from an American friend, we had sent him a recruitment letter through the good offices of a neutral diplomat and proposed using him as a communications channel. He readily agreed, and—once more with diplomatic assistance— we provided him with a complete FSS-7 two-way radio. Within three days he was on the air.

At our request, he sent us a list of his friends and associates whom he considered reliable. Among these was a department head in the Ministry of Defense, whose duties included processing and approving all requests for food for Soviet troops stationed throughout Cuba. Within forty-eight hours of the time these requests landed on the official's desk, we had them in Miami.

The most pressing of these requirements was for "flesh" (fresh meat and some fish). In the summer of 1962 the Soviets began to requisition fourteen thousand kilograms of flesh daily, with the figures rising in the fall of 1962 to between fifteen thousand and sixteen thousand kilograms. While the Soviets did not reveal the number of troops for whom the requisitions were intended, the official said he felt it likely that they were using a target of not more than four hundred grams per day (more than three quarters of a pound) per man and that therefore the Soviets were requisitioning meat and fish for more than forty thousand men.

DDI analysts in Washington were firmly on record that the Soviets had no more than fifteen thousand troops in Cuba. For several days after we submitted the first of many detailed reports from this agent, a strange silence descended over Washington, and we knew that DDI analysts were scurrying for cover.

The first reaction from headquarters was a cautious comment that there was no way of knowing how much flesh the Soviets fed their troops. We replied that we doubted it was in excess of the one pound per man that the U.S. Army had set as a goal in World War II. Although headquarters then found a 1947 Soviet Army manual that gave the recommended meat consumption of three hundred fifty to four hundred grams per man per day, the DDI never fully retreated from its estimate of fifteen thousand troops.

Our methodology was obviously less than perfect, but it had its strengths. Sam Halpern, who had been Bill Harvey's executive assistant before, during, and after the October 1962 crisis, had the benefit of attendance at the 1992 Havana conference on the Cuban missile crisis, where he saw Soviet documents showing there were 42,200 Russian troops in Cuba by October 1962.

Sam's figure of 42,200 was confirmed for me on October 22, 1994, at a meeting of the Association of Former Intelligence Officers. Yuri Pavlov, former Soviet ambassador to Costa Rica and Chile, and—more to the point—translator for the Kremlin during the missile crisis, told us that in October 1962, Russia had between forty-two thousand and forty-five thousand troops in Cuba.

The Soviet buildup in personnel continued in August. Simultaneously, the Soviets were detected moving more of their equipment at night to construction sites in and around Mariel, Havana, and Matanzas. The data on their activities was coming from on-island clandestine sources reporting by radio and SW. Opa Locka was also obtaining a steady stream of sightings from the refugees it was processing. Thus, there was no question about the pace of the movement. At issue was what was being moved.

The agents were now describing the canvas-wrapped equipment as being more in the length category of a royal palm tree. As we tried to sort out what this might mean, we concluded we were hearing about the movement of surface-to-air missile (SAM)–2 missiles. The question was how to clarify this point. We tried to get 35mm photographs of the equipment as it moved on secondary Cuban roads. This was less than a smashing success, for most movements were at night. Unfortunately, none of the film our agents in Cuba could get their hands on was fast enough to handle the challenge of darkness.

At some point in this mad swirl of August, I was in Washington for a one-day trip to review with headquarters the September infiltration schedule for Cuba. DCI McCone was scheduled on that day for an afternoon meeting in the Oval Office with the president, and I was asked to attend on the off chance the president would have a question that the Miami Station had unique insight into. The president did ask me a few questions about agent reporting in which royal palm trees were being used as a unit of measure. He finished his inquiry into this matter with the comment he needed "hard intelligence" on what the royal palm trees were. No one at the meeting had the wit to ask what the president would accept as having met the requirement of hard intelligence. Subsequent events provided the answer. The president wanted clear, unambiguous U-2 photographs of SAM-2s or whatever was being deployed. That, to him, was hard intelligence.

The impetus to resolve this issue came from Julio, who in an SW report disseminated in Washington on September 18, 1962, delineated what has come to be called the trapezoid area bounded by the cities of San Cristóbal, San Diego de los Baños, Consolación del Norte, and Los Pozos. He reported that all Cubans in the area had been moved out and that security was being enforced to prevent access to the area where very secret and important work, believed to be concerned with the missiles, was in progress. This report is credited with targeting the U-2 flight that on October 14, 1962, produced the hard intelligence that President Kennedy had been seeking. And it was here that medium-range ballistic missiles (MRBMs) were found.

Helms, in a reflective mood when talking with Halpern in July 1997, noted wryly that the U-2 flight over the trapezoid area in Pinar del Rio that had been identified by JMWAVE's agent had produced 928 pictures proving that the Soviet Union was putting long-range missiles into Cuba. Helms then permitted himself the caustic evaluation that this agent report was the only positive and productive aspect of the Kennedy–Lansdale Operation Mongoose.

Of course, the ensuing blockade of Cuba had not ended the crisis. There was always the possibility that some Soviet officer, drunk or sober, would fire a medium-range nuclear missile in an action uncoordinated with Moscow. The chances of this were minimal. But prudence dictated that we search for this possibility.

It was clear, too, that if an American invasion were to take place, the Miami Station would have to provide pathfinder teams to help our troops, particularly any airborne units, to move rapidly in the country. Also, we would need to provide the military with counter-intelligence teams for weeding out agents of the Cuban security service (DGI) and other potential troublemakers.

Last but not least, we would be a resource for providing Cuban experts who would get the government functioning at the local level after an invasion. Here the emphasis was on municipal facilities—water, electricity, police, and sanitation. We were equipped to do this as we had been collaborating for months with an exiled former official of the Batista Treasury Department who had been compiling files on Cubans qualified in a variety of municipal skills.

Equally important, we used the time between October 14 and 18 to review all of our boat documentation. This confirmed that all vessels were properly registered with the Coast Guard, met all safety requirements, and were provided with ownership and cover stories. Also, a review of our handling and control of weapons and ammunition satisfied me that our procedures were tightly controlled, everything being issued onboard ship or at loading docks at mission time only and retrieved at the end of each mission before a vessel hit land in the United States or before any personnel were allowed to go ashore.

The purpose of this review, besides confirmation of what we already knew, was a search for a wartime niche. In effect we were working ourselves into becoming the strategic planners for the military command that would invade Cuba if that turned out to be the president's decision. Fortunately, it was not. Consequently, after October 28, 1962, the CIA's mission became one of monitoring the Soviet withdrawal from Cuba. The major part of this task was carried out by photographic resources and the SIGINT community.

By October 30 there was a stand-down order on all sabotage operations against Cuba. We therefore restricted our paramilitary assets to the duty of infiltrating supplies into Cuba to support our ongoing agent-collection operations, improving our clandestine communications, and sometimes exfiltrating agents who had become compromised.

We had begun to recognize by then that the DGI was rapidly improving. Whereas it had been acting up until then primarily as a police force, it was now becoming more sophisticated under the tutelage of the KGB. Once we could have been fairly confident that an agent was still free as long as he was communicating with us. Now we had to take into consideration the possibility that the DGI might have caught and doubled him. Consequently, we had to review the signals by which an agent could notify us of such a disaster. And we had to prepare emergency-evacuation schemes for endangered agents.

By then, we also had two new techniques for communicating with our on-island sources—one-way voice link (OWVL) and "burst" radio transmissions. Both had been invented for the protection of agents from radio-direction finders as they eliminated the long and tedious procedures by which in the old days an agent would establish radio contact with his headquarters and then proceed to tap out his report. In OWVL, all an agent needed to do was tune his receiver to an agreed frequency at an agreed time, copy down a spoken message consisting of nothing but numerals, and then decode it.

"Burst" was a little more complicated. It required the agent to encipher his message in the same numerical system, punch it onto a paper tape, and load the tape into an FSS-7 transmitter. He would then tune his receiver to an agreed frequency at an agreed time, await a go signal, and then feed the tape through the transmitter at a speed so high that no radio-direction finder would have time to lock onto the signal.

Both systems worked well. We equipped more than twenty-five of our agents with OWVL and also had a significant number of two-way circuits using real-time burst transmissions. They formed a useful part of the total collection mosaic after October 28.

A hazard we always tried to avoid was unnecessary contact between agents belonging to different nets as it broke down the compartmentation that we always tried to build into our operations. But in practice this was difficult to avoid. Understandably, our agents belonged largely to the Cuban middle class. As Cuba is a small country and its middle class is also small, the agent pool was somewhat shallow, and on many occasions we would have to warn one of our agents away from one of his acquaintances, not necessarily because we knew the individual to be dangerous, but either because he was already involved with one of our other nets or another friendly intelligence service or was so openly antagonistic to the Fidelista regime that we could confidently assume he was being watched by agents of the DGI.

By mid-1963 one of Julio's subagents, a young woman I remember only as "Betty," fell into this trap. She had begun to frequent the home of "Mongo" and "Polita," more formally known as Ramón Grau Alsina and María Leopoldina Grau Alsina, the adopted children of former Cuban president Ramón Grau San Martín. Their home had become a magnet for disaffected Cubans, and Mongo himself had become involved with one of our other nets.

One day Betty told us by a burst transmission that she was in danger of arrest, so we set up an operation to exfiltrate her from Cuba. Studying photographs taken by the high-altitude U-2, we examined the country roads in Matanzas Province and were able to select a place where Betty could meet the paramilitary team that would be sent for her, a place that could be described so unmistakably that neither party could miss it. We then sent her complete meeting arrangements by OWVL—place, time, recognition signal, and alternate time in case for any reason the first rendezvous would have to be aborted—and dispatched the Rex, one of our mother ships, with a paramilitary team on board.

The team was dropped off in a Boston Whaler and set off for shore, while the Rex continued on its way. Hiding the small boat in a mangrove swamp, they headed for the designated meeting place where they picked up Betty and one other agent, who in the meantime had been added to the operation. But the sea had begun to pick up, and unexpected complications set in.

The paramilitary team with its two passengers on board headed out to sea for its scheduled pickup, but the Rex was nowhere to be seen. Back to the mangrove swamp they went to try again next day, but now conditions were even worse, and still there was no mother ship in the offing.

Betty had brought communications gear along and kept us informed as this drama unfolded. Back in Miami we received a message to the effect that there was enough cryptographic material left for only one more OWVL message, enough battery power for one more transmission, and enough gasoline aboard the Boston Whaler for one more one-way trip to an offshore rendezvous with the Rex.

It was tempting to send the Rex one more time, but this would be to risk all on a final throw of the dice. Instead, we loaded a dinghy with food, water, gasoline, batteries, and one-time pads and arranged to have it anchored in the mangrove swamp at a place that we could clearly describe to our agents in what would have been the last OWVL message that we could send.

Back came the FSS-7 radio message we had hoped for. Our party had located the dinghy and was now well equipped to await the Rex's arrival. The pickup was finally achieved, and our two hunted agents were safe in Florida.

6

TRYING AGAIN

WITH the easing of tension when it became apparent the Soviet withdrawal was real, policy makers started paying attention to cleaning up the battlefield. Robert Kennedy was the attack dog on this issue. He asked in November 1962 that Harvey be relieved from his Task Force W position.

I acknowledge that I am not an unbiased observer of this event as I have always regarded Harvey as a mentor and friend. Furthermore, my first-hand knowledge of it is limited. Harvey told me it was the result of a major confrontation with Bobby. The end result, Harvey said, was that he called Bobby a liar. Obviously, this did not go down well with Bobby, and Harvey had to walk the plank. The issue in dispute revolved around the question of whether Harvey had been acting as a loose cannon by having agent assets, including commando teams, on the water and headed for Cuba in the period between October 14 and 28. Harvey told me this was not a unilateral Task Force W effort but one coordinated with other agencies. Bobby disagreed, tempers flared, Harvey was injudicious in bringing the affair to a close, and his days as Task Force W chief became numbered. That is all I got out of Harvey.

I have been told since by Sam Halpern that Harvey, in response to the needs of the Joint Chiefs of Staff (JCS) Planning Staff for current tactical intelligence on the missile sites, had been planning to use a submarine to put ten Cuban five-man teams on the island to try to cover the newly discovered SAM and related missile sites. Lansdale was also involved in this effort. This was also known to Helms, deputy director of the CIA (DDCI) Marshall S. Carter, and probably DCI McCone. Also, Bobby must have known that the CIA had no submarines, so how could Harvey have been acting on this project on his so-called own authority?

One and all at the CIA's policy levels agreed it was wrong for Bobby to level the charge against Harvey that he had gone "off the reservation" and acted on his own at a critical time. Yet, when Bobby followed up on this false charge and asked that Harvey be removed from his position as chief of Task Force W, there was nothing anyone could or would do to reverse this request. Harvey was screwed. Thus, in January 1963, he was out the door, headed in due course for the station chief's job in Rome. This dismissal was a fatal blow to Harvey's psyche. In my view, he never recovered from it. In effect, this incident ended the brilliant career of an old curmudgeon. The media got wind of Bobby's charges and Harvey's departure. As a result, the open-source literature on the Cuban missile crisis contains totally inaccurate stories about this matter. Once tarred with such material, Harvey found it impossible to shake it off, particularly since he was not an adept practitioner of the fine art of Washington public relations.

In January 1963 we were visited by Harvey's replacement, Desmond FitzGerald. "Des" made it plain that regime change in Havana was still at the top of Washington's agenda and that the preferred means to this end was a military coup. Haranguing the troops, he told us to recruit more sources in the Cuban Army and militia, giving preference to people high enough in the hierarchy to be able to comment on the leaders' political views.

We accordingly reviewed our military assets and found them inadequate to the new task at hand. We had sources that were geared to monitoring Soviet troop movements. Our assets were NCOs, logisticians, and food handlers, useful in the past but hardly what we would need for a coup. We would have to see if these existing sources could put us in touch with tankers and combat infantry units, the elements that would be required by any possible coup plotter.

As we started, we got one small break. We learned that José Richard Rabel Nuñez, a defector from the Agrarian Reform Institute who had flown a small airplane at wave-top level into Key West, Florida, in November 1962, knew a lot of senior army personnel from his own days in the Cuban Air Force, as well as from his close friendship with Fidel with whom he had done a lot of spear fishing in 1960–1962. Consequently, we put Rabel on a special project to build files on the military commanders he knew.

This worked quite well in terms of data collection. The downside was that with each passing month, Rabel became increasingly impatient with our unwillingness to run a high-risk operation to exfiltrate his wife and three children from Havana. We explained to Rabel that his family was under constant DGI surveillance; as we could not get a communications or exfiltration plan to the wife securely, there could be no rescue operation. Rabel tired of this explanation and in August 1965 went back to Cuba in a small boat to get his family. The foolhardy effort failed, Rabel was arrested on September 4, and the work he had done in Miami on military personalities became known to the DGI. That in turn permitted the DGI to conclude that the CIA was looking seriously at the coup option.

The net result was that while we upgraded the quality of our military personalities portfolio, we had no prospects of putting a coup team together. We simply lacked secure access to dissidents and so could not reach an understanding with a potential coup central command. What we were looking for in 1963 did not materialize until mid-1989 when Arnaldo Ochoa Sánchez blossomed into a full-blown military threat to Castro as a result of his exploits in Angola.

When I outlined my conclusion privately to Des in about March 1963, his reaction was to say that my judgment was undoubtedly correct. Yet, given the mandate that had been imposed on the CIA by Bobby, we had to keep hacking away at the problem.

Des then lofted the idea of working at arm's length with one or two Cuban exile groups—led respectively by Manuel Artime and Manolo Ray, also known as Manuel Ray Rivero—to see if they could engage in a dialog with a coup group. This effort, if it moved forward, would be run out of Washington. It would require operational support from Miami in the form of caches put into Cuba, perhaps tutorial training of Artime and Ray on how to run operations, and some guidance on how to maintain a fleet of small boats. I told Des all of this was possible, but working with Ray seemed to be a marginal venture at best. He brushed this cautionary note aside with a wave of his hand and countered by saying he would have Alfonso Rodriguez spend a day or two with me in Miami looking at

Ray's potential. If this project got off the ground, he said, Rodriguez would be its case officer.

I explained to "Rod" that Ray was not rooted in Miami but in Puerto Rico where he worked in some housing agency and was allegedly close to Luis Muñoz Marín, the governor of Puerto Rico. Rumor had it that pressure from Muñoz Marín had moved Bobby to get Ray involved in a new effort to overthrow Castro. There were elements in Miami of Ray's organization, the Revolutionary Movement of the People (MRP). Rod could get a rundown on the group from Dave Morales, Tom Clines, and Bob Wall of the PM branch. I concluded by describing Ray as a far-left ideologue and as much a political and economic threat to American interests in the Caribbean as was Castro. I had no interest, I said, in meeting him.

If I remember correctly, Miami eventually put several caches into Cuba for Ray, which he and his organization never recovered. On the one occasion when Miami was scheduled to have a sea rendezvous with a boatload of Ray's people in order to guide them into a secure Cuban landing site, they did not show up. The explanation they subsequently provided was they had run out of fuel. Talk about the gang that couldn't shoot straight!

Artime was different. He had solid anti-Batista credentials stemming from his early days as a captain in the Rebel Army. He was an early participant in the Movement for Revolutionary Recovery (MRR) and had helped to build the party, although his ambition had then made him a divisive force in the movement. He had prestige in the exile community as a result of having been commander of Brigade 2506 at the Bay of Pigs and as a member of the leadership of the Democratic Revolutionary Front.

So, Des's intention was to subsidize Artime to the tune of $50,000 to $100,000 per month to work from Nicaragua sowing disquiet among the Cuban military as a prelude to an anti-Castro coup; Henry Hecksher would be the case officer for the project. I told Henry that the big unknowns were what the MRR represented in Cuba and what Artime's standing was within the Cuban body politic. Our intelligence suggested that the MRR was not a serious clandestine entity in Cuba, and we had no information indicating that Artime was a popular figure in Cuba around whom a revolutionary movement would rally.

Henry refused to be drawn into this polemic. He said the Kennedys wanted the Artime project to go forward, and go forward it would. We agreed, therefore, that JMWAVE would support the project by helping to equip Artime's troops in Nicaragua, providing operational intelligence on possible boom-and-bang targets in Cuba, tutoring Artime on the management of PM programs, and placing caches in Cuba for recovery by Artime's people.

At some point over the next year, JMWAVE provided Artime's group with all of the above services. This turned out to be a labor of love that produced no tangible results. Artime tried hard to become a player in fomenting a popular uprising in Cuba, but he came to the game too late and without the requisite skills. As a result he was not a success. Thus, after President Kennedy's assassination, the Artime program was phased out.

The third wild card being played in this high-stakes international poker game was Rolando Cubela. We at JMWAVE knew little about him except that he had a drinking problem and wanted desperately to get rid of Castro. This operation was run out of Washington. Nestor Sanchez, an excellent case officer fluent in Spanish, was Cubela's case officer. JMWAVE put some caches into Cuba for Cubela's use. His associates recovered some of these; others they apparently made no attempt to get. In essence this operation was closed down after Kennedy's assassination on November 22, 1963. The CIA formally cut all ties to Cubela in June 1965. While it lasted, however, the operation generated more questions than it answered and produced zero results.

Meanwhile, Bobby Kennedy was still demanding boom-and-bang operations. Dave Morales and I spent many a Miami evening by my swimming pool discussing the problem. It was clear that our paramilitary teams were having no trouble reaching the beach. They could take people in and out of Cuba and make caches, but once they tried to go inland, even a quarter of a mile, the trouble would start. We therefore began looking for ways to enable our teams to hit things that were closer to the water, the theory being that if we could succeed near the beaches, perhaps people inland would burn and destroy what they could to keep the resistance alive and expanding. As a result we started hitting softer targets near the shoreline, targets like small highway bridges, culverts in drainage areas, and so forth.

It also seemed that something always went wrong during these sabotage operations. Was there something in our methodology, we wondered, that was tipping our hand to the enemy? Or, despite the high standards of security at our paramilitary training sites and launch facilities, was our mechanism penetrated somewhere along the line?

Dave and I decided one Saturday afternoon we wanted to create a new, compartmented operational cell that would be kept totally apart from everything else we were doing in the paramilitary field. We felt that with new training facilities, new safe houses, new personnel, and new trainers, we would be in a better position to discover whether something was wrong with our previous methods.

Paramilitary at that time included a former naval officer named Bob Simons. Before joining the CIA, he had reached the rank of lieutenant and then resigned to do other things. Simons had been urging Dave and me for some time to look into underwater demolitions (UDT), a technique in which he had had a lot of experience. This was a high-risk venture, but Dave and I decided to go with UDT, so we put Bob in charge of all aspects of the operation, beginning with selection of personnel. He picked a really good bunch of men, all of them excellent swimmers, of course, and highly intelligent. Some even had engineering degrees. Bob also set up the training program, swam with his men, and taught them all he knew about UDT. When we reached the stage of choosing targets, he played a role in drawing up operational plans.

Assuming these operations were going to be successful, we knew we would have to attribute them to someone, and for that we needed a name different from anything that already existed in the Cuban exile milieu. Next, we needed someone who could front for the group, a man with managerial talent, perhaps with money, and unassociated with any Cuban exile organization.

Dave produced a candidate whom he had known in Havana— Rafael M., a man who had become a multimillionaire in business in Cuba, who had seen all his properties confiscated by Castro, and who was now traveling extensively throughout Central America as a representative of various American companies, including Uncle Ben's Rice.

We ran the usual checks on M., and Dave and I then sat down to talk with him. He was just what the doctor ordered: a discreet, dedicated, patriotic Cuban who wanted to do something against Castro but who, because of his prolonged absences from Miami, had not been drawn into professional revolutionary circles. His very travel patterns made him ideal for our purposes because he could take credit for our operations in press conferences that he could hold in places like the Dominican Republic or Costa Rica, where he would be far from our doorstep.

We recruited him, and he, Dave, and I then put our heads together to try to find a name for the group. We were all in agreement that "Commandos" had to be part of it, but "Commandos *What*"? This was not a question that could be decided lightly, and Dave and M. spent days working on it. Finally, M. remembered that the Cuban resistance fighters against Spain had called themselves "Mambises." There was no need to look any further. The "Commandos Mambises" were born.

But the group was not yet operational because a long period of training was still needed. By the time of the missile crisis of October 1962, part of the group was fully trained, and we thought for a while that we might have to use their UDT skills for marking landing beaches. But the crisis eased, and it was not until 1963 that the UDT operations began.

On August 18, M. walked into the offices of the *Miami Herald* news bureau in Guatemala City to announce that Commandos Mambises had struck the night before at oil installations at Casilda on the south coast of Las Villas Province. Commandos Mambises, he said, was a force of more than one thousand men operating on three different mountain fronts and led by a charismatic figure known only by the war name of "Ignacio." The organization was hemispherewide, he said, with cells in most major U.S. and Latin American cities.

Reporters were used to hearing this kind of stuff. What was different this time was that M. was a known and substantial personality in Guatemala City. His statement that he was resigning his position as credit manager and vice president of the Commerce and Industry Bank of Guatemala to become the Mambises' spokesman lent further weight to the story. But what M. did next was unprecedented: He called the Mambises' next shot. That same night, he said, the commandos would destroy an industrial plant at Santa

Lucía on the north coast of Pinar del Río Province. The Castro government was kind enough to confirm the attack. Its official communiqué claimed that the raiders had missed their target, but it admitted that some damage had been done to oil storage and sulfuric acid tanks and pipelines. When more reliable returns came in, including agent reporting and satellite photography, we calculated the damage as four days' loss of return on capital investment of $15,335,000 for $184,000; 14,000 gallons of fuel costing 10¢ per gallon for $1,400; and repair of 5 fuel tanks at $100 per tank for $500.

Commandos Mambises struck three more times during the year. On October 1 they destroyed a lumber sawmill at Cayo Guin on the northeast coast of Oriente Province for an estimated total damage of $39,000. The mill was the region's largest producer of railway ties, an item already in critical shortage in Cuba.

On October 22 they attacked and damaged government patrol boats docked at Isabela de Sagua, a port in Las Villas Province. The only vessel totally destroyed in this raid was a barge, the value of which we estimated at $75,000. M. said in his communiqué that the attack was revenge for the August 8 kidnapping of nineteen people who had been fleeing Cuba and had gotten as far as Bahamian waters before being captured by Cuban patrol boats.

What influence Commandos Mambises operations may have had on other incidents of sabotage in Cuba was hard to document. We did note, particularly from monitoring Single Sideband radio messages in Cuba, that spontaneous sabotage events tended to occur shortly after a Commandos Mambises operation. For example, on October 24, 1963, a militia unit in Las Villas Province was attacked. The building was set on fire just as M. had recommended. Then, on October 30 a train was derailed in Matanzas Province. On November 5 a truck carrying shoes was hijacked and set on fire near Colón in Matanzas Province.

Commandos Mambises' last operation of the year on December 23, 1963, seriously damaged a Soviet-built patrol boat in Enseñada Bay off the Isle of Pines. According to our assessment, the vessel was half destroyed for a probable loss to the Cuban government of $375,000.

The Cuban government was plainly as sorely stung by the group's panache as by the physical damage it was causing. In

November 1963 Cuban radio and television presented several prisoners who confessed to being Mambises. In fact, we never lost a man as long as the operation continued.

However, the on-again, off-again orders we began getting from Washington in 1964 finally put an end to this operation. This fine group of men was unwilling to sit around doing nothing while waiting for policy makers to make up their minds, so we closed Commandos Mambises down, and its members went their separate ways. This was a sad trend, for the three units we still had that were like Commandos Mambises could have waged an effective guerrilla campaign in Cuba if the strategy from Washington had been more resolute and sustained.

Unsatisfactory as this conclusion was from my point of view, it at least allows one now to address the false notion, still held by far too many people, that the CIA rampages at will, in the words of the late senator Frank Church, like a rogue elephant. The truth is that the CIA cannot use tusk or trunk without the concurrence of some special coordinating committee of the National Security Council (NSC). This means that final approval in the boom-and-bang arena rests, as always, with the president.

In April 1964, President Johnson put a stop to boom-and-bang operations against Cuba. This meant that Cuba, as far as intelligence collection was concerned, was now a typical denied area. To me that meant the war was over. There would be no popular uprising, no pretext American invasion of Cuba, no coup, and no assassination of Castro. The bearded devil had won the war. It was time, therefore, to recognize this reality and move on before some Washington wise man said, "Let's try again."

7

DEFECTORS

DURING the three years and five months that I spent in Miami, many thousands of Cubans fled to the United States, but few of them could truly be called defectors. Fidel Castro was still riding high, and most of the people who occupied high-level positions in his political, economic, or military apparatuses continued to occupy them; those who decided they didn't like what they saw going on were either imprisoned like Huber Matos or died under mysterious circumstances like Camilo Cienfuegos. The outstanding exception was Fidel's own sister Juanita. She had been an active member of his July 26 Movement as long as it was in revolt against the dictator Fulgencio Batista, but when on December 1, 1961, Castro announced that he was a Marxist-Leninist, she openly showed her disapproval. To do him justice, Castro's unwillingness to deal with her as he had with his erstwhile comrades Matos and Cienfuegos may have been due to fraternal affection, although I think it more likely that he wanted to avoid the wave of unfavorable publicity that would descend on him in Latin America for treating a sister so, and finally did descend on him when Juanita defected.

She must have made it really difficult for Fidel, because as the years 1962 and 1963 wore on, she became more and more open in the help she gave to his enemies. We were kept thoroughly apprised of this situation by our on-island sources, and I have little doubt that Fidel's informants were doing the same for him.

We were gradually building a picture of Juanita Castro as a woman who might be willing to defect, partly because of her opposition to the regime, partly because of an increasing likelihood that

Fidel had had about enough of her antics, and perhaps mostly because of the social isolation she was suffering because of her family relationship. Of course, this very isolation meant she would probably have little information of intelligence value, but we felt that the psychological impact her defection would make in Latin America outweighed this consideration.

One of the channels through which we were keeping in touch with Juanita included a State Department officer and the wife of Vasco Leitao de Cunha, the Brazilian ambassador to Cuba. The lady's diplomatic status allowed her to travel at will to Miami, and we took advantage of this fact to send Juanita a message suggesting that she apply for permission to travel to Mexico to visit her married sister Emma, assuring her that she could rely on us for whatever assistance she might need in reestablishing herself. Juanita made her move in July 1964, taking twenty-one suitcases with her. Fidel therefore could hardly have swallowed the story that she intended only a short family visit, but I like to think he was surprised by the consequences of her defection.

I sent Tony Sforza to Mexico City to meet and debrief Juanita. Tony was an experienced street man who had served in Cuba prior to Castro's rise to power. He was fluent in Spanish and had a great feel for the dynamics of Cuban politics. As I had expected, when Tony entered into a dialog with Juanita, it became clear that her access to political intelligence was minimal, although she was able to clarify some past events for us and provide useful information about leading Cuban personalities.

Her greatest value was as a propaganda instrument. Upon arrival in Mexico City, she told a televised news conference that she had "broken all bonds" with her brothers Fidel and Raul and that "Cuba is an immense prison surrounded by water," a sentiment that we were glad to have her share with her Latin American audiences, many of whom were prone to accept the Cuban revolution at face value.

Resettlement was no problem for Juanita, a strong-willed person capable of making her own way. Once on her own in the United States, she expressed her views independently and forthrightly on radio and television programs, in interviews with all the weekly newsmagazines, and finally on June 11, 1965, in testimony before the House Un-American Activities Committee. None of this outpouring was coordinated in any way with us. For one thing, it is against the law for the CIA to make propaganda in the United States. For another, to try to put words into Juanita's mouth—or, for that matter, to take them out—would have been a futile exercise.

In many ways, it is better to have a defector than the average in-place agent. Being under no communications constraints in dealing with him, you can sit down with him and talk by the hour—by the month if need be—and extract the most useful information in the greatest possible detail. He can give you the current positive intelligence, whether political, economic, or military, that he had as of the time that he defected. By talking with you about past history, he can put events and people into perspective and give you a basis for interpreting what happened in the past and perhaps even guidelines to what is likely to happen in the future. Depending upon how wide his circle of acquaintances is, he can provide you with the kind of biographical data that enables you to build up your personality indexes or confirm information that you may have obtained from other sources. If you are lucky, he may be able to come up with the names of one or two other prospective defectors, or even of people who might be recruitable as agents in place. He can help you decide which of these leads are perishable, in the sense that some of the individuals involved may be subject to early recall to the homeland, either in the course of normal rotation or because of known intimacy with the defector; leads such as these obviously must be exploited almost immediately. When the defector himself is an intelligence officer, he can tell you what operations he is running, who his agents are, and in some cases what other officers in his *rezidentura* are doing. In short, a well-placed defector can be a gold mine of information.

And this is not all because you can often get him to do things for you. If plans for his defection are laid on in advance, you can arrange for him to bring documents out with him. Failing that, you can sometimes get from him the information about locks and alarms that will enable you to run a surreptitious entry operation back into his old installation. And once you have decided you can trust this person, you can enlist his help in making recruitment pitches to those people he may have told you were susceptible.

I had the good fortune early in my career to get one of these prizes. His name was Jozef Swiatlo, and in December 1953 he crossed from East to West Berlin and turned himself over to the American authorities. I had just been transferred from the CIA's Frankfurt Operations Base to Nürnberg, but was immediately recalled to Frankfurt and told to take over the debriefing of an individual who was claiming to be a colonel in the UB, the action arm of Poland's Ministry of Security, and who was now in Frankfurt as a resident of the Defector Reception Center.

The word "center" in this context was a misnomer, for there was nothing central about it except that all people defecting in Europe from countries of the Soviet bloc were brought here. The defectors were not kept in one place, however, but were housed individually in villas scattered widely through the city's environs. Swiatlo was kept in a safe house somewhere north of Frankfurt in the general direction of Oberursel, with only CIA security guards and a cleared German housekeeper for company. His daily sessions with me took place at another secure location to which he was driven by his guards.

An essential first step in those days in the debriefing of a defector from a Warsaw Pact country was to inquire whether he had any information bearing on the possibility of an early initiation of hostilities. With that out of the way, I was able to get down to the tedious business of establishing Swiatlo's bona fides, or in other words confirming that he was the person that he claimed to be, that he had enjoyed the access to intelligence that he claimed to have had, and that his reasons for coming over to us were what he said they were.

The CIA has provided its case officers with several tools that are supposed to assist in this process, and to some extent they do. They include the polygraph test, handwriting analysis, and a psychological assessment battery. I have always been willing to use them but never to rely on them as infallible oracles. I have occasionally found them useful, however, for the hints they sometimes provide on how to proceed in face-to-face debriefing. Careful and methodical cross-questioning, checking and rechecking of the answers, and the personal impressions gained in interviews, which in Swiatlo's case spanned roughly five hours a day, seven days a week, for three months, are for me the most reliable ways to establish a defector's bona fides.

One of the first things to be covered in this process is the matter of motivation. Why did he come over? We want to eliminate the possibility that the defector's underlying motive is to feed us incorrect information and thereby cause us harm. But beyond that, understanding what makes this person tick will be vitally important later if and when we undertake to help him build a new life in the West.

When asked why he has come over, a defector may tell you he is ideologically opposed to the system he has been living under and is convinced of the superiority of life in the West. "Choosing freedom" is the euphemism that our own propagandists have coined and is therefore one that many a defector has come out with when first asked. But the facts are generally different. Defectors' motivations tend to run to such things as fear for their personal safety, exasperation with their living conditions, hatred for a boss, marital problems, or a life complicated by alcoholism, gambling debts, embezzlement, or womanizing. Whatever it may be, once you understand what it is, you take the defector as he is.

Swiatlo was deputy chief of Department 10 of the UB, the department that had responsibility for maintaining the purity of the Polish Communist Party. In practice this entailed purging those party members who had somehow incurred the displeasure of Joseph Stalin. Inasmuch as Stalin's bête noire at the time was defined variously as "rootless cosmopolitanism," or Zionism, his victims were disproportionately Jewish. Swiatlo in effect was playing a leading role in a pogrom, and as he himself was Jewish, this fact weighed on his conscience. It also weighed on his instinct for survival, which had already been sharpened by the turmoil into which Polish politics was slipping. Add to this the fact that Swiatlo was having marital troubles and saw his relationship with his superiors, such as Vice Minister of State Security Roman Romkowski, deteriorating, and you have a classic example of mixed motivation.

One day while I was talking with Swiatlo, he suddenly asked if I was familiar with the case of Noel and Herta Field because he had the full story of what had happened to them. The names rang a bell with me, but that was about all, so I stalled, saying I knew the general outlines of the case and would add it to our agenda for discussion at a later date.

Back in the Frankfurt Station later that afternoon, I questioned some of the more senior officers about the Fields, I traced the names in the station's card index, and I looked to see what the Special

Services' library had on them. With what little I got from these sources, I was able to frame a cable to headquarters asking for guidance and requirements. What I got back completed the picture as far as anybody in the U.S. government had it at the time.

In short, Noel Field had been an officer of the State Department from 1926 to 1936 when he resigned to join the staff of the League of Nations in Geneva. Here he stayed, working for various international and charitable organizations until May 1949 when he departed for Prague and dropped out of sight. His wife, Herta, went to Prague in July 1949 to look for him, and in less than a month she too had vanished. Official American interest in the Fields' case derived partly from the normal concern aroused in the bureaucracy whenever it seems that an American citizen has met with foul play when traveling abroad and partly from a desire to clarify certain ambiguities in the couple's history. For one thing, the disappearances occurred within months of the opening in Budapest of the staged Laszlo Rajk trial, one of the communist purges that were beginning to make our friend Swiatlo nervous, and Rajk testified at his trial that Noel Field had once tried to recruit him to carry on espionage in Hungary as a "servant of American imperialism." Assuming that the two events, the Field disappearance and the Rajk trial, were connected, there were two ways to see the connection. One was that the Hungarian authorities expected Field to testify at the Rajk trial, and the other was to assure that Field would never say anything publicly that would contradict Rajk's testimony.

Meanwhile, back in the United States, two former Soviet agents offered an alternative explanation for Noel Field's disappearance. Both Whittaker Chambers and Hede Massing identified Field as one of those Americans in government service who, like Alger Hiss, had joined communist cells in the 1930s and become devoted servants of the Soviet Union. Field's disappearance occurred within two weeks of the opening of the Hiss perjury trial in New York, and Chambers, who was to be the government's star witness in the trial, suggested that Field had been kidnapped to prevent his coming forward to testify against Hiss.

The Field affair was perhaps accorded greater importance than in retrospect it can be seen to have deserved, but at the time it aroused considerable anxiety. In Czechoslovakia, the presumed scene of the crime, communists had overthrown the democratically elected government only a year before. This event was thought in Washington to presage a Red Army invasion of West Germany, and it led directly to the creation of the North Atlantic Treaty Organization (NATO). Anything of an untoward nature happening in Czechoslovakia and involving Americans was bound to be taken seriously, and the disappearance of Noel and Herta Field, whatever it might signify, was so taken. Washington replied to my cable with a list of questions to be answered urgently, and I returned to my debriefing of Jozef Swiatlo with the Field case now high on the agenda.

Swiatlo told me that Noel and Herta Field had been delivered by Czechoslovakia to Hungary, which wanted to exploit them in connection with the Rajk trial and that they were still being held there. Swiatlo said he had interrogated Noel in Budapest. In addition, he had personally arrested Field's brother Hermann in August 1949 at the Warsaw airport for the same purpose. According to Swiatlo, Hermann was still in prison in Warsaw. Armed with this information, the State Department late in 1954 sent notes to both Poland and Hungary demanding "immediate consular access" to all three prisoners, and before the year was out all three had been set free.

Swiatlo was unable to confirm or deny the Chambers/Massing allegation that Noel Field had been a witting espionage agent for the Soviet Union, but he did tell me that he had no doubt that Noel Field had communist sympathies. Not surprisingly then, perhaps, neither Noel nor Herta Field seemed to be in any hurry to return to the bosom of their homeland. Upon their release from a five-year imprisonment in Hungary, they asked for political asylum in Hungary and announced their intention to stay there.

The Field story, plus the wealth of detail that Swiatlo was able to give me about the organization, functions, and misdeeds of the UB, soon made it evident that Swiatlo was uniquely able to provide answers to questions that had long remained unanswered, and I was bombarded by cabled demands from headquarters that I tackle Swiatlo on other subjects. Fortunately, the assignment of Bernice L. to the case soon relieved the additional pressure that this put on me. Bernice is a talented linguist who can take shorthand in Polish, and with her sitting in on my debriefing sessions and taking notes, running the necessary name traces in the Frankfurt Station's card index, and helping to meld everything together for cabled transmission to

Washington, my paperwork load was reduced. This left more time for me at the end of the day to prepare for the next day's debriefing. I was also free now to socialize a little with Swiatlo; I had realized that life had become a bit tedious for him with nobody for company in his afternoon and evening hours but security guards and a housekeeper.

Swiatlo was also able to clear up for us the mystery of what had happened to Wladyslaw Gomulka, the former secretary general of the Polish Communist Party. It was public knowledge that Gomulka, like Laszlo Rajk in Hungary and Rudolf Slánský in Czechoslovakia, had earned the displeasure of Joseph Stalin and that the Central Committee of the Polish Communist Party had obligingly voted Gomulka out of office in September 1948, removed him from the Politburo, and finally in November 1949 kicked him out of the Central Committee. From then on, hard information about Gomulka's whereabouts gradually dwindled to nothing. Rumor had it that he had died in prison.

Our interest in Gomulka's fate had a purely practical basis. If there was an anti-Stalinist faction in the Polish Communist Party, we wanted to encourage it. If there was turmoil in the Polish leadership and the bureaucracy, we wanted to keep the pot boiling. But for that we needed hard facts, and here was Jozef Swiatlo ready to supply them.

Gomulka was alive and in prison, he said. Swiatlo himself was the UB officer who had arrested him on July 31, 1951, at a health resort in the Tatra Mountains and conducted him and his wife, Zofia, to Warsaw where they were incarcerated in a special villa belonging to the UB's Tenth Department. No one in the Polish hierarchy, it seemed, wanted to risk following the Hungarian and Czech examples by subjecting Gomulka to a show trial, for there was no certainty that he would play ball. Nor did they dare release him for fear of bringing down upon themselves the wrath of the Soviets. So, the Gomulkas had been sitting in their prison villa for two and a half years, receiving good food and reading matter, but kept under constant observation.

To get this and other interesting tidbits of news to the Polish people, we enlisted the services of Radio Free Europe. Although covered as a private organization funded by American businessmen and dedicated to the mission of transmitting accurate information to audiences behind the Iron Curtain, in fact the CIA owned and managed RFE. It gathered its news from defectors and refugees and played it back to its target audiences in a low-key and unpolemical way. Its influence was enormous, especially in Poland where, during the revolutionary events of 1956 that brought Gomulka back to power again, the suggestion was actually made that RFE should be regarded as the government's "loyal opposition."

But these events were still in the future in 1954 when RFE went on the air with Swiatlo's revelations, not only about Gomulka but about the UB in general. That these broadcasts helped keep the pot boiling and set the stage for the subsequent liberalization in Poland is beyond doubt. The Polish authorities of the time complained publicly about the broadcasts, calling Swiatlo a traitor and demanding his extradition on charges of murder, but behind the scenes an investigation into the UB's excesses, which was already under way, was accelerated. In September 1954, the Gomulkas were quietly released from prison. This put Polish politics on the slippery path that eventually spawned the Solidarity Movement and the democratization of Poland.

In April 1954, Swiatlo and I traveled to the United States on an old military aircraft that had seen better days and was now configured basically for hauling cargo. Even by the standards of those days, it was a long and comfortless trip. From Frankfurt we flew first to the Azores, spending the night there and then proceeding to Bermuda for another stopover. I was told later by Bill Holtzman and the other interrogators who took over the job of working with Swiatlo that there wasn't much that I had missed in my preliminary debriefing. It made me feel pretty good.[1]

As for Swiatlo, once he had fulfilled his obligations to the U.S. government, he sank quietly into private life as a legal resident of the United States. According to what little I have heard about him, he moved to New York—whether City or State I don't know—and opened a small business. The absence of any news to the contrary gives me confidence that his resettlement was a success.

The immigration and resettlement of defectors like Jozef Swiatlo would ordinarily have been blocked by a paradox, which we were able to overcome only with the help of the U.S. Congress. The paradox was this: To have access to the type of information that would make him desirable as an intelligence source, the defector almost by definition had to belong to the Communist Party; under the McCarran Immigration Act of 1952, Communist Party members were prohibited from entering the United States; however, high among the various motives that caused a defector to come over to our side, stimulated by the success stories broadcast by RFE, was the expectation that he would be allowed to make a new life in the United States.

In 1949 a helpful Congress had passed Public Law 110, which, among other provisions, gave the director of central intelligence authority to bring up to one hundred persons per year to the United States for permanent residence, provided the CIA was prepared to certify that these persons had provided significant political, economic, or military intelligence to the U.S. government and that the CIA would accept responsibility for their successful resettlement.

To get the director's okay, an operations officer had to compose and submit a staggering number of testimonials, and he had to act on the okay, once it was granted and passed along to the Immigration and Naturalization Service, within a very short period. The extra paperwork involved and the compulsion to complete the requirements levied on me by headquarters before expiration of the deadline added appreciably to the pressure I was under.

All directors of central intelligence, as far as I know, have exercised the authority granted them by Public Law 110 most conscientiously, and I have never heard of an instance of the law's fraudulent or frivolous use. I have, however, had occasion to wish that the law had been framed a little more elastically.

František Tišler, a colonel in Czech military intelligence, had never wanted to be a spy. He had always wanted to be an artist, but he had been unable to satisfy his aspirations in Czechoslovakia. The party apparatus had moved him instead into a career path that by July 1959 found him in the Czech embassy in Washington with responsibility for recruiting American citizens as espionage agents.

In the testimony that Tišler gave about a year later to the House Un-American Activities Committee, he said that he had become disillusioned with communism because of the Rudolf Slánský trial. No doubt this was true, but his reasons for defecting were infinitely more complex, including the constant denial of his artistic calling, the fact that he was about to be reassigned to Prague after a less than brilliant tour of duty as an intelligence officer, and marital problems that would probably have prevented his ever getting another foreign assignment once they became known to his superiors, as inevitably they would.

Tišler , in short, had discovered early in his Washington tour that his status as an intelligence officer gave him an excuse for being out at all hours and at the same time absolved him of responsibility for explaining himself in detail to his wife. Thus tempted, he had embarked on a series of affairs, and his wife, Adéla Tišlerová, a member of the Czech shot put and discus team, had caught him out at it. After getting his promise that he would mend his ways and suspecting that he had not done so, she waited one night for him to come home and surprised him with a sound thrashing.

In July 1959, Tišler presented himself at the Washington offices of the FBI and asked for political asylum. Here he had the good fortune to be put into the hands of Special Agent Landon McDowell, a supremely warm and sympathetic human being whose expertise in the counterintelligence arena more than compensated for his relative lack of knowledge about the Czech internal services, military intelligence, and the political scene.

Landon's first move was right out of the book. He persuaded Tišler to return to the Czech embassy and work there as an agent in place, promising his help for the time when Tišler could no longer defer his defection. Then he asked Sam Papich, the bureau's liaison officer with the CIA, to put him in touch with whoever in the agency would be interested in an officer of Czech military intelligence.

I was then chief of the Eastern European Division's section responsible for Czechoslovakia, and I was definitely interested. Landon and I met and started what we both thought was going to be an orderly discussion of how best to exploit this uniquely placed agent. Heading our wish list, of course, was a chance to plant a bug in the Czech embassy, but it was not to be. Taking matters into his own hands one day, Tišler notified the bureau that he would be duty officer that night and would have keys to all the safes. In a rudely effective operation, he bundled the contents of the safes into bags, threw the bags out the window, and departed the embassy for good. I was able to collect him from the bureau later and move him to a safe house.

Rather to my surprise, Adéla Tišlerová had come too. I never knew just what had tilted the balance in favor of her defection. My guess would be that she had realized that her days of international athletic competition would be over if she remained in Czechoslovakia and hoped there might be an opening for her on the U.S. team. Maybe I do her an injustice. Maybe she loved Tišler, but I doubt it.

Although Tišler was now officially a CIA body, I told Landon McDowell I hoped he would continue seeing him as I would have been sorry for Tišler at this delicate stage of his new life to lose the friendship that had sprung up between the two men. Landon and his wife devoted many hours of their free time to making the Tišlers feel at home, and I am sure that they contributed much to Tišler's successful resettlement.

My task now was to supervise the debriefing of Tišler for information on what the Czech embassy was doing and with whom. Tišler's revelations, I must say, were unexciting. As far as the military intelligence *rezidentura* was concerned (that is to say, Tišler himself and the three officers under his command), the Czechs were running no agents out of the Washington embassy. He was able to mention only two U.S. citizens of Czech ancestry, Antonin Krchmarek and Charles Musil, as members of the Communist Party USA with whom members of the Czechoslovak embassy were in contact. Krchmarek indeed had received money from the Czechs for reports he had submitted on the U.S. election process, but Tišler had no reason to believe that any classified information had been passed in these transactions.

If the Czech embassy was not exactly a hotbed of espionage, it was not for lack of trying. Tišler told me that 45 percent of the embassy staff was involved in intelligence in one way or another. This statistic, when repeated to the House Un-American Activities Committee and reported by the *New York Times,* came as a salutary shock to the American public, many of whom were still unaware of the extent to which Eastern European diplomatic installations were serving as adjuncts to the KGB and the GRU.

The documents that Tišler had flung out the embassy window had been examined by our Czech-speaking analysts, précis had been written, and full translations made of those that looked most interesting. These we used as a basis for debriefing Tišler on the whole structure of Czech military intelligence, the interrelationship between military intelligence and the Ministry of Interior, and war plans. Tišler also gave us leads to military-intelligence personnel in various parts of the world. We made pitches to some of them, and—as is usual—some were successful and some were not.

Tišler made a very happy resettlement. He went to art school, got a master's degree, and was then hired by the University of Miami, where I was able to visit him once or twice during my stint as chief of station JMWAVE between 1962 and 1965.

When the MiG pilot Viktor Ivanovich Belenko flew his aircraft to Japan on September 9, 1976, I was associate deputy director of operations and so was responsible for many of the decisions that had to be made in his regard, but I never actually met him until after I had retired. My role in the months that followed his defection was one of coordination with other governmental agencies and departments, seeing to it that the government spoke with one voice in the matter of this important defector.

The arrival of Belenko's new MiG-25 Foxbat interceptor at Japan's Hakodate airport caused a sensation at Langley. James R. Schlesinger, once a director of central intelligence and subsequently a secretary of defense, considered the Foxbat so formidable a weapon that its deployment in the Soviet Air Force would force fundamental changes in Western strategy and weaponry. The things we wanted to know about the Foxbat had long been incorporated into a technological requirements package, waiting for the day when one would be available for study. Now we wanted to go over the plane from nose to tail, and we wanted to pick the brains of the highly trained pilot who had succeeded in penetrating the Japanese defenses.

Achieving our second goal presented no difficulties. Even before taking off from his Siberian airport, Belenko had laboriously scrawled a note in which he asked for asylum in the United States. The Japanese were quite willing, indeed eager, to get him out of their country, and within a few short days we had him en route to Virginia.

Belenko turned out to be a rare bird indeed. Except for his being fed up with his living and working conditions, his motivation turned out to be entirely ideological. Certainly he was in no kind of political or legal trouble, and although his marriage was on the rocks, this circumstance seems only to have removed what would otherwise have been an obstacle to his defection.

Getting access to the Foxbat turned out to be somewhat trickier. In support of their demand that one of their pilots be allowed to fly the plane back home, the Soviets were applying the crudest forms of economic pressure on Japan, including interning Japanese fishing vessels and jailing their crews on charges of fishing in Soviet waters. For the time being, therefore, no American personnel could get anywhere near the plane. Eventually, however, the Japanese hit upon a formula that would at least partially save Soviet face while giving us nearly everything we wanted short of actually getting to fly the plane. Of course the MiG-25 was Soviet property, they said, and of course the Soviets could have it back. Unfortunately, it could not be flown back because for a Soviet military aircraft to take off from a Japanese airport would be a violation of Japanese airspace. The Japanese were sure, they said, that the Soviets would appreciate this fine point of international law. In fact, it had been a violation of Japanese law for the plane to land at Hakodate airport in the first place. A crime had been committed and must be investigated. The plane was evidence and would have to be examined.

Once this point had been made, our technicians were permitted to work in civilian clothes alongside the Japanese, thoroughly photographing the plane, removing small material samples, and literally taking the machine apart. We learned about 90 percent of what we hoped to about the aircraft in this way. Ultimately, the Soviets got their Foxbat back, but dismantled and in crates.

According to an estimate made public by Senator Birch Bayh, the combined value of the plane and the expertise that Belenko brought with him amounted to more than $5 million. My own estimate would run to a considerably higher figure, for Belenko in his own person has become a valuable addition to our country, thanks in part to a thoughtful resettlement program that released him into society inch by inch, so to speak. After successfully completing an intensive English-language course, Belenko was given an opportunity to cooperate with John Barron in writing an account of his life. The Intelligence Committee of the U.S. Senate then introduced a private bill to waive the statutory ten-year waiting period for naturalization normally imposed on former members of the Communist Party of the Soviet Union in order that, as a U.S. citizen, Belenko might be able to help train American Air Force pilots in countering Soviet tactics.

Some three years after Belenko's defection, another Soviet defector told the CIA that much of the pressure on the Japanese government to return Belenko's plane had been coming from Hirohide Ishida, president of the Suprapartisan Parliamentarians' League for Japan-Soviet Friendship. According to the defector, a former KGB major named Stanislav Levchenko, the KGB had been financing the league's activities, a charge that Ishida angrily denied. The agency was unable to establish the truth of the allegation one way or another. It could be sure, however, that Levchenko was in a position to know, inasmuch as he had been a member of a KGB "active-measures" unit in Tokyo whose mission was to nudge Japan away from the United States and toward the Soviet Union using such techniques as bribery and disinformation.

Levchenko defected in 1979 at a time when the CIA was no longer taking the same level of interest that it had in the past to assure defectors of a satisfactory resettlement. The reason for this may have been slumping morale or the actual shortage of dedicated personnel, both lingering consequences of Stansfield Turner's "Halloween Massacre" of October 31, 1977;[2] whatever the reason, case officers were now considering themselves warriors for the working day. Once the 8:30–5:30 bureaucratic day was done, it was hard to find people to sit and socialize with Levchenko or, indeed, to concern themselves much with how he was adapting to his new environment.

John Barron came to the rescue with a book proposal, but by the time *The KGB Today: The Hidden Hand* was published in May 1983, Levchenko was bored and homesick and beginning to drink too much. Recognizing that Levchenko needed a support network and a job, John and I helped Levchenko get a job with a private security company in Oakland, California. Levchenko married the owner's daughter, but the marriage failed and Levchenko moved back to Washington where, after a period of time, he married a Russian lady who had defected from the Soviet embassy. I wish I could record that this ended his difficulties, but from all I hear, that is less than certain.

The Levchenko story is not only a human tragedy but an intelligence failure. There are those at Langley who might dispute this. How can any operation be an intelligence failure, I can hear them asking, when it produces information about the agents and activities of an intelligence service as inimical to the United States as the

KGB was then? All very true, I say, but until a cooperative and valued defector is comfortable in his new life, our work is not done.

In debriefing a defector a case officer must try to establish his bona fides because a false defector, a man or woman planted by the opposition, can cause immense damage. Oversuspicion, however, can also do harm. In the CIA, suspicion of a defector's motives had become institutionalized among the CI staff, which, until Bill Colby fired him, had been headed for thirty years by James Jesus Angleton. In at least one case that I am aware of, oversuspicion has hurt us.

Yuri Nosenko, a KGB officer, contacted the CIA in Geneva in June 1962 with an offer to sell secrets for cash. He has been a source of dispute, dissension, and embarrassment to the agency ever since.

It was not until about fifteen years after Nosenko's defection that his file reached my desk. I was then associate deputy director for operations (ADDO), and it was my job to review an exhaustive study of the case that had just been completed by John Hart, a senior officer of the Clandestine Service, who had recently retired but had been recalled to duty for this specific purpose. The report made horrendous reading.

Nosenko had worked for the CIA as an agent in place until February 1964 when he defected and was flown to the United States. In the intervening years, however, Angleton had formed the conviction that Nosenko was a false defector. One very valid reason for this was that much of the intelligence Nosenko's debriefers had obtained in Geneva simply didn't make sense. Hart was able belatedly to find persuasive explanations for some of the discrepancies. Nosenko was an alcoholic. He had made no attempt to conceal his disease from his case officers. In fact, as he had told them himself, his primary motivation in defecting was that he had embezzled official funds in order to buy liquor. It seems now that much of his debriefing in Geneva took place while he was highly inebriated, a circumstance that must certainly have contributed to a lack of clear understanding. An additional barrier to communication between the agent and his case officer, Pete Bagley, was the fact that the debriefings were conducted in Russian, a language in which Bagley was only moderately proficient.

It can be appreciated that Bagley's reports must have left Angleton with the feeling that there was something wrong in

Geneva. But Angleton's doubts about Nosenko increased when he read that Nosenko had flatly contradicted statements made by Anatoly Golitsyn, an earlier defector and one in whom Angleton had complete trust. Golitsyn had predicted that the KGB would send a false defector to discredit him, and Nosenko seemed to fill the bill. Doubt hardened into certainty when Angleton read that Nosenko had claimed that Lee Harvey Oswald had not been working for the KGB when he shot President Kennedy. This was simply too much for Angleton to swallow. Thirty years of concentration on the KGB had conditioned him to see traces of them everywhere: "Of course the KGB had done it. Of course they would send a false defector to deny their guilt. It all adds up."

When Nosenko arrived in the United States in April 1964, his welcome consisted of a year and a half of abusive confinement, the only justification for which seems to have been the hope that he could be forced to implicate the Soviet Union in the Kennedy assassination. When this hope eventually faded, he was released, but his name was still under a cloud ten years later when Hart completed his review of the case.

Hart's conclusion was that Nosenko was a legitimate defector. I found his report convincing.

The agency has made what amends it could, providing Nosenko with an income for life. When I last saw him, he was married to an American woman and appeared happy. As for Angleton, some say his obsession with the KGB had turned to paranoia. I am not medically qualified to validate that opinion, but I am certain that twenty-nine years is far too long for any one person to be chief of the counterintelligence staff.

8

BERLIN INTERLUDE

BY the spring of 1965, all signs were pointing to the probability that JMWAVE would be redirected against targets in Latin America and the Caribbean, thereby becoming just one more field station under the jurisdiction of the Western Hemisphere (WH) Division. I felt it would be wise for me to get out. During the period when JMWAVE was being given first priority in the allocation of funds and personnel, I had unavoidably bruised the feelings of some of the senior WH officers. As a result, future regional teamwork with the old-timers in Latin America would undoubtedly be burdened with the baggage of the past.

For my next assignment I wanted, and I thought I had earned, a higher rung on the career ladder, an overseas station and preferably a large one. Instead, I found I was being nudged into the job of chief of base, Berlin. I was not keen to go back to Berlin. The place held too many memories for me. It was in Berlin in 1946–1947 that as a fuzzy-cheeked young man doing his military service in an Army Counterintelligence Corps (CIC) unit, I became interested in intelligence as a career. It was there that I had worked under the tutelage of the legendary practitioner of the intelligence trade Bill Harvey.

Also, the move amounted to a demotion. Whereas in Miami I enjoyed direct access to the higher headquarters in Langley, from Berlin I would have to report through an intermediate layer of bureaucracy in Bonn.

I went anyway. To help me make up my mind, they lathered me with arguments and promises: that erection of the infamous Wall had turned Berlin Base into a problem area, its agents cut off and its staff dispirited; that being a German speaker, knowing the territory, and having experience in running denied area operations, I was just the man to revitalize the place. They needn't have bothered. I went because I had never yet balked at an assignment, and I wasn't going to begin now.

Upon returning to Washington in July 1965 to prepare for the Berlin job, I called on the Soviet Division and visited the various country desks in the Eastern European Division and the Western European Division to see what one and all would expect of me in this new job. Very little, as it turned out. Because of the Wall, it seemed, a spirit of defeatism reigned. The mood of the day was that nothing operational could be done from Berlin.

The Berlin of 1965 resembled the Berlin of old in name only. There had been a time when Berlin nightclub comics would ask, "What is the difference between Berlin and the world?" and the straight men would answer "None! Berlin is the world." Those days were gone. I speak now of West Berlin, a city in shock and paralyzed by the Wall. The average citizen took no joy in his surroundings and had no confidence in the future. Businesses were retrenching, and the cream of the professional class had either already left or was preparing to leave for West Germany where jobs were better and the future more certain. Pensioners who could not afford to move constituted an increasingly large fraction of the population. The city was also harboring more and more idlers of military age, a direct consequence of the fact that West Germany's conscription law did not extend to West Berlin. In general, the watchwords were contraction and preservation—preservation of one's own skin, one's capital, and one's privacy. In the space of only seven years, West Berlin had become a dull and stodgy place.

Just as the vibrancy of the earlier Berlin had enlivened the spirits of the agency personnel assigned there, my new staff seemed to have absorbed the lethargy and defeatism that now surrounded it. Instead of a team, I was captaining an assortment of individual personalities, each one conscientiously performing the tasks assigned him but few concerning themselves with the mission of the base as a whole.

High on the list of tasks I assigned myself was the overcoming of this malaise. In hopes of encouraging the growth of something resembling team spirit among the case officers, I announced that I would play volleyball every Sunday morning with whoever cared to join me. We had a pretty good turnout for the first few weeks, but as soon as more pressing matters began to occupy my time, the athletes began one by one to fade away.

If my staff was to concentrate its attention on the mission of the base as a whole, I would have to define that mission in more dynamic terms. As I surveyed the situation, I could see that we had to confront six challenges, four of them stemming directly from the erection of the Wall. First of all, there was the defeatist mood of the population. Could we use covert action to help revitalize West Berlin, give it some feeling of permanence and survivability? There were the German agents whom the Wall had cut off from us, many of them still in good positions. Could we reestablish communication with them? Our Czech, Polish, and other non-German agents in East Berlin could still cross into West Berlin, so contact had not been lost, only confidence. How could we reassure them they were still working for the right side? The recruitment of new agents—never easy at the best of times—had been made immeasurably more difficult by the Wall. How could we overcome its negative impact?

I could only assume that things would get no better. However, the possibility that things might actually get worse did have to be addressed. What if conditions required me to evacuate the staff from Berlin? Could we make advance provision for such an eventuality by developing a stay-behind capability? Could we do so without sending an alarm signal to the population at large? This would be like walking on eggs, but the contingency had to be considered.

I reminded myself that the word "crisis" connotes both challenge and opportunity. I had identified the challenges. Was there also opportunity? The West German government was understandably as concerned as we were about the future of West Berlin and was doing its utmost to influence developments there. Could we then use Berlin as a window onto West German politics?

I decided that highlighting the need to build a stay-behind network would set too negative a mood within the base. Instead, I chose to reinforce ongoing efforts to accentuate the positive by enlisting all our covert-action assets in the campaign to help preserve the idea of Berlin as a viable entity and symbol of anti-Soviet resistance. We used what behind-the-scenes influence we could muster to see that international conferences and seminars were held in Berlin;

and a news service that normally mailed cartoons, fillers, commentaries, and stories with an anticommunist slant to newspapers in Asia, Africa, and Latin America now began including items of Berlin interest. This helped give the Berlin issue worldwide exposure.

By dint of painstaking labor, we also succeeded in reestablishing communications with a number of our agents on the eastern side of the Wall. As a preliminary we had to test each of the ten crossing points between East and West Berlin in order to learn what could and could not be carried through them, how the searches for contraband were carried out, and which categories of traveler were subjected to the most rigorous search. Once this was done, we could risk carrying letters into East Berlin for mailing to controlled addresses in the West. When these letters were back in our hands, experts in the Technical Services Division were able to tell us which had been examined the most minutely by East German censors and what tests had been performed on them. From this information we were able to make informed judgments about where we should locate our accommodation addresses, in the federal republic or overseas, what kind of cover letters would arouse the least suspicion, whether it would be best to use secret inks, microdots, or latent images for the clandestine communication, and if secret inks, what kind? Only after all this work had been done could we decide how best to train our agents in new communication techniques, what concealment devices to use in bringing their materials to them (and in some cases, bringing their documentary material out), and where and by whom to transport these things in and out of East Berlin.

We exchanged views on these topics with the West German intelligence service, the BND. In one such meeting with the Germans in Pullach, where their headquarters was located, I noted how defensive the BND officers were about why their agents had not performed better in alerting Bonn to the building of the Wall. One operational theme that emerged from this session was that we needed to use medium-speed radios extensively in the future to communicate with agents in East Germany.

The work of rebuilding communications with agents was made more difficult for us by freelance body-smugglers, who, of course, were pursuing their own agendas of profit or principle. Although we could sympathize with the idealists who were risking their own lives and freedom to help others escape from the communist East, this was small consolation when a clumsily executed bolt for freedom caused the security barriers to come clanking down at Checkpoint Charlie. Despite this, we did successfully build a capability to help people escape from the East. A Middle Eastern diplomat whom we recruited for this work was to have his finest hour in 1968 when he would exfiltrate Lieutenant Colonel Eugen Runge from East Berlin. Runge was the KGB illegal[1] who had run Leonore Heinz as a significant penetration of the West German Foreign Office, and the opportunity this case gave the CIA to talk to him underscores the reality that building agent resources is like putting money in the bank. You have it, and you use it when it is needed.

It was a source of real satisfaction to me that while working in this unfavorable environment, we were able to train an East German ship captain living in Rostock in the use of the medium-speed burst transmission radio, the RS-7, and infiltrate a set for him into East Germany. The concept inherent in this operation was simple. The captain was in a position to see early warning developments involving troop or equipment movements. If he eyeballed such events, he could alert us to them rapidly via the radio. And, if we should ever recruit an agent better able than the captain to give us early warning on the imminence of hostilities, we could use dead drops to get the intelligence to where the captain could pick it up and relay it to us by radio. The captain was unusual in that his job gave him daily access to the Rostock area land mass, and he could service dead drops in a wide area if required.

This preoccupation with early warning was born of a determination to have no surprises during my tenure in Berlin. One of the influences that had contributed to this attitude was my participation in a war game sponsored by the Rand Corporation and held at Camp David over a pressure-packed weekend in September 1961. The game had a Berlin scenario in which the challenge was to figure out the alternatives for dealing with a major-power confrontation over the divided city. Some of the key players were Henry Kissinger, then an academic, Carl Kayser of the White House staff, John McNaughton from Defense, and David Henry from the Department of State. I was on the control team to help the Rand people keep the game real world in its Berlin orientation. The insight I gleaned from the exercise was that policy makers do not like "short-fuse" surprises. The shorter the time for reaction to an unexpected event, the poorer the chances a decision will be based on a sound strategic rationale that the enemy will understand.

After getting to Berlin and reviewing all available files, talking to officers who had served in Berlin in the months immediately preceding the erection of the Wall, and hearing the views of German politicians and British, French, and German liaison contacts, I could not help wondering why the media and the congressional watchdogs on intelligence had not called the building of the Wall an intelligence fiasco. If they had done so, it seemed inevitable to me that they would have created a cause célèbre. In that atmosphere, one had to be prepared to show not only that lessons had been learned, but that they were being applied. Two such lessons, in my view, were that the CIA needed radio-communications capability in East Germany and that we wanted more agents with the access and guts to report early warning data.

The ship captain's radio came up on the air at just about the time I was being transferred from Berlin. This was the first medium-speed radio activated by any Western service in East Germany. It was a bittersweet accomplishment, however, because it earned me a reprimand from Bronson Tweedy, the Eastern European Division chief. I had sent him a cable setting forth in detail what we planned to do and how we planned to do it, and when, after a considerable interval, we had no comment from him one way or the other, I assumed that silence meant consent, as it had done in JMWAVE operations, and went ahead and executed the plan. Then, when I reported that the deed was done, I did get a reply, a critical one.

I never learned what fault Tweedy found with putting an RS-7 radio into precisely the kind of place it was designed for. Various explanations are possible, one being that Tweedy felt a need, for policy reasons, to coordinate such an operation with the Department of State. His rationale might have been that the novelty of the operation might have upset the Russians had they ever known of it, and that the delicate balance in Berlin might thereby have been damaged.

Another possibility has to do with management style. Perhaps headquarters wanted rigid decision-making control on all matters, whereas I was operating on a theory of decentralized control, which called for headquarters to set policy, provide people and funds to field stations, furnish support when collection requirements or equipment were asked for, and provide coordination among field units, but to let the field run operations on a daily basis. In this scheme of things, headquarters had a review function designed to measure field-unit productivity at periodic intervals rather than at every move. Years later, when Tweedy visited me in one of my Asia postings in order to orient himself on the Vietnam War, I gently probed him on this radio event, seeking to educate myself on why we had been worlds apart on such a fundamental issue. Tweedy responded in Delphic terms. He said, "You are clearly more at ease with the decentralized conduct of the Vietnam War than you were in Berlin."

A question that was occupying the minds of the policy makers back home was whether the federal republic would continue to align itself with the noncommunist West or whether it would increasingly find common ground with the East. We in Berlin had to be alert for any signs of a tendency for Bonn to accommodate itself to the needs and desires of East Germany. Unfortunately, there was such a sign right under our noses, one that had been becoming ever more evident since 1962 when the Soviet spy Rudolf Abel was swapped for U-2 pilot Gary Powers at Berlin's Glienicke Bridge, one that in the period 1964–1989 was to result in the transfer of more than $2.4 billion from West to East Germany in return for the release of 33,755 East German political prisoners and the family reunification of 215,019 people who joined their loved ones to live outside of East Germany.

Involved here was ransom money, the payment of hard cash in exchange for the release to West Germany of political prisoners being held in East German jails. The exchange was clearly to the net benefit of East Germany, which badly needed this infusion of hard currency and would not be inconvenienced in the least by the loss of mostly elderly "antistate elements," some of whom had been out of circulation since 1945. West German public opinion, on the other hand, was sharply divided about the morality of these transactions. Some denounced them as an infamous trafficking in human beings, some hailed them as acts of pure humanitarianism, and others quietly welcomed them for the links that they forged between the two Germanys.

John Mapother, the senior reports officer at the base, told me that these deals were being cut in Berlin by two lawyers, a West German named Juergen Stange and his East German associate,

Wolfgang Vogel; Mapother said we needed a better understanding of their activities, and I agreed. Subsequently, in reading the files on Vogel and Stange, I learned that West Berlin socialists Willy Brandt and Dietrich Spangenberg had once supported their commerce in human beings, using cash from a welfare account that Brandt had access to. When this source of funds was exhausted, it was replaced by a labyrinth of channels whose highly personalized lines of communication often ran without coordination on parallel tracks and involved such players as Brandt, Vogel, Rainer Barzel (a then up-and-coming member of the Christian Democratic Party), and the Hamburg media giant Axel Springer. Eventually, the federal government, as represented by the Berlin office of the federal All-German Affairs Ministry, joined the game, as did the Evangelical Church, which made its own payments through Stange and Vogel in exchange for the release of its parishioners.

Vogel's backing was murkier. He let it be known that he had first approached the East German authorities with the delicately floated West German proposition that a busload of repentant East German dissidents be swapped for an envelope full of cash. This was true, but it dodged the question of who were Vogel's masters. It was clear that he had a dialog with the East Germans both at the political level and among the state security groups. That explained in part the lavish lifestyle that Vogel was able to enjoy in East Berlin. He also had ties to Moscow as was proven by the Abel–Powers exchange. We felt therefore that we had to regard him as a suspected KGB or MfS agent and needed to keep a close eye on the network of vested interests that he was building in West Berlin.

High on the list were Willy Brandt and his close associates in the Socialist Party of Germany (SPD). During the brief time that I remained in Berlin, Brandt's *Ostpolitik* was still tentative and modest, but by the time he became federal chancellor in 1969, he was advocating major concessions to East Germany. Also on the list was the Berlin office of the All-German Affairs Ministry. We blanketed these targets with sources both human and technical, and although in the period 1965–1966 we never resolved to our satisfaction the question of whether Vogel was a Soviet agent, we did stay abreast of the scope and direction of the ransom payments and were able to monitor the growth of Brandt's *Ostpolitik*. Washington policy makers therefore experienced no surprises on these issues.

By 1966 Washington was trying through normal diplomatic channels to get Bonn to take a public position in support of the Vietnam War effort but was not having much success. The Eastern European Division then called on us to see what we could do through unofficial channels that had been built up by Ralph Brown, a German-born case officer attached to the Berlin Base. When Brown discussed Vietnam with German politicos, he was told that officialdom was on the horns of a dilemma. The government wanted to show solidarity with the United States but was anxious to avoid the wrenching internal dissension that it was sure would follow any public display of hostility to Hanoi or the Vietcong. Brown's interlocutors said they would be most grateful if Brown could suggest some gesture they could make that would achieve the one thing and avoid the other. Brown, acting on a previously agreed-upon CIA strategy, suggested that they equip and dispatch a hospital ship. The idea was seized on, and when I arrived in Saigon in 1968, the former North Sea ferry *Helgoland* was cruising off to Indochina in its new role as an angel of mercy.

Our major excursion into Soviet operations was a bitter disappointment to me. At just about the time that I arrived in Berlin, one of our men recruited a field-grade Soviet officer. As there is a very good possibility this officer is still alive, I must be cautious in what I say about him, but I think it is safe to note that his specialty concerned neither intelligence nor politics but rather was technical. We worked hard to authenticate him, and from my point of view we succeeded. He was who he said he was, he worked where he said he worked, he lived where he said he lived, and the level of information he gave us was commensurate with his position. His motivation for working for us was sound: Like so many other Eastern Europeans posted to within sight and smell of the West, he had become dangerously overextended and needed money.

I expected headquarters to be pleased with this development, if not actually congratulatory, but its reaction was querulous and picky. Our authentication procedures were brushed aside as of no importance, and we were assured we could never trust our new agent.

It was hard to counter these arguments because I couldn't be quite sure where they were coming from, the Soviet Division, the Eastern European Division, or the CI staff. I thought the latter alternative was the more likely, given Jim Angleton's known bias against Soviet agents.

I tried, though. I cabled back in effect, "Well, okay, let's say that the guy isn't turning out a product that's of vital interest, but let's train him and so forth, so that when he goes back home and into what may be a better position, we'll have an agent in place. Let's see what happens, and in the meantime use it as a training exercise, a confidence-builder for our officers to let them know that they've successfully recruited the most difficult of targets, a Soviet."

It was no use. Everything that I got back from headquarters on this case started with the presumption we had blundered into a Soviet trap, and for us to train this new agent in anything would simply be to reveal our modus operandi to the other side. Admittedly, the CI staff, or whoever it was that I was corresponding with, might have had information to buttress its argument, information from a source so sensitive that it couldn't be shared with me, but nary a hint of this did I get from the cable traffic with which I was constantly pounded. Instead, the recurring theme was, "The guy's a Soviet, Soviets can't be trusted, and therefore your operation is sour from the beginning." Finally, to avoid having to hear any more variations on this theme, we ended our relationship with this agent. I still think it was a waste.

In January 1966 I got a cable from Des FitzGerald, who by then was DDP, saying in effect, "We realize that you have been in Berlin a very short period of time, but we'd like you to go to Laos. How about it?"

I jumped at it.

9

LAOS:
THE IMPERATIVE OF CHANGE

IN preparation for my new assignment, I went to the Special Services library to get everything they had on Laos. All they had was one book, which gives some idea of the importance the U.S. Army attached to Laos. Then, I had a stroke of luck. My counterpart in the French intelligence service, the SDECE, Colonel Clemenceau, had served in Vietnam and had some knowledge of Laos. He was gracious enough to spend many evenings with me, telling me in detail how to deal with the Indochinese tribal people and the Vietnamese.

Agency travel regulations limited Hazel and me to one shipment of forty-five pounds of excess baggage and 150 pounds of unaccompanied air freight. The rest of our material possessions then in Berlin were to be stored in Bremerhaven until a post-Laos assignment made it cost-effective to ship the household goods to our next post, wherever that might be. Hazel began weighing items that might go into the forty-five-pound shipment. It quickly became apparent that this portion of our weight allowance had to be dedicated to our daughter Suzanne's most prized possessions—a Raggedy Ann doll, a teddy bear, and children's books. Unfortunately, there was no room for Bobo, a rocking horse that at the time was Suzanne's greatest treasure. Years later as a teenager, Suzanne still recalled Bobo's loss as one of several negative aspects of Dad's wanderings around the globe with the family in tow.

With our travel and other administrative plans settled, Hazel and I made the appropriate round of Berlin farewell parties. Our German contacts were perplexed by my abbreviated tour. They saw little merit in Washington's moving what they saw as an experienced German hand to the Southeast Asian jungles. One liaison contact, the West Berlin police chief, who knew of my anti-Castro experience with paramilitary operations, was more perceptive. As we talked one evening over farewell drinks, he said, "You are going to be in Southeast Asia for years. In that time you will work both sides of the street. At some point you will be directing guerrilla operations. At others you will be trying to defeat irregulars. As you face those challenges, bear in mind my experience as a young German officer on the Russian front in World War II. I fought the partisans. We Germans suffered more damage in Russia from guerrillas than from any other type of combat. We learned that irregulars are a cheap way to sap an enemy's fighting strength. If you can make use of guerrillas in the war against Hanoi, do it."

Once I arrived at headquarters, it was clear that everything possible was being done to have me in Laos by early July 1966. My outprocessing with the Eastern European Division was perfunctory at best; Berlin issues were being subordinated to the priority of the war in Indochina.

My first point of contact in the Far East Division was Bill Colby, the division chief. We had not met previously. All I knew about him was what I had heard of the corridor gossip. He had been in OSS during World War II and had parachuted into Scandinavia where he had performed heroically. After the war he had served with distinction in Rome and Saigon as a CIA officer. In Washington he was jokingly referred to as Langley's Jesuit-in-residence specializing in liberation theology, an allusion to his commitment to nation building in places like Vietnam and Laos. Last but not least, it was speculated he was a future deputy director for plans and even a possible director of the CIA.

He told me I needed to make a special effort to lay on a quiet Washington evening with Vint Lawrence who had just returned from Long Tieng, Laos, where he had been the principal day-to-day point of liaison with Vang Pao, the key guerrilla leader among the Hmong. Vint would be joining Colby's personal staff in a matter of days for his next assignment. He was a gold mine of information on Laos that I should work, he said, for the nuggets I would need.

In the days and weeks that followed I came to work early and stayed late in order to read NSC position papers on Laos, review decision memoranda of the 303 Group, which had authorized an increase in the number of paramilitary troops in Laos, and look at program files dealing with budgets, personnel, and programs. In addition, I started reading the positive intelligence that was flowing out of the Vientiane Station, as well as monitoring the station's operational traffic that dealt with the nuts and bolts of current operations. I spent lunch hours, coffee breaks, and whatever free time I could squeeze out of the schedules of officers who had served in Laos to discuss their experiences and their knowledge of the country, its peoples, and its problems.

Vint Lawrence devoted several office sessions to briefing me on how things worked in Laos. He also took the initiative in arranging a social evening at his apartment where we could discuss the dynamics of Hmong life in anthropological terms. When I probed gingerly on what else could be done from Laos to contribute further to winning the Vietnam War, Vint expressed the opinion that little more could be done from the Hmong area in North Laos. The focus would have to be on the southern panhandle, and there Vint did not feel he knew enough about tribes like the Kha to provide any useful advice. This was a candid appreciation of the situation and was one shared by many of the agency people who had previously served in Laos.

I then started my series of courtesy calls on key Washington officials. This involved meetings at the Pentagon and the State Department and with NSC staffers. What emerged from this round of visits was everyone's preoccupation with the imperative that there be an increase in the level of military activity against Hanoi's forces in the Lao panhandle. Policy makers such as William P. Bundy, the assistant secretary of state for the Far East, told Colby and me they clearly considered such action critical to the protection of U.S. forces in Vietnam. There were then about three hundred thousand American ground troops and Air Force personnel in Vietnam, with two additional divisions slated to get there by December 1966. This, coupled with the other unit deployments that were in progress, meant that American troop strength in Vietnam was forecast to be at the four-hundred-thousand level by the end of the year.

I found no interagency disagreement on the fundamental need to do more against Hanoi's use of the Ho Chi Minh Trail. The unsolved riddle was what could be done by whom and at what political price. My sense of the turf battles that were about to emerge was

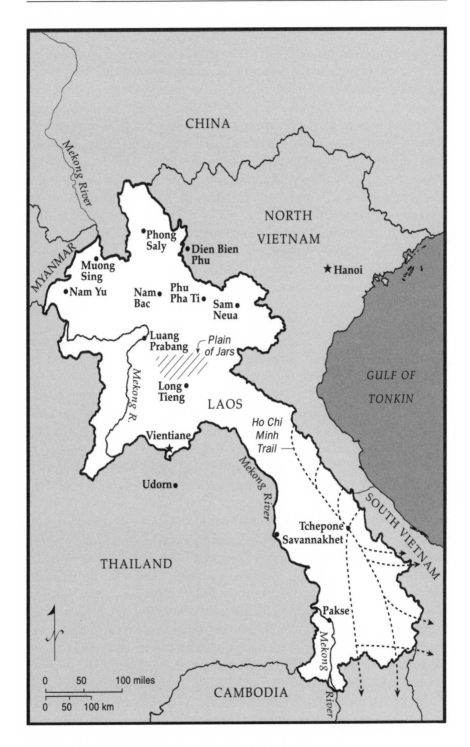

that the Department of Defense wanted to run penetrations in force by American troops into the Ho Chi Minh route structure to disrupt it as much as possible. The State Department, on the other hand, wanted to preserve the illusion of Lao neutrality. One way of doing so was to have the Lao do what they could against the Vietnamese forces in the panhandle. One and all conceded that the Force Armée Royale (FAR) was not up to this challenge, which left only one other option predicated on the assumption that the CIA could use indigenous paramilitary forces in South Laos to achieve the same levels of success that had been attained in North Laos. Should the passage of some undefined but brief period of time prove that the CIA's contribution did not meet expectations, a widening of the war was inevitable. What form it would take was not clear. This created an environment in which the pressure on the CIA to do more was nothing less than intense.

In my farewell meeting with Colby, I was urged to think about alternative pools of manpower for panhandle operations. I said I had talked with others about using Thai or Nung on a selective basis. This had produced generally negative responses. The Thai had been characterized as good artillerymen but were not seen as aggressive enough for the raid and ambush tasks. The Nung, while reliable soldiers, had been corrupted by city life in South Vietnam, and were seen as "Cholon cowboys" more suited for static defense activities rather than hit-and-run operations in tough jungle terrain. If we could overcome the expected State Department opposition to the use of nonindigenous forces in Laos, perhaps Gurkhas might be the answer.

Having saved what I thought would be our most controversial topic for the last agenda item, I noted that the level of station effort devoted to nation building seemed excessive. What we needed to emphasize, I suggested, was the economic well-being of those tribal elements that worked with us. Other aspects of what was being done in the nation-building arena seemed more of a U.S. Agency for International Development (USAID) task than one properly carried out by the CIA, particularly since American aid to Laos in 1966 was programmed at about the $50 million level for nonmilitary assistance.

To my surprise, Colby said that the demands on the CIA's resources had become so heavy that fine-tuning was required in some of our covert-action projects. "See what you think once you have looked at this effort on the ground," said Colby. "If cuts appear warranted or programs need to be transferred to other agencies like USAID, let's do it."

That was more of a mandate for change than I had expected. It underscored for me the obvious resource crunch in terms of money and manpower that the Vietnam War was imposing on the CIA.

My final briefing was by the director of central intelligence, Richard Helms, who made it clear that his primary concern was the Vietnam War. He said he knew I understood the nuances of the schizophrenia about Laos being an integral part of the war in Vietnam. On one hand powerful policy-level voices wanted the fig leaf of neutrality as provided by the Geneva Accords to prevail in Laos. Other equally influential policy formulators were demanding a greater contribution from Laos to the successful conduct of the war in South Vietnam; that is, the CIA had to do more from the Lao panhandle against North Vietnamese Army (NVA) forces. In walking the fine line between these divergent groups as I tried to devise a strategy for the Vientiane Station, Helms noted it would be prudent for me to enlist Ambassador William Sullivan as a supporter for any new initiative rather than engage in polemics with him.

I realized at once that Helms was telling me not to fall into the trap of being at odds with the ambassador, as an earlier chief of station in Vientiane, Henry Hecksher, had been with Ambassador Winthrop Brown. Puzzled and somewhat troubled by what might be the true significance of this guidance, I said Hecksher's record was well known to me. While I admired many of Henry's talents and could not hope to be the fountain of knowledge on German history and politics that he was, I was persuaded that my past experience in working harmoniously with ambassadors had developed my sensitivity levels to the point where it was unlikely I would end up in a hostile relationship with Ambassador Sullivan. Having made his point, Helms said it was his view that Sullivan and I would get along just fine. With that, our meeting came to an end. I said my good-byes. Helms said he looked forward to seeing what my program recommendations would be for Laos sixty days hence.

En route to the Far East, I stopped in Honolulu to make a courtesy call to Admiral Ulysses S. Grant Sharpe, commander in chief, Pacific (CINCPAC). He was a man short in stature, slight of build, and quiet in demeanor. A natural gentleman's civility exuded from him. He asked about my family, our schedule for getting to Laos, and most importantly about my agency experiences. It was clear he was taking my measure. Equally visible was the admiral's concern that, with a widening of the Vietnam War as reflected in the ongoing American troop buildup in South Vietnam, there had to be a corresponding push by Hanoi to put more logistics and manpower into its battle plan. That seemed to be the objective of General Nguyen Chi Thanh, Hanoi's senior general in the south. How to impede such a move was of paramount strategic concern to CINCPAC.

The admiral then treated me to a *tour d'horizon* of the possibilities of limiting Hanoi's logistics options. First on his menu was the need to mine Haiphong's harbor and to use submarines to keep the harbor bottled up. This would stop the flow of Russian and Chinese matériel to North Vietnam via the cost-effective sea routes. Second, a sustained air campaign needed to be mounted against North Vietnam's railroad system, particularly against chokepoints along routes entering North Vietnam from China and then moving southward. Third, the Red River dikes should be bombed; the resulting floods would divert some of Hanoi's time and attention from the war. The cumulative impact of this strategy would do two things. It would curb Hanoi's logistical ability to seek a decisive battlefield victory against Saigon in the near term. Additionally, it would force General Vo Nguyen Giap, Hanoi's senior strategist, to revert to a protracted war option where infiltration of men and matériel would be focused exclusively on the Ho Chi Minh Trail. In time the "attrition price" imposed on Hanoi for its use of the trail, by American airpower and ground operations launched from both South Vietnam and Laos against the trail structure, had a chance of causing either a battlefield stalemate or enough of a victory for Saigon that a longer-term political solution could be negotiated. After outlining his views, the admiral added that Washington had thus far put its money on a selective bombing campaign against North Vietnam known as Operation Rolling Thunder. This operation did not use smart bombs, however, so it was not as effective as it might have been, for iron bombs did not produce the desired results against bridges. The Ho Chi Minh Trail was also being attacked with both airpower and limited ground operations mounted from South Vietnam by a special American unit known as the

Military Advisor Command Vietnam (MACV) Studies and Operations Group (SOG). The latter was allowed to operate only in shallow penetration in an area of Laos designated as Prairie Fire. Admiral Sharpe thought Ambassador Sullivan had been instrumental in placing too many restrictions on MACV SOG operations into the Lao panhandle. The admiral asked that I bear in mind his views that more could be done by MACV SOG in the panhandle as I formulated the new CIA program for South Laos. I said the ambassador's views on this topic were not yet known to me as we had not met. On a personal basis, however, I assured the admiral that his point of view would be factored into CIA planning for future operations against the Ho Chi Minh Trail structure.

After intermediate stops in Tokyo and Bangkok, Hazel and I got our first glimpse of the Vietnam War when our small agency aircraft set down in Udorn, a bustling military airfield recently carved out of the flat red soil of rural Thailand. As we rolled down the runway, camouflaged American jets of various types were getting into position for takeoff. One look at the bomb racks told me that these birds were being launched for air strikes connected with the war in Vietnam. If one needed a reality check, this was it. No one was talking theory here.

It was on this short flight that I got acquainted with Colonel Dhep, the head of Headquarters 333. He exuded charm, intelligence, and intensity, was obviously comfortable with Westerners, and had an extroverted personality that did not fit the profile of what I had been led to believe in Washington briefings was typical for Thai military men. Dhep wanted to know what the prospects were for change in Washington's policies on the Vietnam War, the struggle in Laos, and the North Vietnamese–supported insurgency threat to Thailand. In fielding these very legitimate questions in a preliminary way, I said Washington wanted battlefield results in Vietnam that would lead to a political solution favorable to free-world interests. In this context the war in North Laos could be expected to proceed in the future as it had in the past. The Lao panhandle was a different subject. Washington wanted more done in that area in order to raise the cost for Hanoi's violation of Lao sovereignty. This was a topic, therefore, that Dhep and I needed to address in detail over the coming weeks when his ideas would be most welcome. With regard to the emerging threat in Northeast

Thailand, I said that my Washington briefing had not touched on that topic. Dhep seemed pleased with the frankness of my remarks, and we agreed to meet soon in Udorn for further discussions.

In Udorn we were introduced to Jim Lilley and Pat Landry. The two men contrasted sharply in appearance, dress, and manner. Lilley, who was the deputy chief of Vientiane Station operating under diplomatic cover, was tall and athletic in appearance, with hair that was beginning to show flashes of gray. He wore a tropical suit and looked "diplomatic." I knew from reading his file at headquarters that he was an experienced Asian hand, having already served in the Philippines, Cambodia, and Thailand. Born in China as the son of an oil company executive, he was fluent in Mandarin and could also speak French. Washington viewed him as a rising star.

Landry was deputy chief in Udorn. He was a stocky, suntanned, powerfully built man with close-cropped dark hair and dressed in a short-sleeved, tan-colored sport shirt, light-colored cotton slacks, and thong sandals. He looked to me like an ex–college football player, one who probably had played at the guard position. The striking feature about him was a swagger stick, which he kept flicking against his pant leg. I knew that Landry was a Texas A&M man who had spent his career in Asia in paramilitary operations. He and Bill Lair were the Lao paramilitary equivalent of the famous West Point football players Doc Blanchard and Glenn Davis, known as "Mr. Inside" and "Mr. Outside." Landry looked like "Mr. Inside," and that was his reputation. He moved people and matériel while Lair handled tactics and relations with Vang Pao and the Thai.

The Shackleys and Lilley then boarded a twin-engined Dornier aircraft for the fifteen or twenty-minute flight to Vientiane. Upon landing in Vientiane we met a number of people in a blur of faces— Air America personnel and people from the station. One stood out—Sally Lilley—not only because of her erect posture, engaging smile, and elegant manner, but because she quickly and efficiently took Suzanne and Hazel in tow and got them into Jim's Volkswagen. Jim and I followed them promptly, for it was hot in the late afternoon sun.

With Jim driving, we left the airport and were soon on a road that was described as the main route into Vientiane. As I was looking to the side of the road at the corrugated tin siding and roofs on what passed for shops, and saw Indian, Chinese, and Vietnamese merchants hawking bolts of cloth, pots and pans and rice, it struck me that we were entering an environment more primitive than what the Washington briefings had portrayed. Just then my attention was seized by an accident scene, a child of five or six years having apparently been killed by a truck. As a crowd gathered, Hazel diverted Suzanne's attention to the other side of the road where there were chickens, ducks, water buffalo, and horses. Spotting the animals, Suzanne said, "Mommy, Mommy, what fun! Laos is a farm." With that I knew one member of the family would have no trouble adjusting to life in Laos. The Lilleys took us to their home, pointing out en route Vientiane's one stoplight, the morning market, and other noteworthy sites. After a brief break for coffee and a chance for me to freshen up, Jim said he wanted to take me to the office to meet outgoing station chief Doug Blaufarb. The latter was finishing up some paperwork at the embassy, had a farewell dinner engagement that evening, and was leaving Laos the next day. In view of that, we needed to get on with the passing of the baton.

Once in the embassy we went directly to the station premises, for the ambassador was out and there was no need to attempt to pay a courtesy call on him. Jim introduced me to Blaufarb and diplomatically excused himself in order to complete some tasks in his own office. Lilley obviously sensed that whatever time was available for Blaufarb and me to exchange views on the station was best utilized without the presence of a third party.

Blaufarb had a haggard look. When he spoke his voice had no bounce. The impression he made was that of a tired man who needed some time at a luxury beach resort. I vowed to myself that I wouldn't let the Vientiane job wear me down.

As we talked, I went through my mental checklist, focusing first on potential problems.

"Are there any issues outstanding with the ambassador?"

"No."

"Does the station have any turf disputes with other members of the country team?"

"Yes. The USAID Director Joe Mendenhall is unhappy with some aspects of the station's Sedone Valley pacification project, but it isn't serious."

"Should I be concerned about any personnel issues such as alcoholism?"

"No."

"Can I assume the station's finances and logistics are in proper shape?"

"Yes."

"Are there any problems with liaison?"

"No."

I could see that Blaufarb was getting restless, so I asked how much time we had.

"Not much," he said. He had to be at a farewell dinner being given in his honor by a foreign diplomat, so at the most we could talk for another thirty minutes before he had to leave for home to change clothes and pick up his wife.

"Okay," I said icily, "when do we formally transfer command?"

Blaufarb picked up on the shift in my tone of voice. "I know you have done everything humanly possible to get here in order to have a reasonable overlap with me. It just didn't work, due to circumstances beyond your control, but I must leave on schedule. My plans can't be changed."

I knew from headquarters that the pressure was not connected to Blaufarb's next assignment. Whatever was driving him had to be something personal. "So be it," I thought.

Our time was now up. Blaufarb suggested I ride with him to his residence so that we could continue to talk and work out a schedule for the next morning, the program of which included such absolutely essential items as an introduction to Ambassador Sullivan and cabled notification to Washington that I had taken over command of the station. After an uneventful ride to Blaufarb's residence, I met a very uptight Mrs. Blaufarb. This lady was keen to get the Lao experience behind her. We chatted briefly and I then excused myself and had the Blaufarb driver take me to the Lilleys' where I rejoined my family. Suzanne had found a friend in the Lilleys' youngest son, Jeffrey, and Hazel was learning from the Lilleys about life in Laos.

The next day was pressure packed. The station had a car pick me up at 7:15 A.M. and take me to the embassy. In the bright sun of an early Asian morning, the embassy compound located on a side street not far from the morning market looked dilapidated. In fact, as I gazed over the embassy grounds and had a chance to take a better look at the interior of the building, I concluded this was the shabbiest American embassy I had ever seen. Jim Lilley introduced me to the handful of people who were in the office—secretaries, communications personnel, the reports officer, and one or two case officers. With that icebreaker behind me, I found a chair in Blaufarb's office, drafted the change of command cable, and had it typed up ready for Blaufarb's signature. I then plunged into the stack of cable traffic that had come into the station overnight.

Later that day I had my first long talk with Ambassador Bill Sullivan, a man I knew only from what I had gleaned from my friends in the State Department, at the Pentagon, and at the agency. Sullivan was a Brown University graduate, had been an officer in the Navy, and upon entering the Foreign Service had consistently come to his superiors' attention for his wit, his ability to write interesting diplomatic reports, and his willingness to speak his mind with a degree of frankness not characteristic of most midlevel American diplomats. The latter trait had occasionally caused him grief by earning him postings to backwater assignments. On the other hand, this same characteristic had caught Averell Harriman's attention when the latter was involved with the Geneva Conferences on Laos in 1961–1962. Sullivan had worked closely with Harriman there and had won the older man's confidence and respect. As a result Harriman, who then was appointed assistant secretary of state for Far Eastern Affairs, became Sullivan's mentor and patron. This boost, coupled with Sullivan's considerable diplomatic skills, had resulted in his becoming America's youngest ambassador at the time that he arrived in Laos in 1964.

Sullivan was an acknowledged expert on Laos. He was credited with having an excellent relationship with Prime Minister Prince Souvanna Phouma, an alleged neutralist; he knew the Pathet Lao leader Prince Souphanouvong; and he could get the attention of the unsociable rightist Prince Boun Oum na Champassak. He was also known to be dedicated to preserving the tattered fig leaf of Lao neutrality. He therefore had forcefully articulated the position that the American military, particularly MACV, had to be kept out of Laos. Clearly, Sullivan's view had prevailed thus far in Washington's policy formulation circles.

Sullivan said he was familiar with my record and that he knew I was on a fast-track career-development program within the CIA. His colleagues in the State Department who had worked with me in the past said I was a straight shooter, a hard worker, a skilled practitioner of the craft of intelligence, and a very determined advocate of the CIA's positions in interdepartmental forums. The latter trait had caused some to question my ability to be a team player in the complex environment of Laos. Because of that, Sullivan wanted to clear the air on two points. First, he as ambassador was America's senior representative in Laos.

I said, "That principle is well codified in interagency agreements and I've no thought of challenging it."

Sullivan replied, "Fine, but please sign this statement saying we have discussed this matter."

The paper he placed before me broke no new ground in the area of CIA–State Department relations. I signed it but remarked I thought it was unnecessary, given the interagency agreements already in force.

Sullivan, sensing my irritation over this gambit, quickly moved to his second point. In essence it was an admonishment to stay away from Prime Minister Souvanna Phouma. The task of conducting liaisons with the prime minister was defined as being exclusively Sullivan's turf. Simply put, Sullivan said he did not want a situation to develop similar to what existed in Thailand where the station chief had equal if not better access to the prime minister than did the ambassador.

"Fine," I told him. "Dealing directly with heads of state is not an integral part of my strategy."

Having made his points, Sullivan asked how I planned to proceed on the priority task of getting more paramilitary operations functioning against North Vietnamese forces operating in, from, or through the Lao panhandle while preserving the spirit of Lao "neutrality." In response I outlined my preliminary ideas for developing new operations by modifying and expanding the concept of road-watch teams. Ten-man teams, I said, made up of indigenous personnel—Lao or Kha—would be selected, trained, and dispatched into the Ho Chi Minh Trail area to find a prominent terrain feature from which they could find the enemy and report on his movement by radio, thus providing us with a basis for taking air or ground actions against the North Vietnamese/Pathet Lao personnel or logistics. In addition, it was my intention to draw on the lessons learned from successful operations that had been conducted in North Laos

by Vang Pao's forces. This meant we would use twelve-man reconnaissance teams to find the enemy, engage him in firefights, take
prisoners, and search enemy dead for documents. Additionally, we
would plant mines along North Vietnamese infiltration routes in
the Lao panhandle and—on a highly selective basis—mount raids
against enemy command posts, communications facilities, or storage depots. We would hope that as a result of these programs a constantly increasing number of Hanoi's forces would be tied down in
flank security tasks in South Laos and thus kept out of combat
against American forces in South Vietnam. An expansion of existing CIA facilities at Savannakhet and Pakse would naturally be required, but I would be unable to discuss specifics before consulting
further with my associates at Udorn, Savannakhet, and Pakse.

Sullivan paused for reflection. He then asked if we could have
these programs in place by the end of the rainy season in November
1966.

I told him the program would be functional by then but just
barely. As an example of our problems, I pointed out that once we
recruited personnel for road-watch teams, we would have to give
them six to eight weeks of training.

The ambassador said, "You don't have a Vang Pao to work with
in Savannakhet. General Bounphone Makthepharak, the Military
Region-3 (MR-3) commander, is a political general more interested
in business and making money than fighting a war. You can't count
on him to help you with finding recruits. In Pakse you have General
Phasouk as MR-4 commander. He is highly regarded as a conventional soldier but has shown little sympathy for guerrilla-warfare
concepts. That, and the fact that his relations with the ethnic groups
in his region such as the Kha are poor, does not augur well for the
prospects of quick success."

In response I noted that while our options were not open-ended,
the files in Washington suggested Phasouk had been a key player in
making the Sedone Valley development project a pacification success. Perhaps, with that experience under his belt, Phasouk could
be persuaded by our man in Pakse, Brandy Carlon, to be more supportive of a more aggressive paramilitary program, particularly
since it made sense for us to try to build our road-watch teams on
the Kha tribal groupings. In Savannakhet we might have to recruit
Lao teams unilaterally or see if we could get Thai volunteers for our

programs. If that failed we would have to look at using Nung from South Vietnam or Gurkhas demobilized by the British.

Sullivan winced at the mention of Gurkhas. He said that their use in Laos would shred the concept of Lao neutrality. Because of that he asked that I not pursue the idea of using Gurkhas until all other options had failed. That was an easy request to honor, for as I told the ambassador, we would need policy approval from Washington to use Gurkhas in Laos.

Sullivan asked what pressure we could expect from the Pentagon to gain a license for MACV to expand ground operations into Laos. I told the ambassador that a major buildup of U.S. forces in South Vietnam was continuing and that Washington policy makers had consequently decided that more had to be done from Laos against Hanoi's use of the Lao panhandle. The question was how. The preferred solution would be to achieve this objective while preserving Lao neutrality. The option deemed best for doing that was expanding the CIA paramilitary program. My evaluation of the Washington mood left me with the sense that the 1966–1967 dry season (December–April) would be the testing time. Either Laos would make an enhanced contribution to inflicting pain on Hanoi's forces in the panhandle or someone else would take over the job. That someone would be MACV and/or a Southeast Asian Theater command run out of what was now MACV.

Late in the afternoon, Jim Lilley and I went to the commercial terminal at Vientiane's Wattay Airport to participate in a champagne send-off for Blaufarb. I was impressed by the size of the turnout and asked Jim if Blaufarb had been an unusually popular member of the diplomatic community. Jim said it would be a mistake to read too much into the size of the send-off. There was very little to do socially in Vientiane, so Westerners and Lao alike always turned out in numbers for these affairs where one could socialize as well as engage in diplomatic information gathering. However, he added, Blaufarb had been active socially and was well liked.

It was at this affair that I met Brigadier General Oudone Sananikone, the chief of staff of the Royal Lao Army, and Colonel Etam Singvongsa, the G-2, or head of military intelligence. The most memorable encounter, however, was with Major General Kouprasith Abhay, commander of MR-5, which included Vientiane. Kouprasith was regarded as the strong man of Vientiane for he had the troops required to make or break any coup that might take place there. He was not on good terms with the station, however, for he still brooded over General Vang Pao's past association with General Phoumi Nosavan, a former Lao defense minister now living in exile in Thailand, and resented the support the CIA was giving to Vang Pao. In addition, Kouprasith was a Francophile and, as such, was a believer in French military doctrine, which called for the Royal Lao government (RLG) to have enough military power to keep it on a par with the Kong Le neutralists and/or the Pathet Lao. Under this estimate of the situation, Kouprasith as MR-5 commander believed he would get the lion's share of the French military assistance effort, particularly any tanks scheduled to be given to the Lao. That is what he lusted for because tanks made or broke coups.

When we were introduced and Kouprasith learned I had been transferred to Laos from Berlin, he asked why. My response was blunt. I said that the Vietnam War was entering a new phase, one that would affect Laos significantly. Because of that and because of the professional skills I had acquired in other limited wars, my government had seen fit to post me to Vientiane.

Kouprasith's English was not up to grasping that, so he had the nearby General Oudone Sananikone translate into Lao. Kouprasith's response was, "Interesting, we must talk further at another time." He then stalked off.

Oudone said, "You got his attention. Follow up on that for there needs to be a better American dialog with Kouprasith."

As Blaufarb prepared to board his aircraft, General Oudone remarked, "It is auspicious according to Lao folklore to start a long journey cleansed by the rains."

"Yes," replied Blaufarb, "it is a good omen."

Oudone went on, "With the rains that we have had and what is forecast in a few weeks time, you might be saying in Paris *après moi le deluge.*" Oudone laughed at his own joke, but as he turned toward me he noted there was barely a smile on my face. Ever the gentle Lao, Oudone quickly explained he had not meant to suggest that Laos would suffer major battlefield losses now that Blaufarb had departed. Instead, his remark was intended as an expression of real concern over the prospects of a flood in August as the up-country rainfall worked its way southward. The general's remarks were my first early warning indicator of a possible flood in Vientiane and points southward. I thanked Oudone for his clarification while making a mental note to see what our contingency plans would be for continuing operations if indeed we were confronted with a flood.

10

A FLOOD AND A COUP

I checked with the station's chief of support, Jerry Ferrentinos, and his deputy, Allen Elkins, and both confirmed that we were likely to experience the deluge that General Oudone Sananikone had referred to. I asked them to work up a station contingency plan, one that would fit into any plan that the embassy might have for dealing with a flood. Essentially, I wanted a scenario for coping with the evacuation of CIA families to Udorn or Bangkok, the prepositioning of food and water supplies at our embassy offices, an emergency communications plan tying all station personnel into a voice radio network, and the selection of alternative locations on high ground where the hard core of the station could function despite the flood. Ferrentinos, Elkins, and our chief logistics man, Joe Nolan, turned to and developed an excellent plan that included prepositioning rubber rafts at key locations for use in a possible emergency.

By late August of 1966 we could be sure we were going to have flooding in Vientiane. The daily monsoon cloudbursts—awesome because of their frequency and intensity—surpassed anything that my family and I had experienced during hurricane seasons in subtropical southern Florida. Reports from the USAID technicians charged with monitoring rainfall in areas north of Vientiane, together with anecdotal reports from CIA officers working throughout North Laos, left no room for doubt. In fact we could see that entire areas of Laos along the length of the Mekong River below Vientiane were going to be affected. The still unanswered questions were how high the September floodwaters would rise and how long the major population centers, particularly Vientiane, would be inundated. With no answers readily available and given my responsibility for the safety of CIA employees and the security of agency facilities in Vientiane, Savannakhet, and Pakse, I deferred my plans for a quick trip back to Washington. A station chief simply did not leave his post in time of potential crisis.

In a matter of days, the Mekong overflowed its banks, and numerous tributaries suddenly flowed through Vientiane. In the heart of the city in the area of the morning market, sections could be crossed only in small native boats—pirogues—or rubber rafts of the RB-10 category powered by small outboard motors. The waters were so swift in some areas that livestock would float by before anyone could rescue them. After a few days the swift currents carried down all sorts of debris from dead pigs to logs and an occasional human body. Fortunately, there was also high ground, particularly in the residential areas where most foreigners lived. This meant that Vientiane had become a city of floodwaters mixed with islands of high dry spots.

The house that I then occupied—Blaufarb's former residence—was on high ground. To make the daily 9:00 A.M. country-team meeting with the ambassador and his staff, I had to traverse a rather complicated route. My journey started at 6:00 A.M. when an American three-quarter-ton, four-wheel-drive military vehicle known as a weapons carrier picked me up at my residence. It took me on a ten-minute ride through a sea of humanity—Lao, Thai, Vietnamese, and Chinese—seeking high ground and food and shelter. The vehicle dropped me at a rubber raft pickup point manned by embassy Marines who ferried me over a treacherous stretch of water to another high spot of land about five minutes away. There, another vehicle—a military two-and-a-half-ton truck—would take me across this island to another Marine-controlled rubber raft that would bring me up to the embassy courtyard. Here I would disembark by 7:00 A.M. and walk in wading boots in knee-high water to the embassy building, which had at various times six to ten inches of water on the ground floor. I would then proceed to my second-floor office, where I would read the overnight cable traffic from Washington, Saigon, Bangkok, and Udorn. By 8:00 A.M. I would start the return journey to get by 9:00 A.M. to the bit of high ground where the country team was meeting under Ambassador Sullivan's chairmanship at the residence of an embassy officer.

The station's flood contingency plan functioned perfectly. A few wives and children went out of Laos on leave to Bangkok. Other families moved in with friends. For example, Sally and Jim Lilley provided shelter for various Americans, like Mark Pratt and Bill Manes and his wife, as well as for various Lao friends. Our emergency radios performed as expected, and we were able to keep in touch with all station personnel. The support staff led by Jerry Ferrentinos, Allen Elkins, and Joe Nolan did an outstanding job of keeping things running by supplying everyone with life's necessities. The communications people at the station also performed superbly.

We were never really isolated, for the high ground around That Luang served as an excellent helicopter pad. This permitted me to go to Udorn for a few hours of meetings whenever required. The helicopter ride from Vientiane to Udorn over a rampaging Mekong was indeed a sight to behold.

The flood gave me an early insight into how the gentle land of Laos really functioned. Its Buddhist orientation was on display when I raised with General Oudone Sananikone the need to do something for the sake of public safety about the packs of wild dogs that were roaming the high-ground areas, attacking what was left of chickens, cats, and other small domestic animals. Several packs menaced young children and older people. With food getting scarcer among the Lao, it seemed only a matter of time until these packs started attacking humans. Rabies was also a growing concern. The police had refused to address the wild dog issue, claiming this was a matter for the military.

Oudone asked what I would suggest. My initial and somewhat flippant response was that a few expert marksmen with M-1 carbines ought to be able to thin out the packs without endangering the public. This was politely rejected as not in keeping with Lao Buddhist values. We then kicked around a variety of other approaches. Finally, Oudone decided to set pellets of a meat-type mixture out where wild dogs could get them, every third pellet being laced with poison. Which dog ate which pellet would then be a matter of fate and thus more in keeping with Lao traditions. In the days that followed, the wild dog packs began to diminish. Some of our American cynics suggested this was the result of hungry Lao imitating the Vietnamese practice of killing and eating dogs. Others were willing to credit Oudone's pellets.

In line with our contingency planning, we had prepositioned large quantities of rice in Vientiane for the emergency feeding of our local employees and station personnel. It was good that we had done so, for as the floodwaters surged, most of the indigenous population soon ran out of rice. Although the Lao custom is to buy food each day for only the day's needs, rice as a staple of life is held in quantities large enough to last several days.

The rice trade in Vientiane was primarily in the hands of the overseas Chinese. This group, seeing the flood as an opportunity to enhance profits, started raising rice prices exorbitantly. The Lao complained. The Chinese shrugged and played hardball, keeping prices ridiculously high. This information reached us promptly and was soon a topic for discussion at the country-team meeting. Plans were developed to let the Chinese know that USAID had or could get plenty of rice and would bring it in to help the RLG counter price gouging.

The station had a backup role in this drama. We instructed our logistics people to move about one ton of rice in one-hundred-pound bags into my house. This movement did not escape local attention, which was precisely what we wanted. When the local laborers (coolies) finished stacking the bags, the pile virtually reached the ceiling of what was our living room. As soon as the rice was in place, extra guards were put around my residence to protect the cache. We also brought in cartons of paper bags capable of holding about a pound of rice. When I came home that evening, Hazel dressed in old slacks, sandals, and a long-sleeved shirt, was sitting near the top of the rice heap. I asked if she was playing King of the Mountain.

"No," she said sweetly, "I'm just wondering how a gal from Coffee County, Alabama, ends up sitting on a ton of rice in her living room in a flood in Vientiane, Laos."

I explained that this was part of a coordinated embassy strategy to force Chinese rice merchants to be reasonable. Hazel said, "I hope it works. If it doesn't, I trust you also know how to get this rice out of here."

The next day we did two things in a timed sequence. First, station officers called on a handful of Chinese merchants whom they knew quite well and let it be known that the embassy was dissatisfied with rice price gouging. Ah, yes, observed the Chinese, they had heard of that from USAID personnel. The station officers then said the embassy already had significant supplies of rice at various secure sites around Vientiane. Starting at midday these stocks would be drawn on as a test to see how an orderly distribution could be made to local employees of the embassy and USAID. If this worked well, the distribution system would be expanded the next day to give free flood-relief rice to Vientiane's populace. The second part of the plan could be abandoned, however, if normal distribution systems began to function at reasonable market prices. After the appropriate sipping of tea, the discussions broke off, and the station officers proceeded on to other tasks.

That same day we gave out a few hundred pounds of rice in one-pound brown paper bags to local employees of the embassy and USAID. The next day rice prices on the open market dropped back to preflood standards. The Chinese merchants had obviously decided that accepting a safe profit was better than risking a total loss of market share. Economic reality had its place even in Laos.

When the floodwaters receded and while a major cleanup was in progress, coup rumors began to circulate. As Jim Lilley had lived through a Lao coup or two, I leaned on him to put together a plan for addressing this problem. Essentially, we identified potential coup leaders, the units that would be needed to pull off a coup, and those it would take to thwart one. This proved educational for it showed we needed one or two more penetration agents in key FAR units to provide us early warning of any coup planning. We then turned to the related issues of keeping the station functioning while a coup was in progress, maintaining emergency communications, and evacuating dependents while cutting the staff to a hard-core nucleus.

For guidance we studied the case of General Siho Lamphouta-koul, the former head of the Lao police. This man had fled from Laos to Thailand on February 3, 1965, with General Phoumi Nosa-van in the aftermath of a failed coup. Siho had been outmaneuvered in that coup by MR-5 commander General Kouprasith Abhay, his mortal enemy. For reasons best known to Siho, after consulting with a fortune-teller in Thailand, he decided to return to Laos in June 1966 to carve out a new niche for himself. Siho infiltrated back into Laos across the Mekong in the Pakse area and opened a dialog with MR-4 commander General Phasouk Somly.

The latter persuaded Siho to turn himself in, and he did. Phasouk then left Siho to the tender mercies of his enemy, Kouprasith. The latter had Siho incarcerated at Phou Khao Khouai in MR-5. This was an ironic twist of fate, for when Siho was in power, Phou Khao Khouai had been his main base of operations.

The Siho story was always a mass of ambiguities. Key issues were never resolved. There were no convincing answers as to why he had returned, why Phasouk put him into Kouprasith's hands, and what Kouprasith hoped to get out of interrogating Siho in Phou Khao Khouai. Siho was shot and killed in September 1966, allegedly while trying to escape. The embassy and the military attaché tried to sort out this story, and we tried to help by querying appropriate agents, but as far as I know no one ever came up with hard evidence about Siho's demise. The persistent rumor that reached the station was that four enlisted men who reported directly to then lieutenant colonel Thonglith Chokbengboun, the chief of staff in MR-5, had killed him. The motive attributed to those responsible for the murder was the elimination of the possibility that a dangerous enemy might escape in the confusion of the flood. So much for the image of a gentle land.

The chief plotter this year was said to be Brigadier General Thao Ma, head of the Royal Lao Air Force. Other alleged conspirators were MR-4 commander General Phasouk Somly and Vang Pao. Rumor had it that Ma was incensed over the corruption of generals Ouan Rathikoun and Kouprasith Abhay and brooding over what he saw as an attempt to split up the Lao Air Force into two parts, one to be a tactical command covering the Lao T-28s, which he would control, and the other a transport command under which the Royal Lao C-47 aircraft would be available to support the smuggling operations of Generals Ouan and Kouprasith. Finally, Ma was said to feel himself under unreasonable political pressure to move his headquarters from Savannakhet to Vientiane. As the Royal Lao Air Force T-28s were trying to hit targets in the panhandle, Ma felt it made more sense to stay in Savannakhet. That would put him closer to his area of operations and keep him out of what he felt was the political cesspool of Vientiane.

Colonel Paul "Pappy" Pettigrew, the Air attaché, chatted regularly with me and Jim Lilley about Ma. Pettigrew said Ma was erratic as ever but gave no evidence of coup plotting. In fact,

Pettigrew said he was impressed that in the period from late July to early August 1966, Ma's energies had been consumed in providing tactical air support for FAR operations in the Nam Bac valley. This had proven successful, and the FAR had gained territory for the Lao government that had been out of its control since 1961.

The station had no agent in Ma's entourage. I had met Ma once or twice very briefly in Vientiane, courtesy of Colonel Pettigrew, and had thought him one uptight guy. Pettigrew began to say that Ma suffered from combat fatigue and that no one could figure out how to get Ma to take a break. Ma evidently thought that if he took leave or loosened his control over the T-28 planes and pilots, he would never regain command.

We queried Vang Pao and Phasouk about Ma's attitude, and both assured us they were not involved in any coup plotting. According to what Vang Pao told Bill Lair, the people to watch in connection with Ma and any possible coup were Colonels Thao Ly and Bounleut Saycocie, but that was hardly startling intelligence, for this trio had been involved in other coups. At the time that we were trying to sort out these rumors, only Thao Ly had control of any troops, and unfortunately for Ma, these were in MR-4, far removed from the Vientiane scene where coups are made or broken. Our collection antennas were tuned to the possibility of a coup, but none appeared to be in the making.

On the morning of October 21, 1966, around 8:30 A.M., I got a big surprise. As my driver was starting to ease my car out of the dirt road on which the embassy stood, I saw a T-28 flying down the main street and firing its machine guns, a few rounds of which skipped in the road two or three feet in front of my car. So, Ma was trying his luck after all. I told Lum, the driver, to turn around and drive back to the embassy. While this maneuver was being completed, I heard a distant explosion in the area of my residence and the FAR general staff headquarters at Phone Kheng.

Now headed back to the embassy, I was startled to hear and see a single T-28 above us headed toward the Pathet Lao headquarters building farther down the road. Flying past us at treetop level, the T-28 straddled us with a burst of machine gun fire that hit both shoulders of the road. It was like a second-rate B movie dealing with World War II. The pilot either wasn't trying to hit us, simply wanted to give us a scare, or couldn't hit a sitting duck. In any event

Lum and I were thankful for our blessings as we pulled into the embassy compound. As I exited my car, I could see a cloud of black smoke billowing up from the area of Phone Kheng and my residence. I gave a silent prayer that the fire would be at Phone Kheng and not my house because Hazel and Suzanne were at home.

Upon entering the embassy I told the Marine guard that a coup was in progress and that he should take the prescribed emergency measures. I then ran up to my office and told our duty officer to contact the ambassador and give him the word. Next stop was the communications center where I put the "commo" people in the picture and told them to activate our emergency radio net and advise all employees that if they were not already headed to the office, they should stay put and report what they could see and hear.

My next move was to contact Udorn by telephone, alert them to the coup, and ask them to consult SIGINT for indications of troop movements in MR-2, -3, and -4. With that behind me I went to the station's air operations office, which was located just across the street from the embassy. While crossing the embassy courtyard, I stopped and told Lum to drive to my residence, tell Madame to turn on the radio, and do what he could to help at the house.

With that I went into the air operations office and had the officer then on duty use the Single Sideband radio to get me Tom Fosmire, the Savannakhet chief. The latter, in response to my question about what was going on, said six T-28s had taken off from Savannakhet early in the morning for what looked like a routine operation into the panhandle area. Since then it had been learned via the Lao radio in Savannakhet that a coup was in progress. Ma was on the radio saying his planes had struck targets at FAR headquarters in Phone Kheng, Kouprasith's base in Chinaimo, and Wattay Airport. Fosmire said Ma seemed to be in control of the Savannakhet airport, but no major ground-force units appeared to have joined him. I told him to let us know when the original strike aircraft returned and to report to us anything that might indicate what they would do next, as well as any signs of ground-troop movements that might be supporting Ma or counterattacking his position.

I then reached out on Single Sideband to Jonathan R. at Long Tieng. He reported that there were no unusual troop movements in his area. While R. and I were talking, Vang Pao appeared at R.'s office, and he and I had a chat, the essence of which was that Ma was indeed acting on his own. Vang Pao had no plans to be involved in this fiasco, he said.

Next I contacted Pakse and found that all was quiet on that front. The base had been in touch with Phasouk, who had said that the first he had heard of Ma's coup attempt was when one of our officers contacted him. Phasouk said he saw this as a Vientiane matter, and he would be doing nothing until he got orders from the FAR general staff.

This coup clearly was going nowhere. I returned to the office and learned from Jim Lilley that no troops were moving in Vientiane. With that I telephoned Udorn and exchanged information with Pat Landry. Everything indicated that Ma was acting on his own. His coup was based on airpower alone and had no chance of success.

It was then about 10:00 A.M. I dictated a message to Washington outlining the start of the coup. Results to date, I reported, were that thirty-one people had been killed and sixteen wounded, that a fire was in progress at Phone Kheng, and that we still awaited damage reports from Chinaimo and Wattay. I stressed that the coup had no support from ground troops and was destined to fail. Still, we could not predict how it would end (i.e., with Ma fleeing to Thailand or ending his life in some dramatic fashion).

Just as I finished the message and sent it on its way, I was advised that the ambassador was now in the embassy. I quickly went to his office and gave him a rundown of what we knew. The ambassador said he had just learned from the Lao that Ma's planes were back in Savannakhet readying for another mission. The ambassador asked that our people in Savannakhet try to keep on top of what Ma was doing.

Returning to my office I telephoned Hazel and got no answer. I tried our emergency radio and made contact. Hazel and Suzanne were fine, Lum was back at the house, and the servants were panicking but were still in place, although it was clear they wanted to flee to Thailand. Our house had been used as a reference point for the bombing runs on Phone Kheng. As a result, some of our windows had been blown out, and flares were still smoldering in our front yard. A fire was burning at the Army base, but no tanks could be heard moving from Phone Kheng to downtown Vientiane.

At that point I went back downstairs to see the ambassador. In the embassy lobby I found General Oudone Sananikone entering the building. He spotted me and asked, "What does it look like?" I gave him a status report. Oudone was both pleased and relieved to learn that neither Vang Pao nor Phasouk was involved in the coup. We then went in to see the ambassador, and I told the latter of my hallway exchange with Oudone. With that I excused myself in order to get back to where the intelligence was flowing into the station. I thought it interesting that the chief of staff of the Royal Lao Army was coming to the American embassy to get hard intelligence on the scope of the coup and its prospects for success or failure.

Later in the morning Ambassador Sullivan held a country-team meeting where each agency head reported what he knew was happening. The CIA contribution was based on American eyewitness accounts. Ma's T-28s were all back in Savannakhet; they had been reloaded with fuel, bombs, and rockets and were ready to launch. But would they? Who knew. Ma and his associates were in control of the airport but had received no ground-troop reinforcements that CIA officers in Savannakhet could identify. Our officers in the other regions—MR-2, MR-4, and MR-1—saw no troop movements that could be interpreted as help for Ma. All of these observations were backed up by SIGINT; thus, it was clear Ma had maneuvered himself into a box canyon.

Colonel Pettigrew had some hard facts from one of his men in Savannakhet, to wit, that Ma and his associates were not going to be captured. They had plans to do something, and the odds seemed to favor it being another bombing run on selected Vientiane targets.

Ambassador Sullivan said he had been talking with senior Lao political figures such as Minister of Finance Sisouk na Champassak and President of the National Assembly Phoui Sananikone, Prime Minister Souvanna Phouma being then in Paris. Sullivan said that in all of these discussions, he had asked how we could negotiate Ma out of his untenable situation. What eventually emerged from these soundings was that British ambassador Fred Warner, Ambassador Sullivan, and Prince Boun Oum na Champassak should meet with Ma in Savannakhet to see what kind of a face-saving scenario could be crafted to bring the coup to an end.

Ambassadors Sullivan and Warner subsequently flew to Savannakhet and, joined by Boun Oum, reached what they thought was an understanding that Ma would take no further action. Under that plan Ma would review his situation with the prime minister when the latter returned to Laos on October 23. With that, the American and British ambassadors flew back to Vientiane. The crisis appeared to be over. The embassy dispatched cables to that effect to Washington, London, Bangkok, Saigon, Paris, and Honolulu.

For our part we in the CIA put a discreet watch on the Ma forces in Savannakhet as we closed down for the day. Our instincts told us that Ma was still under tremendous pressure, was emotionally unstable, and at any moment could do the unexpected.

Arriving home at dusk I saw the burned-out flares in our front yard, and in our back yard I found fragments of 500-pound iron bombs that had been dropped on Phone Kheng. Hazel and Suzanne had been in a hot spot. Hazel then told her war story. When the first plane flew over the house, she thought it was a Soviet MiG breaking the sound barrier, something she had frequently experienced in Berlin. Other runs caused her to realize it was more serious. Searching for Suzanne she found her in an upstairs bedroom trying to get under a bed to escape the noise. With our baby in her arms and her face turned away from the windows and any glass that might be flying, Hazel dashed down the stairs. She called for Wantana and Wat, the two servants in the house, and heard a weak response. Tracing the sound of their voices, Hazel found them crouched next to a toilet in a ground-floor powder room, which, being under a staircase, was the best bomb shelter in the house. Hazel pushed Suzanne in and told her to stay with Wantana.

"Madame," said Wantana. "It is a coup. We must go to Thailand. Let us hurry."

Hazel said, "No, stay put."

Wantana, a devout Buddhist, answered "We will pray."

"Mommy, Mommy," cried Suzanne, "who should I pray to—God or Buddha?"

"Both!" Hazel said, closing the bathroom door and hastening to secure the rest of the house. This meant getting the Lao guard to understand that shutters should only be partly closed in order to cut down on flying glass, but not closed up tight so that explosions would create vacuums. After some preventive breaking of glass windows in key areas, all that could be done was completed. According to Hazel, the first attack plane was followed by two or three others, and she saw bombs falling, heard explosions, and saw smoke billowing out of Phone Kheng. Once Lum appeared on the scene, Hazel said, he helped calm Wat and Wantana.

After an exchange of war stories and a brief dinner, we decided an early retreat to bed was in order. In a matter of moments I was asleep. At about 10:00 P.M. I was jolted out of my slumber by a telephone call. The station duty officer was letting me know that Tom Fosmire had just reported from Savannakhet that some T-28s under Ma's command were lining up on the runway fully loaded for combat and ready for takeoff.

"Going where?" I asked.

"No one knows," said the duty officer.

Quickly examining my alternatives, I told the duty officer that I would notify the ambassador. The duty officer himself was to get the word to our people at Udorn and tell them to alert 7/13th Air Force in case the ambassador decided there had to be a show of force by American fighter aircraft to keep Ma from bombing Vientiane. He then should notify the Air and military attachés. Our liaison officer to Generals Ouan Rathikoun and Oudone Sananikone should be told to contact these worthies and let them know the state of play. Presumably, they in turn would contact General Kouprasith Abhay, the MR-5 commander. Our liaison officer should also be asked to find out where General Ouan and the others planned to be in order to deal with the crisis implicit in Ma and his followers' taking off from Savannakhet at this late hour. In addition, the senior air operations officers should be called and told to come in to activate the Single Sideband network to Savannakhet. Jim Lilley must also be called, and he should activate our emergency communications network in order to put all station personnel on alert. With that done, the duty officer should send out an immediate cable to Washington, Bangkok, and CINCPAC saying Ma's aircraft were on the runway ready to launch. Having placed that full plate of duties in front of him, I closed the conversation with the duty officer.

My next move was to telephone Ambassador Sullivan at his residence. He, too, had been in a sound sleep when I called, and it took a few seconds to get us on the same wavelength. "Let me know when Ma takes off, where he is headed, or if he decides to stay put in Savannakhet," he ordered.

"We have officers at the airfield," I told the ambassador, "and they'll let us know everything they see happening. I'm heading for the embassy now where I can sit on communications from our centers in Savannakhet and Udorn."

"Fine," said the ambassador. "I'll be working out of my residence, at least for now."

While I got dressed, Hazel went to find Lum and get the other servants up and dressed. That done, I told Hazel to keep her emergency radio on. Ma appeared ready to launch his aircraft from Savannakhet, I told her, and if he did so, we had to assume he was either headed for exile in Thailand or on a suicide mission. While I did not think the latter likely as the T-28 pilots had no nighttime combat capability, it could not be excluded. Should he head for Vientiane my guess was that Ambassador Sullivan would have the 7/13th Air Force put up a show of force by Udorn fighters, which would cause Ma to abort. If he did not, it was my intent to get General Ouan to pull the plug at the Vientiane power plant and, in so doing, black out the entire city. That too should deter Ma as it limited his reference points for any bombing or strafing runs. If it did not, my guess was that he would go after Chinaimo in an attempt to get Kouprasith. In view of this mixed bag of options, the best bet was for Hazel and Suzanne to stay put, get water stored in the bathtubs for emergency use, and have our emergency evacuation kit at hand in the unlikely event that we would have to use it.

Dashing out of my house I headed for the embassy. When I got there about twenty-five or thirty minutes after the duty officer had first contacted me, I found the situation well in hand. Udorn had notified the 7/13th Air Force, it was in contact with Fosmire in Savannakhet, and SIGINT showed no movement of any Royal Lao ground forces. Ma was still the Lone Ranger.

An immediate-precedence cable had been sent to Washington and the other usual addressees, the station emergency net had been activated, and the Vientiane air operations officer was also in direct Single Sideband contact with Fosmire in Savannakhet. General Ouan had been contacted at his Vientiane residence by a station officer and given his first information on Ma's current status. Ouan said he was alerting Kouprasith and Oudone, and they planned to meet at That Luang shortly to set up an informal command post out in the open, the thinking being that Ma would try to hit Chinaimo or Phone Kheng if he launched a night attack. The Air and military attachés had been put into the picture. Colonel Pettigrew had subsequently told the station duty officer that his people in Savannakhet had confirmed that Ma's planes were on the runway and that it looked as though a takeoff was a certainty.

No sooner had I digested all of these facts than Fosmire was on the telephone saying he had just seen nine T-28s with Ma in the lead aircraft taking off from Savannakhet and headed north. This would put them on a heading to reach Vientiane or Udorn in thirty or forty minutes. One guess was as good as another as to what Ma was doing. In essence, it was a crapshoot. The dice were rolling. Fosmire had just passed the same word to Pat Landry in Udorn, and we could be confident that it would be relayed to the 7/13th Air Force. In a quick exchange of speculation, Fosmire agreed with me that Ma was unlikely to bomb at night, but who could be certain?

I shared the information with those who were in the office. Either Jim Lilley or one of the reports officers started writing up a situation report for Washington and other interested addressees. I, in turn, got on the telephone to the ambassador. He obviously felt no joy in learning of the launch. We reviewed the options quickly, once again, and concluded that a flight to Udorn was most likely, but that a raid on Vientiane could not be ruled out. Sullivan said he was working his communications contacts from home and would stay there to be in touch with the 7/13th Air Force. Where would I be? I told him I hoped to link up with Generals Ouan and Oudone at That Luang to see if we could be of any help to them with communications. "Okay," said Sullivan, "keep in touch."

Leaving the embassy I had Lum take me to That Luang. There was no traffic on the streets, and we made the trip in about five or six minutes. I quickly spotted Ouan and Oudone and headed for them.

Oudone asked, "Anything new?"

"Yes," said I, "Ma and his boys took off from Savannakhet about ten or twelve minutes ago headed north. The nine T-28s are loaded for combat, and we could be hearing them soon if Vientiane is the target."

Kouprasith and Colonel Thonglith emerged from the shadows at that point. While Oudone was translating for Kouprasith what I had said, Ouan took me by the arm and walked a few steps away from the others. "What do you think we should do?" he asked, adding "What is the ambassador doing?"

I answered, "If I were the MR-5 commander, I would throw the switch of the Vientiane power plant now. That would put Vientiane in a blackout situation. The T-28s have no nighttime bombing capability, so this would reduce Ma's options. Additionally, I would put a platoon of my best soldiers around the power plant to see that no one puts the power back on."

Oudone came up as I was finishing and asked what the ambassador's view was. I said, "When I talked with the ambassador a few minutes ago, he was in touch from his residence with appropriate power centers including the 7/13th Air Force. What he may have done since we last talked, I don't know. I have my radio with me and can contact Sullivan through my duty officer. Is that what you want?"

Getting no immediate reply, I glanced at my wrist watch and said, "Time is short. You do something—pull the power plant switch—and cut Ma's options or leave all the choices to him."

Kouprasith edged closer to us. How much he had heard or understood of the last part of the exchange I did not know. To my surprise Kouprasith asked me directly, "What would you do?"

I said again, "Put out all lights in Vientiane."

A fast exchange in Lao then followed between Kouprasith and Ouan. Kouprasith then turned to Thonglith, barked some orders, and the latter moved out on the double. A few seconds later one could see two jeeps headed back into town, and Thonglith was on a radio to someone.

With that the tension eased somewhat and Ouan and Kouprasith moved away from me to talk with some of their subordinates. Oudone lingered on and whispered in a stage voice, "Kouprasith sees himself as a man of action. He is going to black out Vientiane."

"Good," I said. "That is a Lao decision no one can fault."

Oudone paused, smiled, and looking me straight in the eyes said, "We Lao can be quite clever at times."

Oudone joined the other Lao. Left to my own devices, I got on my radio to contact the duty officer. I instructed him, "If you aren't already on emergency power, go to it now for communications purposes. Vientiane may be blacked out in a matter of minutes."

The duty officer said, "Okay." His only information for me was that the 7/13th Air Force had Ma on radar, and his heading was still such that his destination could be Vientiane or Udorn or both; that is, he could bomb Vientiane and then seek asylum in Thailand.

This latest tidbit was passed to Ouan, Kouprasith, and Oudone. As we talked, Vientiane suddenly went black. "Good!" was my initial reaction. Then, as I took a second look at the Vientiane skyline from the high ground at That Luang, there to my shock was one beam of light shining like a bright star in a clear night. "What is that?" I asked Oudone incredulously.

Oudone and the other Lao talked briefly. Oudone said it had to be Ambassador Sullivan's residential compound. Then it hit me: Sullivan was on emergency power and no one had turned off his perimeter lights. Now he was a bright shining point of reference for Ma. What bad luck!

I quickly got on my radio to the duty officer and told him to call Sullivan's residence and tell them to cut the lights at the ambassador's compound. Just as that conversation was completed, we could hear the drone of aircraft in the distance. The moment of truth had arrived. In seconds the sound faded, and there was silence. No one talked or moved. Seconds turned into minutes and still nothing. The spell was eventually broken, and we started to assume that Ma had decided not to hit Vientiane. As we chatted, someone from the Air attaché's office came up and said Ma and his group had just landed in Udorn. Big smiles broke out on the faces of Ouan, Kouprasith, and Oudone. That was my cue to ease out of the situation, get back to the embassy, and see what was likely to happen next. As I paid my respects to Ouan and started to leave, Kouprasith stuck his hand out, shook mine, and said in his broken English, "You are a friend. Good night."

Back at the embassy the teamwork for which CIA people are known had been in full play. Connie Ettridge had sent out situation reports to Washington, Bangkok, Saigon, and CINCPAC as events unfolded. Udorn had done its thing in keeping the 7/13th Air Force briefed and our units in Long Tieng and Pakse in the loop. The latter in turn kept Generals Vang Pao and Phasouk in the picture. There had also been a steady dialog between Jim Lilley and the embassy staff, the attachés' offices, and key USAID people. A final check with Udorn revealed that the Thai had Ma and his fellow pilots in custody and would be talking to him further tomorrow to consider his asylum request. We therefore closed down and went home.

In the end Ma and his men were detained by the Thai in a type of house arrest while the Lao tried to extradite him to stand trial. With the passage of time, Ma and his group were given political asylum in Thailand. Ma then disappeared into obscurity. One would hear from time to time that he was flying C-47s for some airplane entrepreneur. About a year later his pilots were granted amnesty and permitted to return to Laos where they again took up flying combat sorties for the Royal Lao Air Force. This decision was a judicious blending of Lao forgiveness and the military's needs for good, experienced pilots.

After the Lao T-28s landed in Udorn on October 21–22, Thai-Lao-American negotiations started on October 22 to have these airplanes returned to Laos. Instead, for a while Royal Thai Air Force pilots known as the B Team flew them out of Udorn. The latter flew T-28s with Lao markings. They were part of the Water Pump project started in April 1964 in which the United States agreed to train Lao and Thai T-28 pilots. These helped fill the shortfall created by Ma's aborted coup and flight to Thailand. Unfortunately, the reality of life was that Ma was a great tactical air commander, and after his departure the Lao T-28 program was never as combat-effective as it had been under his leadership in mid-1966.

11

PLANNING FOR A
TWO-FRONT WAR

FLOOD and coup delayed, but couldn't halt, planning for the two-front war that headquarters was demanding of us. As the Mekong was rising, I flew to Udorn to confer with Bill Lair and Pat Landry, the two officers primarily responsible for the station's paramilitary activities. Landry I had already met. Lair was a new face. A man of medium build, he was dressed in a sport shirt, khaki pants, and comfortable walking shoes. Projecting the aura of a man at peace with himself, he spoke with a soft, low-key voice that had a touch of the American Southwest.

In the order-of-battle (OB) briefing that followed, I learned that the combined Pathet Lao/North Vietnamese force in Laos was seventy-two thousand, of which ten thousand were North Vietnamese combat infantry troops organized into pure North Vietnamese battalions and about six thousand were North Vietnamese troops spread among forty-two battalions of Pathet Lao troops in order to give the latter an iron backbone.

Some inescapable conclusions came out of this briefing. First, it was believed that the Pathet Lao, left to their own devices, were not a military threat to the RLG. Second, the validity of the intelligence on enemy units in North Laos was much more solidly based on multiple-source reporting than that in the Lao panhandle. This was no surprise, considering that the major thrust of the station's paramilitary effort had been in North Laos.

It was then my turn. I outlined the policy makers' view of the war, stressing that more had to be done from Laos to contribute to winning the war in Vietnam while helping cut American manpower losses. It was my impression during this session that Lair and Landry did not like much about the inevitable expansion of the effort in Laos into a two-front war; perhaps they anticipated the damage it would do to the Hmong people. Still, both clearly understood that the sole factor driving this change was U.S. national interest. In that context they also knew both from my comments and from the kudos they had earned in the past that their work in North Laos with Vang Pao and others was regarded as a magnificent achievement. The imperatives of policy were simply forcing change.

Gossip, based on who knows what, would have it that I told Lair and Landry at this session that their past effort had been like the outstanding management of a very successful country-store operation that was now going to be turned into a supermarket as part of a chain called the Vietnam War. This supposedly ruffled Lair and Landry's feathers. I have no memory of making such a comment; nor do I normally speak in simile. If I did say it, so be it, for it would be an accurate portrayal of the then existing realities. Lair and Landry, in my view, would have seen that as a compliment, had the remark been phrased in that way. These were mature men with extensive experience in dealing with the brutal dynamics of war. They did not wear their hearts on their sleeves.

Meanwhile I was engaged in extensive correspondence with Langley on the burning question of how the Vientiane Station should respond to the requirements levied on it by the Washington policy makers, and by early September 1966 we had agreed on a program with six clearly definable operational parts. The first part called for the collection of intelligence on the strengths, weaknesses, and intentions of North Vietnamese and Pathet Lao forces operating in, from, or through Laos. This consisted of three distinct efforts.

1. *Road-watch teams.* The objective was to put trained indigenous forces onto prominent terrain features or in close proximity to the roads and trails used by the North Vietnamese and Pathet Lao for moving men and matériel to South Vietnam.[1] Besides the insight into enemy strengths, weaknesses, and intentions that we hoped for from this deployment, we saw the road-watch teams as potential forward observers with ground-to-air communications who could direct friendly airpower onto enemy

personnel concentrations or storage facilities. The teams were also envisioned as a means of obtaining early-warning intelligence on Pathet Lao or North Vietnamese operations against Royal Lao forces or CIA paramilitary units. We put our first priority on the entry routes into Laos from North Vietnam. As a result, we focused on Route 7 in Vang Pao's MR-2. In MR-3 we were concerned with the Nape Pass and Route 8, the Mu Gia Pass and Routes 12 and 23, and the Ban Karai pass. The area of interest in MR-4 relative to Cambodia was primarily Route 110. Unfortunately, in mid-1966 we were not clear on how much matériel was flowing to Hanoi's forces in South Vietnam from Cambodia or to what extent Cambodia was a sanctuary for North Vietnamese forces.

2. *Reconnaissance patrols.* Our interest here was to use guerrilla forces as a reconnaissance screen in front of government-held areas. Patrolling continuously and aggressively, they would be expected through visual observations of enemy forces on the move to obtain intelligence and through firefights to capture enemy documents or prisoners for interrogation. We believed this task had to be carried out in all military regions.

3. *Refugee exploitation.* We felt that a more organized effort to screen the refugee flow out of the area held by the Pathet Lao and their North Vietnamese masters was required. This was expected to produce OB intelligence on hostile forces, political and economic intelligence from enemy-held areas, leads to people who might be recruited as in-place agents, and data to sharpen the aim of air strikes on enemy concentrations of men or matériel.

The second part of the program required us to take the war to the enemy. Simply put, we wanted to inflict damage by harassment operations and air strikes in order to compel the enemy to commit more forces to flank security tasks. Under the harassment heading we envisioned raids by twenty-man guerrilla units on personnel concentrations or supply depots and an active campaign of ambushes using mines and fifteen-man firefight teams. We also wanted to make use of booby traps. In the air-strike area, our goal was to use the all-source intelligence approach to identify targets suitable for attack by Royal Lao Air Force T-28s or the A-1Es or F-104s of the 7/13th Air Force.

In the third part of our program we undertook to prevent Laos from falling under Hanoi's control, directly or indirectly, via the Pathet Lao. To pursue this objective we intended to use indigenous paramilitary assets, primarily the special guerrilla units (SGUs), to help government forces hold those areas of Laos already under their control. Such actions were designed to help the local inhabitants feel physically secure, thereby encouraging them to lead relatively normal lives and contributing to the development or maintenance of a spirit of resistance to any Pathet Lao/North Vietnamese incursion into government-held areas.[2]

We also considered using paramilitary forces and guerrilla tactics to wrest areas of Laos from enemy control without provoking a major North Vietnamese response. In this way, CIA resources could be used to help the RLG expand its control over contested or enemy-held areas of Laos. This was essentially the selective use of salami-slice tactics, taking things one small step at a time, to attempt to gain and hold terrain and population.

The fourth part called on the station to cultivate a sense of national identity in the tribal elements that worked with the CIA in the paramilitary field so that in time they could be fully integrated into Lao society. This was a response to our mandate to engage in nation building.

The fifth part was our host-country operations, a national insurance policy, so to speak, in protection of America's investment in Laos. Here the objective was to obtain and maintain penetrations of the Lao power structure so that we could be confident that the Lao would do what they said they would do. In addition, we had to maintain a political-action capability to shape events and influence public opinion in Laos.

The sixth part was a classic installation-penetration effort targeted against the Soviet, Chinese, North Vietnamese, Polish, and Pathet Lao installations in Vientiane.

Having defined the program, my next order of business was to see that our organization, manpower, and budget were adequate for quick development of road-watch and raid-and-ambush capabilities in the panhandle. Station headquarters would obviously remain in Vientiane. Udorn needed to retain first-echelon control of the war in North Laos through the major outposts in Luang Prabang, Long Tieng, and Nam Yu. The panhandle war had to be run out of units in Savannakhet and Pakse. The unresolved question was how most effectively to tie these two latter units into the rest of the station. In other words, should they receive first-echelon supervision from Udorn or Vientiane?

It was now time to regroup and head for Washington to nail down manpower and budget levels with the policy makers. Organizationally, I felt the flood had both tested the station and shown that we had a flexible, responsive, and productive structure. Equally important, the Ma coup had shown we could handle the unexpected. In addition, the clock was ticking, and if we were to field a productive panhandle operation by December 1966, we needed to expend all of our energy on getting operations rolling rather than making organizational changes. My decision therefore was to leave panhandle operations under Udorn's first-echelon control in a matrix management system where Vientiane could play an activist coordinating role in a triangular dialog—Vientiane, Udorn, and Savannakhet for example. This formula would also permit Bill Lair and Pat Landry to retain appropriate comfort levels on the interchangeability of their roles. In other words, when they were both in Udorn, Lair's primary responsibility was North Laos and Landry's was South Laos. When one of the two was away from Udorn on days off, family visits, and so forth, the other was the first-echelon supervisor for both wars.

This decision was reviewed with Lair and Landry. Both endorsed it and seemed pleased that our relationship had developed in a manner that made such a solution workable. Colonel Dhep was also briefed on my future plans. He expressed confidence that this signaled the start of a new period of harmonious Thai-American relations. In fact, he said, he now felt that we had an integrated command for the first time and that the results could only be positive. With this behind me, the journey to Washington was laid on.

Colby's first question to me was, "Tell me how you are going to cover the panhandle with road-watch teams."

My response was that our initial deployment of Thai road-watch teams into the panhandle had been less than a smashing success. Consequently, we had decided to concentrate in the future on

Lao teams recruited along purely ethnic lines—all Kha, Lao, Lave, or Lao Thung. We had also agreed on a prototype ten-man team, which would comprise one team leader, an assistant team leader, a radio operator, a medic, and six riflemen. Experience had shown that a team's success depended mainly on the team leader and the radio operator.

Our manpower for this program would have to come from units already in existence, such as the *auto-defense de choc* (ADC) groups that were defending villages, SGU battalions, and special operation teams (SOTs) that had been trained for raids and ambushes. This meant that our ideal road-watch team candidate was about twenty years old, had been in our paramilitary program for over a year, had received sixteen to thirty-two weeks of previous training, and was combat tested.

We already had an array of ethnic teams in the pipeline, I told Colby. They were receiving eight weeks of training and would be deployed into the panhandle by December 1966. Thus, while we had a handful of teams already in action in the panhandle, our program would kick in on a sustained basis in December. From that point on we planned to increase deployment until by mid-1967 we would be able to cover key parts of the Ho Chi Minh Trail virtually continuously with forty teams at a time. This plan called for Savannakhet and Pakse each to have a contingent of thirty-five teams, of which at any given time twenty would be deployed, ten would be resting, and five would be in training.

Hazarding a guess, I told Colby that Savannakhet would meet its goal sooner than Pakse because we wanted coverage of the Mu Gia Pass area as soon as possible and so were giving Savannakhet priority over what resources we had. Additionally, the Savannakhet area was less burdened by its Lao military region commander than was Pakse. General Bounphone Makthepharak in MR-3 cared little about what our paramilitary effort did as long as it did not provoke the North Vietnamese or Pathet Lao into attacking his FAR units. In MR-4, on the other hand, General Phasouk Somly believed that any new CIA program would detract from his pacification effort in Wapikhanthong Province, and he therefore tended to hinder by nonaction rather than actively participate in plans to move our road-watch effort forward. This was not an insurmountable problem, for as the station helped Phasouk to secure the Bolovens Plateau through our camps at PS-4 and PS-22, its relations with Phasouk were improving. I was confident that Phasouk, a French-trained conventional soldier and pacification enthusiast, would in time be won over to our paramilitary package because it would actually expand his total operational capabilities. That was something Phasouk could not turn down, for in the final analysis Phasouk was both a realist and a survivor.

The budget and manpower ceilings set during my November 1966 visit grew as Hanoi's and Washington's respective pursuits of what they saw as their policy objectives in Indochina led over the next two years to an increase in the intensity of the war. Without full access to government records, I am unable to detail the way the program grew during my stay in Laos. As Senator Stuart Symington said in Udorn in the fall of 1966 when I briefed him on Laos, "We spend in one year in Laos what it costs us to fight in Vietnam for a week. The CIA is running a cost-effective war in Laos."

Yet, given Hanoi's sustained pressure on American Marine units in the five northern provinces of South Vietnam's MR-1, Washington policy makers were clamoring for more action to impede Hanoi's use of the Lao panhandle. The Washington view was growing that if North Vietnam was able to use the Ho Chi Minh Trail structure at rates that not only replaced combat losses in South Vietnam but enabled the enemy to build up new units and supplies in the western highlands of Vietnam's MR-2, the war had no immediate end in sight. That was an unacceptable vision of the future for American policy makers from the president on down to Cabinet secretaries and department heads. Thus, the CIA simply had to do more "right now" to slow down the Hanoi juggernaut.

In short, separate meetings with Des FitzGerald, the deputy director for plans, and Dick Helms, the DCI, I was reminded that manpower and money were available for productive operations in Laos, as was evidenced by the support my operational proposals had engendered during my current trip to Washington. The message was clear: You asked for and were given the tools you wanted. Now we need instant results. With those thoughts racing through my head, I returned to Vientiane.

12

WATCHING THE ROADS

W HEN our training program turned out its first batch of road-watch teams in early December 1966, we prepared them for infiltration, our objective being to get at least ten teams into the panhandle area south of the Mu Gia Pass as soon as possible. We decided to try two different infiltration techniques. One was to have the team trucked or flown to a launch site in an area under RLG control but adjacent to disputed areas or sectors held by PL/NVA forces. From there the team would walk into the jungle, taking days to get to its assigned target area, where it would set up its base camp and command post (CP).

Our second infiltration technique was to lift the team by helicopter from a place like Savannakhet to a preselected landing zone (LZ) close to the assigned operational area, using Air America H-34s and U.S. military CH-3s or CH-53s out of Thailand for this purpose. From the LZ the team would move to a base area and set up a CP.

In either case, the subsequent procedures would be the same. To guard against the possibility of being surprised and overrun at the base camp, sentries would be posted, tripwires planted, and mines laid. This done, the team would select an observation post (OP) from which a fixed portion of a road or trail could be monitored.

The OP would be manned from dusk to dawn, typically from 7:00 P.M. to 5:00 A.M. Anything moving along the road, whether trucks or troop units, would cause an entry to be made in a notebook. Each notation would include the number of units observed, the time of observation, the direction in which they were headed, and anything else thought worth recording.

At dawn the guerrillas—usually two men—who had manned the OP would work their way cautiously back to the base camp while constantly alert for enemy patrols. At the CP the team leader would debrief his men, check their notebook entries, and prepare a report. Depending on the skill of the radio operator, the report would be sent by manual Morse (RS-1 radio) or a medium-speed tape-transmission radio system (MSRS-48) back to the unit from which the team had been dispatched—Savannakhet or Pakse. From there the report would be relayed to Udorn. The latter would immediately pass the perishable tactical intelligence on to the 7/13th Air Force for possible action by strike aircraft. Then, upon receipt at Udorn of reports from all teams deployed in a particular Ho Chi Minh Trail sector, a report would be prepared for forwarding to Vientiane. The latter would review it quickly, add comments if appropriate, and release it for transmission to addressees such as Washington, Saigon, Bangkok, and Honolulu.

After a few months of this, we drew certain tentative conclusions and faced some hard questions:

- We were producing timely intelligence by trained observers on areas that had not been previously covered by friendly forces. It served as a useful adjunct to the SIGINT that MACV was using to measure enemy troop strengths, supply levels, and intentions.
- We needed better continuity of coverage. In order to evaluate bomb damage to roads, trucks, or military units, we needed daylight operation. The question was how to cover the period 5:00 A.M. to 7:00 P.M.
- A related issue was how to extend the scope of coverage. The early teams were staying in their operational areas about two weeks. When they exfiltrated there was a gap in coverage. This hurt the analytical process of estimating enemy throughput along the Ho Chi Minh Trail. More importantly, it hampered the effective targeting of air strikes by making it more difficult to be certain where our teams were at any given time. We did not want to bomb our own troops.
- Intelligence collected on activities in the Ho Chi Minh Trail area or in North Laos was not merely an analytical

tool. It was a war-fighting instrument. If it was to be of maximum utility, it had to be available as close to real time as one could make it. Our initial intelligence product was timely, meaning it was between six and twenty hours old by the time it reached those who targeted tactical aircraft. This made it moderately useful, but it was not real time. Those who were doing the job of taking airpower to the enemy were clamoring for real-time intelligence, and it became our objective to provide it.

- Authentication was a matter of concern. How could we be certain a team was in its assigned area when it said it was? The quality of a team's intelligence was a litmus test of sorts, but the Air Force planners put more stock in electronic validation. We were constantly asked whether we could use some mechanical device to confirm that a team's reporting was actually coming from its road-watch position.

We also discovered some weaknesses in our methodology and equipment:

- When teams walked the full distance from launch area to a base-camp site, their time in the assigned operational area became limited to two weeks. Furthermore, the walk of ten days or more in the bush exhausted the men and consumed precious food supplies that could more profitably have been used on site. We should not have been surprised to learn that the motivation of tired men from primitive backgrounds subsisting on Spartan rations while operating behind enemy lines, could slip away quite quickly.
- Infiltrating men by helicopter to LZs relatively close to the trail structure heated up an operational area. The North Vietnamese were quick to associate helicopter activity with subsequent increases in air attacks on the same segment of the Ho Chi Minh Trail and to suspect enemy long-range reconnaissance patrols. This caused them to step up their own patrolling, which, in a way, was what we wanted inasmuch as it burned up manpower that could otherwise have been deployed in South Vietnam. On the other hand,

it increased the odds that our teams would be detected, driven from the area, captured, or killed in firefights.

- Our communications package was both cumbersome and heavy. We needed something lighter than the existing RS-1 or RS-48 radios. The gear also had to be simpler to operate than an RS-1 if we were going to train radio operators quickly.
- Communications ground-to-air had to be improved if we were to handle emergency helicopter exfiltration of teams being pursued by North Vietnamese forces.
- We had to beef up the training of our road-watch teams in map reading, clandestine movement, and communications.

Some corrective actions were easier to take than others. We quickly focused on training. We revised our road-watch-team training syllabus. We improved the quality of our American staff by bringing in career paramilitary instructors like Horace D. to run our training centers. We also improved the quality of the Thai and Lao instructors.

Our eight-week road-watch training course then broke down into the following blocks of time: map reading and compass navigation, 40 hours; weapons (M1 rifle, carbine, M-3 submachine gun, and .45 caliber pistol), 36 hours; clandestine movement, 50 hours; OB reporting, 60 hours; caching, 30 hours; sketching, 20 hours; ground photography, 12 hours; leadership, 50 hours; communications, 80 hours; air-reception operations, 30 hours; jungle survival, 40 hours; first aid, 40 hours; reading and writing, 48 hours; and field-training exercises, 100 hours.

By working our students twelve hours a day, seven days a week, we turned out a better product after January 1967 than we had previously. That was true for both North and South Laos. In the following years we could see that we were getting as much out of our indigenous manpower pool in the pursuit of the road-watch mission as could be expected. Others shared this view; for example, Lieutenant Colonel Hartley in an Air Force oral history is on record as saying, "The Road-watch teams . . . were well trained, used their binoculars, counted trucks, counted troops, determined where they were moving, and got hard intelligence. They were effective."[1] What else did one want?

As we turned to our communications package, our review revealed that equipment changes could be made to improve the teams' ability to maintain communications between the OP and the CP without sacrificing security. We therefore added more hand-held tactical radios like the HT-1 and HT-2 to each team's list of equipment. That enhanced the teams' ability to stay in touch while reducing the rate of clandestine movement in enemy territory. It also improved ground-to-air-communication capability.

No easy solution was at hand, however, for the command radio net. That was the one item that was slowing down our road-watch teams more than anything else. Sitting in Udorn late one afternoon in December 1966 and discussing the radio situation with Bill Lair and Pat Landry, I said we needed an idiot-proof device that was handheld. A Kha tribal type had to be able to learn to operate it with ten hours of training. That meant it had to be something he could talk into and that generated a tape and that, upon his pressing a button, would transmit a message to Udorn. As another possibility I suggested a counting unit with pictures of trucks and soldiers that could be pressed when these items were seen. The device could store the data, and at fixed times the push of a big red button would result in the accumulated information being transmitted in a burst transmission to Udorn.

Bill thought about that for a few seconds and said a device with pictures on buttons would be the better solution. Half jokingly, I said that we had inadvertently designed a new device that was worth discussing with our communications experts. We then moved on to other topics.

Teamwork and the CIA's can-do spirit then came into play. A few days after the Udorn session, two Technical Services Division representatives visited me in Vientiane. This was a periodic trip to see what our needs were likely to be in future months for products that they provided—concealment devices, seismic and pneumatic sensors that could count trucks if properly deployed along the Ho Chi Minh Trail, and starlight scopes. We chatted about our future requirements. Then, one of the visitors asked what our most pressing equipment need was. I responded by saying our technical wish list was headed by the critical need for an idiot-proof reporting device that could be used by road-watch teams in lieu of an RS-1 radio. Such a device would enable us to get more teams out onto the trail faster. Additionally, it would bring us closer to our goal of real-time reporting. I then went on to describe what had emerged from our Udorn brainstorming session. The technicians were told we wanted pictures on buttons that described various items of enemy equipment. We also had a need for counting soldiers.

Expecting to be told I was dreaming of Buck Rogers technology that was not at hand, I was pleasantly surprised to have one of the technicians say he thought something might be put together with off-the-shelf technology. That was an exciting prospect, to say the least. When I pressed for a guess as to when the prospect might become a reality, both men said they would be in touch with me soon. They needed to do more homework on the task.

True to their word, in a short period the technicians returned to Vientiane. They had in hand a device with pictures on buttons that could be depressed to count what was being seen by the road-watch teams. A modification of a survival radio which the Air Force had in its inventory, the device also permitted the teams to put a date and time group on their observations. It also had the capability to identify its point of transmission, obviously a plus in terms of authentication.

There was one flaw. The device, which the technicians had dubbed HARK-1, did not have the power to transmit from the trail area to Savannakhet, Pakse, or Udorn. Due to this limitation the system would have to be supported by an orbiting aircraft, which would become a relay platform. This, I could see, posed technical and budgetary questions: What aircraft could we task to fly the orbit pattern, how many orbits would we need, and what would they cost?

With these problems before us, the technicians and I flew to Udorn where Bill and Pat were brought up to date on the project. They were as excited about the prospects of harnessing this tool as I was. Acting on Bill Lair's advice, it was arranged that Jim Rhyne of Air America would seek solutions to the aircraft platform problem. What eventually emerged was a Volpar Turbo 18 aircraft modified to increase its loiter time in its assigned orbit area by adding wing tanks and putting a fuel bladder into its cabin. By March 1967 we were using three such aircraft. One orbited in support of road-watch teams working for Savannakhet and covering the Nape Pass, Mu Gia Pass area, and the road structure around Tchepone. The second flew in support of Pakse teams covering Routes 92, 96, 165, and 110. The third aircraft was a backup.

This proved to be an effective, but expensive, project. With the HARK-1 device in hand, we could train and deploy more teams because we had eliminated the ponderous and lengthy training of radio operators. With lighter gear, and thus a smaller load for team members to carry, we could amend our infiltration tactics by having helicopters take teams from places like Savannakhet halfway or two-thirds of the way to their target area. The teams could walk in the rest of the way, have better infiltrating security, and stay longer on target in the trail because they had more food and took less of a physical beating from long overland marches to the target area. Teams under this system could stay in the operational area for four to six weeks and on occasion for up to three months.

The HARK-1 device enabled us to expand rapidly. By December 1, 1967, approximately one year after the program started to get into high gear, we had a total of 168 road-watch teams. Of this number, eighty-three teams were deployed in the panhandle and eighty-five in the north. These teams in the aggregate produced a monthly average of one hundred reports covering all major routes in Laos used by North Vietnamese/Pathet Lao forces. These reports were multipage documents and were of primary use to OB analysts in Saigon, CINCPAC, and Washington.

The road-watch teams also contributed to truck kills on the Ho Chi Minh Trail. In December 1967 it was estimated that the combined U.S. effort in the panhandle was destroying seven hundred enemy trucks per month while some three hundred trucks were getting through. Hanoi was obviously paying a heavy price in trucks and supplies in order to keep its logistics pipeline into South Vietnam flowing.

As we gained experience with the HARK-1 system we continued to modify its use. By July 1967 a typical road-watch operation might have proceeded as follows: An observer in an OP south of the Mu Gia Pass would see thirty-nine trucks heading south on the Ho Chi Minh Trail. Within two minutes of its being noted by the team, the HARK-1 device would shoot the intelligence to an orbiting Volpar, which would relay it to Udorn, which in turn would pass it orally to the 7/13th Air Force. The latter, through its Airborne Command and

Control Center in C-130s flying over the panhandle, would divert a flight of aircraft to hit the trucks.

We found that trucks were being brought under fire within seven to eight minutes of their sighting. The results were then measured in a variety of ways. First, the most reliable was a post-flight debriefing of the attack airplane crews on the number of secondary explosions they had seen after the trucks were hit, indications that gasoline or ammunition had been hit and destroyed. Second, photography the next day by reconnaissance aircraft would produce pictures of destroyed trucks at the exact location where they had been hit. Third, North Vietnamese communications frequently confirmed the effectiveness of a particular air strike. Finally, the road-watch team would report the strike, the fireball explosions it could see, and the secondary detonations it could hear. When we were regularly obtaining this type of work product, we knew we had achieved real-time reporting.

It was also clear we were doing our job. The men who ran the road-watch teams in South Laos like Walt Floyd, Gene Norwinski, Tom Hewitt, Will Charette, Ray D., Chuck Kleebauer, and Mike L., to name a few, took pride in knowing they were key players in a team effort that was producing the type of results that American policy makers wanted.

It was curiosity that first caused us to take a look at Route 110. MACV had suspected for some time that the North Vietnamese were using this road for hauling significant quantities of war matériel from the Cambodian port of Sihanoukville across Laos into South Vietnam, but analysts in the CIA's Intelligence Directorate had discounted the idea, so we were inclined to assign a low priority to this particular road system. Still, we thought it useful to know what was going on in the area, so Pakse assigned the task of monitoring Route 110 to Doug Swanson, a former Army sergeant major. Operating out of a base at Kong My with occasional support from units on the Bolovens Plateau, Swanson confirmed that MACV was right.

By April 1967 people had begun calling Route 110 the Sihanouk Trail. Pakse's efforts from the Kong My base had identified sixty-three hard targets on Route 110 warranting air strikes. These targets were storage areas, bunkers, and bivouac sites. Collateral sources such as refugee debriefings, information from reconnaissance patrols, aerial reconnaissance, and signals intelligence confirmed the road-watch-team reporting. As a result Udorn, in conjunction with Pakse, was drawing up a strike package to present to the 7/13th Air Force. Just at that juncture the gods of war smiled on our efforts. We obtained access to Second Lieutenant Nguyen Khac Thanh, a North Vietnamese who had just defected to the FAR.

Thanh was a noteworthy source, for he had been assigned to Binh Tran 5, an NVA unit of regimental size that handled security and transportation functions along sections of the Ho Chi Minh Trail. Thanh had worked on building and maintaining Route 110. We learned from him that twelve hundred metric tons per month of rice, salt, fish sauce, sugar, condensed milk, coffee, tobacco, medicine, and ammunition moved over Route 110. Of this total, seventy metric tons stayed in Laos. The tonnage was moved by 140 trucks in the dry season and by 2,000 bicycles in the rainy season. Thanh said his unit also had sixty small boats at its disposal for use along the Se Kong River. It was also determined that Hanoi had started to build the Route 110 structure in early 1965 and regarded it as completed by April 1967.

Thanh was a fountain of new information. We debriefed him and blended his intelligence into our previous holdings. Our planning then went forward to run a series of air strikes against Route 110. The first operation, called SHOCK-1, covered April 27–30, 1967. When the 7/13th Air Force finished its rumble over the selected targets we had recorded 121 secondary explosions, 27 secondary fires, 15 road cuts, 5 fords and underwater bridges destroyed, and 6 bunker complexes destroyed.

When we had these results in hand, we briefed Major General Phasouk Somly, the MR-4 commander. After viewing extensive photographic coverage of the area that had been bombed, an impressed Phasouk told our Pakse unit chief, Dave Morales, "This is an important tactical victory over the North Vietnamese."

After reflecting further on the briefing, Phasouk then somewhat cynically added a footnote to his original comment. He said, "This operation reminds me of an old Lao proverb: 'When elephants fight the grass suffers.'" Morales thought Phasouk was expressing a concern that this American success would trigger a North Vietnamese military response that would hurt the Lao population in Phasouk's military region. Somewhat later it became clear that Phasouk was concerned not with the broader issue of the security of the population but with the specifics of how this operation would affect the rice trade that one of his relatives was conducting with the North Vietnamese.

As the enemy regrouped from the original blow, we updated our intelligence. By mid-May we were ready to hit them again. SHOCK-2 was run in the period May 20–27, 1967. It used 148 sorties by the 7/13th Air Force and 41 by the Royal Lao Air Force T-28s. The results were 27 secondary explosions, 8 secondary fires, 20 road cuts, 23 military-type structures destroyed, 5 trucks destroyed, and 30 boats sunk on the Se Kong River. More importantly, it strengthened Washington's and Saigon's determination to confront the issue of the logistics support that Hanoi was getting for its forces in South Vietnam from the duplicitous Cambodian ruler Norodom Sihanouk via the port of Sihanoukville.

Our road-watch activity was not limited to the panhandle. In North Laos various Hmong and Thai assets functioning as forward air guides (FAGs) not only collected intelligence but sent their observations directly to U.S. aircraft searching in MR-2 for strike targets. They were especially effective against the North Vietnamese 316th Division and its use of Route 7. Other successes were scored along the Route 6 structure that ran from North Vietnam to Sam Neua in Laos and ultimately tied into Route 602 as it moved westward toward the important Hmong operational base at Phu Pha Ti.

One particular FAG sticks out in my mind. His code name and radio call sign was "Red Hat." He spoke good English, was a Thai national, and from various prominent terrain features would use an HT-1 ground-to-air radio to talk with U.S. Air Force forward air controllers (FACs). Also known by their code name "Ravens," the FACs were a small unit of about twenty-four pilots flying a mixed fleet of O-1s and occasionally T-28s from which they spotted and marked targets for strike aircraft. In a typical real-time operation, Red Hat would spot a five-truck convoy on Route 6 and radio his observations to a Raven, who would validate the target and direct a strike aircraft or two to hit the trucks. Elapsed time from observation to air strike could be as little as five minutes if all systems were working as they should. In the end, four of the five trucks would have been destroyed.

Sometimes the Ravens would fly with a Lao or Hmong backseater. On these occasions the backseater would validate the targets signaled by the FAGs, thus freeing the pilot to look for patterns in the incoming intelligence and actively seek out targets himself. While Ravens worked out of Lao airfields at Vientiane, Long Tieng, Luang Prabang, Savannakhet, and Pakse, during my time in Laos they seemed to be most effective when working with Hmong backseaters in support of General Vang Pao's operations in MR-2. This was due to a variety of factors, primary among them being that the Hmong backseaters had an intimate knowledge of the terrain, had a good feel for the local OB situation, were not prone to panic when the Ravens went low to confirm a sighting, and saw the air strikes as an integral part of Vang Pao's battle plan of the day. This merger of airpower and guerrilla battle plans was a novel development that gave the irregulars an unprecedented degree of firepower.

Later in the war, AC-130 gunships were brought to bear on North Laos for night flights over the Route 6 and 7 areas. This, combined with a FAG talking to the AC-130s and pinpointing truck targets that he had identified on the ground using a night-vision device, parried the Vietnamese tactic of moving trucks only at night with no visible lights. The first time we brought this combination of guerrilla reporting and AC-130s operating at night to bear on Route 7, we ended up with more than thirty secondary explosions.

13

Raids, Ambushes, and Battles

In pursuit of our second mission of inflicting damage on enemy forces operating in, from, or through Laos, we employed raids, ambushes, and mines to harass North Vietnamese and Pathet Lao units. The cutting edge of this program was the reconnaissance team, generally a twelve-man unit. The team's mission was to go out on patrol, use available intelligence to find the enemy, ambush a small enemy force, engage the enemy in a firefight, kill them or take prisoners, and search for documents that could be of intelligence value. By December 1, 1967, we had sixty-seven action or reconnaissance teams on our rolls. All told they ran about one hundred long-range patrols a month, thirty or so raids a month on small supply depots, truck parks, and bivouac areas, and some fifty ambush operations against enemy patrols operating throughout Laos. The favorite ambush was to mine a trail area, wait for an enemy unit to walk into the mines and suffer the resulting shock and casualties, and then complete the ambush with heavy automatic-weapons fire before fading away.

On one occasion during a visit to Savannakhet, I concentrated on reviewing the unit's road and ambush operations. This included a discussion with the Thai officer who headed the Headquarters 333 unit in the area. Toward the end of our meeting, the Thai said, "Our training doctrine teaches the teams to run these operations at night whenever possible. You have to remember this effort is like a good love affair. The best actions are carried out at night."

The efforts of all of the reconnaissance teams, combined with the fighting carried out by the SGU battalions throughout Laos, resulted by December 1967 in our inflicting an average of 541 casualties per month in killed and wounded enemy forces. The ratio here was about three killed for every one enemy soldier wounded. This effort, while impressive, was achieved at a cost. There were also casualties on our side. The guerrilla forces suffered an average of seventy-seven men killed or wounded per month. In statistical terms this is a 7:1 ratio in favor of the guerrilla forces. That is an effective combat-loss ratio in terms of the type of analysis that is conducted by those engaged in war games at military staff colleges or academic think tanks. Unfortunately, in the context of Laos it was a tragedy, for the Hmong suffered a disproportionate share of the friendly losses.

This sad reality of Hmong combat losses also carried over into our third operational program. In that effort we used SGU units to serve as a counterreconnaissance screen designed to help the Vientiane government hold those areas that were under the RLG flag. Additionally, we used the SGUs, operating as independent battalions but utilizing guerrilla tactics, to take terrain from the Pathet Lao and North Vietnamese. The SGUs were also tasked to inflict damage on enemy forces by engaging them in firefights whenever a company of SGUs could mount a guerrilla attack in force. On occasion, by marrying FAR's conventional ground operations to the guerrilla tactics of the SGUs, we would engage in joint operations designed to take and hold terrain.

In December 1967 we had a guerrilla-force-level ceiling of forty thousand men. This ceiling, as well as all the other increases that had been made in the force structure during 1961–1967, had been approved by the Washington policy-level body known as the Special Group (5412 Committee) or its successor organizations. Our actual onboard strength for the guerrilla-force structure broke down as follows:

Nam Yu (northwest)	6,843
Luang Prabang (north central)	2,502
Long Tieng (north)	21,741
Savannakhet (central)	3,535
Pakse (south)	4,232
Total	**38,853**

Within this overall force level we had twenty-one SGU battalions, each with a table of organization and equipment that called for five hundred fifty men. Rarely was any SGU battalion up to full strength. As a result, to appreciate what these units could do, one should visualize a five-hundred-man battalion of paramilitary irregulars who were rarely committed to combat as battalions.

The SGUs were the elite of our fighting units. We developed them out of the *auto-defense ordinaire* and *auto-defense de choc* militia units that defended villages and the surrounding territories. This meant the average SGU rifleman had eight weeks of previous light-infantry training, three to six months of service in the CIA's paramilitary force, and a smell of some level of combat. In order to keep ethnic tensions at a minimum within each battalion, we organized the companies along ethnic lines—all Hmong, Yao, or Lao Theung. The officers at company and battalion level were mostly Lao, being professional soldiers taken from the FAR and assigned to SGU duties by the military region commander in whose area the SGU was located. Once formed into an SGU, the entire battalion was sent as a unit to locations like Phitsanloke, Thailand, where Royal Thai Army NCOs and officers conducted three months of training in battalion-level tactics, small-unit tactics, and the use of all weapons up to the 4.2 mortar and the 75mm recoilless rifle.

Typical of an SGU operation designed to hold terrain was what happened at Na Khang (Site 36). One SGU battalion was always at this outpost. The site located south and west of Pathet Lao headquarters at Sam Neua and about 150 nautical miles west of Hanoi had multiple purposes. First, it was a launch site from which roadwatch teams could be sent to cover Route 6 and reconnaissance patrols and SGU units could be dispatched on their attack missions against Pathet Lao/North Vietnamese forces. It was also a forward supply depot from which helicopters or short-takeoff-and-landing (STOL) aircraft could drop supplies to guerrilla units or evacuate them in emergencies from hot spots in forward areas. Equally important, it was a staging base for U.S. Air Force "Jolly Green Giant" Sikorsky HH3E helicopters. Based in Thailand, these aircraft were brought forward every day to Site 36 so that they might react the more quickly to search and rescue (SAR) calls from American fliers downed over North Vietnam or Laos. This effort saved a number of

American pilots and was a tremendous morale booster for those who had to fly over North Vietnam.

Two CIA officers were assigned to Site 36—Jerry D. and Mike L. In addition, AID had a refugee-affairs specialist working out of this position. On January 6, 1967, at dawn a Hmong trooper in a perimeter observation post spotted a North Vietnamese sapper unit advancing to clear a path for the main body of an attack. The Hmong opened fire, alerting the site to what was about to happen. Although the element of surprise was lost, the attack proceeded. It consisted of advancing infantry supported by mortar fire and what was described as 120mm rockets.

Mike L. and a USAID employee, Don Sjostrom, were at the site that particular night. When the attack started, L. got on the radio in the site command bunker to call for air support. Sjostrom went outside to provide security for the entrance to the bunker and to keep L. posted on the flow of the battle to the extent that he could observe it. After L. raised Udorn and knew aircraft were on their way, he went outside the bunker to contact Sjostrom. As he approached the USAID man, the latter was hit by a bullet and killed instantly. L. saw that the Vietnamese were at the north end of the site and the SGU troops were facing a shrinking perimeter. At that juncture F-105s arrived and buzzed the site. The boom from their afterburners caused the Vietnamese to stall their attack. Before they could reorganize, two A-1Es appeared over the site. L., during his ground-to-air conversations, acted as a FAC and directed the close-support air strikes that stopped the Vietnamese attack. Other aircraft subsequently appeared to replace the initial A-1Es, and for the rest of the day and that night, airpower drove the Vietnamese out of the area with heavy casualties. The site remained operational and in the control of its Hmong defenders, but the Vietnamese did not forget it. They subsequently made other attempts to drive the SGU out of this area.

Operation Samakhi is a good example of SGU–FAR cooperation. I got my first intimation of it in early June 1967 when General Oudone Sananikone stopped me at a Vientiane cocktail party to say he would like to come by my residence at an early date for one of our periodic chats. Experience had shown that when Oudone raised an item that obliquely, it meant he wanted to talk sooner rather than later. My immediate response therefore was to lay on a luncheon for the next day at my home.

When Oudone appeared for the scheduled meeting, it was clear he had an agenda. The issue that surfaced over a gin and tonic was interregional FAR cooperation. Succinctly put, the question was whether I would intervene with Vang Pao on General Kouprasith's behalf so that MR-5 and MR-2 could cooperate along their regional boundaries in a joint operation to clear the area northeast of Vientiane of residual pockets of Pathet Lao/North Vietnamese troops. Oudone noted quite frankly that success in this operation would be first and foremost a net gain for Kouprasith, MR-5, and the security of Vientiane. It would, however, also contribute to securing Vang Pao's southeastern flank around Tha Thom and the Moung Nham valley. Additionally, Oudone made it clear that it could be a confidence-building step designed to reduce the past levels of tension between Kouprasith and Vang Pao, which stemmed from their age-old differences over the now deposed and exiled General Phoumi Nosavan.

This proposal was music to my ears. For months Bill Lair, our senior representative at Long Tieng, Jonathan R., Colonel Dhep from Headquarters 333, and I had been cooperating in pursuit of two goals. One was to get Vang Pao to fly the flag periodically and spend a few hours on any given day in Vientiane. We pressed him to visit FAR headquarters, to do some politicking with the National Assembly, and to let it be known by his presence in the city that he had no reason not to be in Vientiane. The other was to try to spread some salve on the old wounds that stood between Vang Pao and Kouprasith. These centered essentially on the fact that Kouprasith hated the now exiled General Phoumi Nosavan, whereas Vang Pao had backed the latter during various internecine struggles. The past had proven difficult to overcome despite our best efforts. Colonel Dhep had worked on Kouprasith, and the American trio had urged reconciliation on Vang Pao. I had also urged General Ouan to play a peacemaker role in this drama. Now Oudone, acting either on Kouprasith's behalf or under instructions from his boss, General Ouan Rathikoun, FAR commander in chief, had set the chessboard for an irresistible, bold move.

Oudone was told that while I was prepared to broach the subject with Vang Pao, even if it meant flying to Long Tieng that very afternoon, life was not that simple. There was the issue of FAR troops. My assumption was that Kouprasith and Vang Pao would both want to use FAR troops on this operation. If so, it would be more appropriate for the Army attaché to handle this intermediary role. Then, there was the question of drawing up an operational plan and coordinating the details of whose troops were to do what, in which operational area, and on what timetable. That was a matter best left to direct contact between Vang Pao and Kouprasith. My suggestion therefore was that I pave the way for a Kouprasith visit to Long Tieng to talk with Vang Pao. The latter had at least four operations in progress, whereas Kouprasith's military region was quiet. This made the logic of a Kouprasith visit to Long Tieng quite compelling.

Oudone obviously did not like this idea. It showed on his face. Pausing to regroup his thoughts, Oudone munched on a few olives and a piece of paté. He then countered with the proposal that Colonel Thonglith Chokbengboun, the MR-5 chief of staff, visit Vang Pao at Long Tieng. My immediate response was that when Kouprasith visited Long Tieng, Thonglith had to be an integral part of the team as he would be the ramrod who would make MR-5's part of the operation a success or failure. We discussed this further over lunch. Oudone finally said he would explore this possibility with others and let me know.

That very evening Kouprasith appeared at a cocktail party where I had not expected to see him. I walked over to him and asked pointblank when he wanted to go to Long Tieng. Kouprasith, whose English had improved in the past eleven months as a result of daily tutoring, said, "I will go. My conditions, however, are that you go with me, we use your airplane, and you personally guarantee my safety."

"No problem on all three points," I assured him. "When do you want to go?"

"Thonglith and I would like to stop at your house tomorrow morning around 10:00 after we finish a meeting at FAR headquarters at Phone Kheng and are on our way back to my headquarters at Chinaimo."

"Fine," I said.

Thonglith stopped at my residence at daybreak the next morning. He was by himself, apologized for calling on me without an appointment, and said he was en route to a meeting at FAR headquarters. As he was passing my house en route to Phone Kheng, he decided to stop in. I invited him in for breakfast. He said he could not stay that long. We went into my study, therefore, to drink coffee. Thonglith was a tough, no-nonsense soldier. He came to the point quickly. The question was, Did I truly understand Kouprasith's concerns about going to Long Tieng? Was I confident I could really guarantee Kouprasith's safety while at Long Tieng?

My answer to both questions was an unequivocal yes.

Thonglith paused, got up, saluted, and said, "Your word has been good so far. I trust that will continue, for my future is linked to Kouprasith's." With that the meeting was over.

At the embassy that morning I had a private chat with Ambassador Sullivan. He was briefed on the prospects of a quick but quiet Kouprasith trip to Long Tieng. The ambassador endorsed the plan and asked that I keep him posted on developments.

At around 10:15 A.M. Kouprasith and Thonglith appeared at my home. Thonglith made a point of saying it was nice to see me after a period with no chance encounters on the social circuit. I got the message: Our early morning meeting was a nonevent insofar as the record went.

Kouprasith wasted no time. He spread out a map and had Thonglith brief me on the operation. After we talked for a few minutes, Kouprasith gave me the map and some written papers in Lao and asked that they be sent to Vang Pao. It was then agreed that Vang Pao could study both items before we went to see him. Our meeting was soon over and we parted company.

Upon returning to my office, I cleaned up some pending business and flew to Udorn. The Kouprasith papers were given to Bill Lair and Pat Landry, and they were hand-carried to Long Tieng that same afternoon by one of our officers who was going up country. Lair agreed to fly to Long Tieng the next day to work with Vang Pao on an early VIP visit for Kouprasith.

A few days later I was at Wattay Airport early in the morning waiting for Kouprasith and Thonglith. The trip to Long Tieng was scheduled, and a Volpar was standing by. When Kouprasith was fifteen minutes late, I started to wonder if this adventure was going to abort.

Suddenly the Kouprasith caravan of five vehicles pulled up, flags flying and security outriders in full battle gear. Out of one car stepped Kouprasith in a very neatly pressed and slightly starched khaki uniform. He was followed by his beautiful wife. That was unexpected; no plans had been made for her going on the trip. Thonglith appeared out of a second car dressed in jungle fatigues.

After exchanging greetings I said to Kouprasith, "If you and Thonglith are ready, let's board the aircraft. We have a full day planned."

At that point the Volpar engines started turning over, as we had arranged for the pilots to start engines as soon as they saw Kouprasith's caravan. Kouprasith turned, spoke to his wife, and motioned to me to lead the way to the aircraft. I quickly moved to get us aboard because I wanted to leave a minimum of openings for a change of heart.

Once on board, Thonglith moved to the back of the aircraft. Kouprasith and I sat across the aisle from each other. As I motioned to the pilots to take off, Kouprasith said, "My wife wanted to see with her own eyes that you were with me."

I said, "We have two pilots today as an extra security precaution."

No further conversation was possible over the engine roar, so we all relaxed and had coffee as the airplane went airborne. We then took note of the terrain and had what for me was an uneventful flight to Long Tieng.

Upon landing in Long Tieng, the Volpar was maneuvered to a disembarkation spot where out of the aircraft window I could see a red carpet, honor guard troops, what appeared to be a band, and a massive civilian welcoming committee. "Vang Pao is obviously putting his best foot forward," I thought. "Bill Lair and Jon R. have put some time and effort into this show," was my second thought. My third reflection was, "Where did the band come from?"

Glancing out of the corner of my eye, I could see Kouprasith clutching a gold Buddha that hung from a gold chain around his neck. He was muttering something that sounded like a prayer. As one of the pilots started to let the exit ramp down, I told Kouprasith he had to get off first as the honored guest. He balked initially and wanted me to go first for security reasons. I said no, told the pilots to let the ramp down, and nudged Kouprasith into the exit. With my hand on his back, pushing ever so gently, Kouprasith started his descent. The band struck up a tune, and Vang Pao moved to the foot of the ramp to greet Kouprasith. Vang Pao also had his dress khakis on and looked every inch the conventional Lao flag-rank officer. When Kouprasith reached the ground, Vang Pao saluted smartly, Kouprasith returned the salute, and by then Thonglith and I were standing respectfully behind Kouprasith. Seeing us all in place, Vang Pao spoke to Kouprasith in Lao and wheeled, whereupon we moved to the troop line to review the honor guard. After reviewing the troops, Vang Pao steered us to the civilian dignitaries. A Hmong district chief (*tasseng*) uttered some greetings, two Hmong girls in their finest silver-bedecked costumes presented flowers, and we moved to a waiting fleet of vehicles that took us to Vang Pao's headquarters.

Once at headquarters, Vang Pao introduced his staff to the visitors. A Lao staff officer responsible for intelligence gave a briefing on the enemy and friendly situation in MR-2. Kouprasith took notes and asked a few questions. By then it was time to adjourn to Vang Pao's house for lunch. The food was plentiful, and we washed it down with warm Thai beer. When lunch was served, Kouprasith as the honored guest obtained his plate first. Knowing of his concerns about being killed, I was quick to sample each dish. Once I had tasted an item, Kouprasith would pick at the same thing.

After lunch we went back to Vang Pao's headquarters where Kouprasith laid out his battle maps. At that point Bill Lair and I faded to the back of the building while R. stayed in the close proximity of Vang Pao. Thonglith in turn shadowed Kouprasith. In my view it was best that we senior CIA types keep a low profile while the two generals sorted out their Royal Lao Army problems in Lao with minimal concern about losing face before the foreigners.

A couple of hours ticked away before the meeting was concluded with a joint agreement to proceed with Operation Samakhi. At that point we started to disengage from Long Tieng, for I could see that Kouprasith was tired from tension and the lack of his customary Lao midday nap. We therefore moved back to Vang Pao's house for a traditional shot or two of Scotch as a substitute for a local brown-colored spirit mix called Mekong. From there it was back to the Long Tieng airfield, a farewell to the local dignitaries, and a passage through a bank of honor guards on each side of the red carpet as we boarded the aircraft. Kouprasith saluted Vang Pao as he boarded and thanked him for the courtesies of the visit. Vang Pao returned the salute, smiled broadly, and turned to bid Thonglith farewell. With Kouprasith and Thonglith on board the Volpar, I was able to whisper to Vang Pao, "Good show! Number one!" as we shook hands and I boarded the airplane.

Our flight to Vientiane was uneventful. Kouprasith went to sleep as soon as we were airborne. Thonglith whispered two brief messages to me: that the visit was outstanding, and that Kouprasith hated to fly.

Upon landing in Vientiane, Kouprasith was greeted by his cavalcade of cars and his wife. After exchanging greetings with his wife, Kouprasith turned back to me saying, "Thank you. The trip was very good, I am back home safely, and your record of keeping your word remains good." Kouprasith then entered his car. Thonglith saluted me and said, "Thanks." With that the adventure of the day was over.

By the next morning there was no doubt that the visit had been a success. R. reported from Long Tieng that Vang Pao was pleased with the trip as were his community leaders. General Oudone visited me at my residence early in the morning and said Kouprasith was now convinced that one could work with Vang Pao and that the heritage of past animosity was best forgotten. Ambassador Sullivan also heard from Kouprasith that the latter regarded the Long Tieng visit a success.

The best part, however, was that on June 14, 1967, an MR-5 task force choppered into the Phou Lawek area on FAR's French-supplied equipment and, according to plan, pacified the area. Vang Pao in turn executed his part of the operation by using three battalions of irregulars to move into the Moung Nham valley. The combined operation achieved its objectives, and Vientiane's security was improved. The effort also had inherent covert-action overtones, for it brought two important power factors in the Lao political equation—Kouprasith and Vang Pao—closer together. This in turn advanced the nation-building part of the station's mission.

Not all of our combined operations ended happily. The attempt to wrest the Nam Bac area from Pathet Lao/North Vietnamese control was one that did not.

This operation found its genesis in a buffet dinner party in Vientiane around December 1966. Colonel Clarke Baldwin, the Army attaché, and I were sitting on the staircase of our host's home, enjoying the food and a glass of wine, and reminiscing about earlier days in Germany. We talked about the Fulda Gap, the attack route that the Group of Soviet Forces Germany (GSFG) were expected to use if they moved into West Germany, and from there our conversation drifted to Soviet combined-arms operations during World War II. The subject that interested us both was the Soviets' use of guerrillas in conjunction with regular Army units when the latter were on the attack.

In this context Baldwin said he was quite pleased with what the FAR had done on a combined-arms basis in MR-1 in the Nam Bac valley during July and August 1966. Knowing that I had just arrived in Laos at that time and that my mind had been on other things, Baldwin outlined on a napkin the deployment of two mobile groups (GMs) (each GM consisted of three battalions) and the use of four or five volunteer battalions (BVs) and Lao T-28s to retake an area that FAR had retreated from in 1961. It was Baldwin's view that the conventional GMs had been the key to victory and that Vang Pao's MR-2 units had contributed. This prompted Baldwin to propose that his office and mine should try to find other opportunities for combined-arms operations.

Not wishing to reject the idea out of hand, I cautioned that the MR-2 irregulars could not afford the high casualty rates that came with set-piece battles and that their primary function would have to be reconnaissance out in front of or on the flanks of any FAR line of attack. Baldwin agreed. It was left that he and his staff would look for opportunities for joint operations. In fact, Baldwin said, his team was wondering if FAR could move out from Nam Bac in late 1967 to further expand RLG control of the surrounding rice-growing areas.

I had no answer to that. We agreed that if Baldwin had a good proposal for such an operation, he would bring it up in a country-team meeting.[1]

The Vientiane Station went about its work, concentrating on building assets. In MR-1 our emphasis was on Luang Prabang. Here the job was to get road-watch teams deployed to report on Route 19 and what was moving into Laos from supply depots in Dien Bien Phu, North Vietnam. We also wanted to run operations designed to inflict damage on the supplies that the North Vietnamese were pushing down the Nam Hou River from Route 19 toward their forces south of the royal capital in Luang Prabang.

In this scheme of things, our new chief at Luang Prabang, Eli

Popovich, used Nam Bac, which was about sixty-five miles south of Dien Bien Phu, as a launch pad from which to leapfrog teams into areas from which they could cover Route 19 up along the Lao/North Vietnamese border. Popovich was an old-timer. He was a former steelworker, a veteran of OSS operations in Yugoslavia in World War II, a longtime trainer of the CIA's junior paramilitary officers, and a distinguished gentleman whose hallmark was a handlebar mustache. Pop, as he was affectionately called, saw the Lao war as his last hurrah. This caused him to work hard, particularly with the Lao Theung, to get the job done.

There were successes, particularly when we started using M-79 grenade launchers in our attacks on the boat traffic. There were also disappointments and moral difficulties. When our sinkings of North Vietnamese/Pathet Lao supplies on the Nam Hou River increased, the Pathet Lao started carrying their families or local hostages in their boat convoys. Popovich and his units took such care to avoid killing or injuring noncombatants that the attacks on river cargo never achieved the tactical goals that had been laid out for this specific program.

After the North Vietnamese ran a very successful sapper attack on Royal Lao Air Force airplanes parked at the Luang Prabang airfield in July 1967, we decided in conjunction with the FAR general staff that more emphasis had to be placed on running reconnaissance patrols north of Luang Prabang. Our goal was to contribute more to enhancing the fragile security around the royal capital.

If memory serves me correctly, it was around early February 1967 that Colonel Baldwin reported to the country team that he and the Lao general staff were looking at a multibattalion FAR operation designed to link up MR-1 with MR-2 at the Nam Hou River and to expand RLG influence toward Muong Sai in the west and toward Nam Tha in the northwest. Baldwin saw this as at least a six-battalion operation augmented by SGUs and lots of Lao and U.S. air support.

A key reservation put forth by Baldwin in the country-team meeting discussion was who on the Lao side would be given command of the operation. This was like throwing a cat in among the pigeons. Unfortunately, there was no agreement because there were only three or four Lao colonels or generals who could do the job. All of these officers were considered unavailable for the assignment.

I spoke up to say that guerrilla unit support would be thin if provided at all, for Luang Prabang was in the early phase of recruiting and training road-watch and harassment teams. Additionally, I noted that Vang Pao was fully committed in MR-2 and had few if any guerrillas he could throw into the fray to expand territorial gains around Nam Bac.

Others, like Joe Mendenhall, the USAID director, had reservations concerning refugee flow and a lack of resources to help incorporate liberated areas into the RLG social structure. It was left, however, that Baldwin should continue his dialog with FAR on the potential operation. This was not a commitment to proceed; nor was it an agreement that the country-team agencies would provide a fixed level of either air sorties or guerrillas in support of a Nam Bac offensive. It was simply a mandate to study options.

I used the first opportunity after the meeting to discuss the matter with Lair. I said that at the country-team meeting the Army attaché had raised the possibility of a Nam Bac offensive operation. If it went forward there would be requests for specific levels of support from CIA assets. Based on that, what were Lair's views on the critical questions? Was such an operation tactically sound and within FAR's capabilities? What support from guerrilla units could the CIA program contribute to the operation? And who in FAR could provide the required combat leadership for this attack?

Lair's initial reaction was that this was an ambitious undertaking. He thought that it would be, if successful, a major territorial gain that would improve Luang Prabang's security. On the other hand, while it could be successful, the nature of the accomplishment might provoke a disastrous Pathet Lao/North Vietnamese response. In essence, FAR theoretically had the manpower, logistics, and tactics to make the operation a success if it had the required command structure committed to the operation. Lair said Vang Pao could obviously handle the operation successfully. The FAR power elite—generals Ouan, Kouprasith, and Oudone—would however never give this opportunity to Vang Pao. While generals Ouan, FAR commander in chief, and Phasouk, MR-4 commander, could manage the operation, it was out of the question that they could be spared from their current duties to handle this task. This meant the task force commander had to be a Lao colonel who was destined for a brigadier general's stars. (The Lao order of rank assigned two stars to a brigadier general and three stars to a major general.)

I interrupted Lair to say that Colonel Bounchanh Savadphayphane was being touted as the likely choice for the position of overall commander of the Nam Bac offensive. Lair said he knew Bounchanh from the days when the latter had headed a GM. This knowledge persuaded Lair that Bounchanh was no tiger. He would have trouble controlling the operation, said Lair.

What about Colonel Thonglith Chokbengboun? I wanted to know. Did he have the ability to run the operation?

Lair said that he doubted General Kouprasith would release Thonglith from MR-5 for the period required to run the operation, but that Thonglith could do the job. In essence, a lack of command leadership made the proposed Nam Bac operation questionable, according to Lair. If, however, Vang Pao or Thonglith could run the operation, there were reasons to believe it could achieve near-term success.

When we looked at what CIA assets could be brought to bear in a Nam Bac offensive, Lair agreed with what I had previously outlined at the country-team meeting. Our Luang Prabang unit could provide some increased reconnaissance activities north of Luang Prabang, more attacks against traffic on the Nam Hou River, as well as expanded road-watch intelligence reporting along Route 19 up to the Lao/North Vietnamese border. Beyond that, the level of combat in MR-2 would determine what resources Vang Pao could divert into the Nam Bac package on a target-of-opportunity basis. Lair said Vang Pao was stretched thin coping with his region's tactical situation and could not be expected to make an ironclad commitment of resources to a Nam Bac operation.

At the end of this exchange of views, it was left that I would share our thoughts with Colonel Baldwin. Subsequently, if the Nam Bac proposal moved forward toward reality, at the next country-team meeting I would mention the questions of leadership and CIA resources as factors limiting the operation's chances of success. I told Lair that I regarded the Nam Bac operation as something the Vientiane Station preferred not to be bullish on. However, if FAR supported by the Army and Air attachés decided to go forward, we in the CIA should be as helpful to the country team in support of this operation as our other responsibilities would permit. Lair agreed.

A few days later, well into the evening hours, Colonel Dhep visited me at my Vientiane residence. This was one of our spontaneous unprogrammed meetings that were made possible by Dhep's frequent forays into Vientiane to talk with Prime Minister Souvanna Phouma, General Ouan, or General Kouprasith. Dhep would close out a Vientiane day with a brief exchange of views with me on political and military matters. These exchanges were very useful to both of us. Dhep had insights into Lao thinking that frequently added a new dimension to the American perspective. Conversely, I had hard intelligence on Lao political gyrations that Dhep could benefit from. I valued his opinions. Thus, on this particular evening I surfaced the possibilities of a FAR-directed and-controlled operation out of Nam Bac designed to strengthen RLG control of terrain, population, and rice crops in the MR-1 region westward from Nam Bac toward Muong Sai, in a northwest direction toward Nam Tha, and eastward toward Muong Ngoi. Dhep said he had not heard much about this operation but knew it was a gleam in General Ouan's eye. When I asked Dhep which FAR colonel could run a six-battalion-plus operation out of Nam Bac, Dhep thought for a moment and then said Colonel Thonglith. Immediately following up on that evaluation, Dhep said Kouprasith was not ready for Thonglith to get his stars just yet, so he would not make him available for the job.

While the planning moved forward within FAR for a Nam Bac offensive, and while Colonel Khamphai Sayasith, the FAR commander at Nam Bac, began trying with salami-slice tactics to expand his area of operations, Hanoi responded with a counterattack aimed at both Nam Bac and the FAR forces deployed on Kou Mountain, a strongpoint in the defensive scheme of Nam Bac. The March 1967 fighting cost the North Vietnamese 110 dead, whereas FAR had about 31 men killed.

FAR reacted by reinforcing Nam Bac with GM-27 and GM-25, an incremental buildup significant by FAR standards. While Colonel Khamphai remained the actual on-site Nam Bac field commander, Colonel Bounchanh with the support of General Ouan emerged as the officer in de facto control of the Nam Bac salient. This was not a popular decision with either the FAR or the

American embassy. In fact, various channels were used by Ambassador Sullivan to let Ouan know the Americans did not regard Bounchanh as the man for the job. It was not surprising, therefore, that General Ouan told me at one of our cocktail-party encounters when I raised the Bounchanh issue that he had no basis for relieving Bounchanh of command. That remark did not, however, address why Bounchanh had been permitted to obtain this critical post in the first place.

In conjunction with the buildup by FAR at Nam Bac, the area of RLG control around the Nam Bac valley was expanded. On August 16, however, the North Vietnamese pushed troops from GM-27 out of positions some fourteen kilometers northeast of Nam Bac. This set off alarm bells that the Vietnamese were planning to retake the Nam Bac area one position at a time in a methodical meat-grinder operation.

General Ouan was determined not to lose Nam Bac; thus, more FAR reinforcements were sent there in September 1967. Subsequently, one unit of reinforcements advanced some ten kilometers southeast of Nam Bac and occupied positions up to the Nam Bac River.

In October 1967 FAR had about four thousand troops in the Nam Bac area and was attempting to launch an offensive with the support of some guerrilla units conducting harassment operations against enemy forces located along FAR's line of attack. The FAR troops made few sustained gains. The CIA irregulars, working out of Luang Prabang, however, made a modest contribution to the security of Nam Bac by taking the village of Nam Thuam, about eighteen kilometers southwest of Nam Bac. They also made some very short-term gains around Muong Sai.

With the dry season upon us, reporting started to flow in that the North Vietnamese 316th Infantry Division supported by an independent regiment was deploying from Dien Bien Phu toward Nam Bac. This was a good news–bad news scenario. The good news was that if the 316th was tied up in Laos, it could not contribute to the fighting in South Vietnam. The bad news was that if the 316th was committed to Nam Bac, the FAR and its guerrilla supporters were in for big trouble. By the early part of December 1967, FAR still had about thirty-eight hundred troops in the Nam Bac area supported by about eight hundred guerrillas scattered throughout MR-1 and trying to contribute to FAR objectives in the Nam Bac valley. This combat ratio gave little comfort to FAR. The OB analysts in Udorn were making it clear that the arrival of the 316th would change the battlefield equation in Hanoi's favor if FAR opted for a static defense posture.

The critical question in country-team meetings became how to avoid a Dien Bien Phu–type siege of FAR at Nam Bac, as well as a possible major defeat. Colonel Bounchanh had moved into Nam Bac by this point in the saga and was the day-to-day battlefield commander. It was clear to one and all, based on his on-the-ground performance, that Bounchanh was not the man for the job. This point was made repeatedly to Ouan by me and Dhep, among many others. Yet, General Ouan would not relieve him.

Instead, efforts were stepped up to resupply Nam Bac by air as a prelude to trying to expand the Nam Bac perimeter and break out of a situation that was lending itself to a set-piece battle of the Dien Bien Phu type. While FAR held the high ground around Nam Bac, if it lost those positions it could be squeezed into a valley-type defensive position. Ouan was reluctant, however, to order an overland withdrawal, knowing retrograde operations are difficult for even the best of armies. He also knew history had shown that attempts at organized retreats by FAR usually turned into undisciplined routs. Trying desperately to avoid a battlefield disaster, Ouan opted for a limited offensive that would expand the FAR presence in the Nam Bac area.

After a major resupply effort by Air America C-123s and RLAF H-35 helicopters onto the twenty-six-hundred-foot airfield at Nam Bac, in the period around December 20–24, 1967, Bounchanh tried to expand his perimeter with some limited success. Vang Pao, in trying to take some pressure off of Nam Bac, sent an understrength battalion of irregulars to take the village of Muong Ngoi as part of what was now called Operation Linkup. This feint and other Vang Pao operations, like the attack on Muong Sai west of Nam Bac, were designed to distract the North Vietnamese/Pathet Lao from Nam Bac. The short-term tactical success by Vang Pao did not reduce the enemy's concentration on Nam Bac. Hanoi saw Nam Bac for what it was and would not be deflected from the main prize. Nam Bac had to be eliminated in order to reopen the threat of a Vietnamese advance on the royal capital at Luang Prabang. Additionally, Nam

Bac now had most of FAR's mobile reserve pinned down where it would be bloodied if not destroyed.

In reality, FAR had already been bled at Nam Bac. Bounchanh claimed in early January 1968 that since April 1967 his forces had taken one thousand casualties in the Nam Bac area. This reflected an attrition rate of about 25 percent. No army can sustain that.

Despite a valiant effort by RLAF T-28s to provide close support to FAR forces in Nam Bac, as well as USAF strikes against North Vietnamese forces and matériel moving to the Nam Bac battlefield, a FAR defeat began to emerge as a real possibility by late December 1967. Tactical air strikes and guerrilla attacks in support were keeping FAR on life support, but the patient was dying. The Vietnamese simply inched up on Nam Bac day by day, squeezing down the defense perimeter, denying Bounchanh the use of the airfield, and forcing his supplies to come in by airdrops from C-123s, which are never as effective as deliveries by landed aircraft.[2]

The best way to describe the final aspects of the Nam Bac defeat is to draw on a report I wrote on January 30, 1968.[3] It said,

> FAR units involved in the Nam Bac salient broke under moderate but sustained enemy pressure and fled in disorder. The collapse of the FAR positions at Houei Ngat, Nam Bac and Phoukou started on 13 January and the rout was completed by 14 January 1968. This defeat, in a tactical sense, was due to FAR's inability to move out from its defensive perimeter and in so doing to eliminate those enemy gun positions which were putting continuous harassing mortar fire on the entire FAR perimeter and in so doing were denying FAR the use of the Nam Bac airfield. As FAR units would not eliminate the enemy's mortar positions by infantry assault operations or well-placed air strikes followed up by ground attacks, FAR was pushed into a tighter and tighter defensive perimeter. This squeezing down of FAR's salient subjected its troops to sustained mortar fire harassment and sapped the troops' morale which had never been too high in the first instance. The net effect of this attrition by fire was a crumbling of the FAR salient under moderate pressure.
>
> When the FAR units started retreating, it was a disorganized effort with the main guidelines being every man for himself. This resulted in men fleeing with little or no unit integrity. This in turn complicated any attempts to mount an organized rescue effort which was designed to regroup the fleeing FAR forces. As a result by 29 January only about one third of the 3,278 men committed to the Nam Bac salient had been

recovered and regrouped. Unless significant numbers of troops are re-covered in the period prior to 14 February, FAR will have taken signifi-cant manpower losses at Nam Bac.

In another part of the report, I wrote,

In retrospect it is clear that the single most important factor contribut-ing to the fall of Nam Bac was that the lack of leadership essentially negated all of the plans that had been designed to save the Nam Bac situation. The second most important factor was the inability of General Ouan Rathikoun, Commander-in-Chief of the Lao Armed Forces, to recognize that Colonel Bounchanh Savathphayphane was not up to the job, that the job was beyond Bounchanh's span of control and that he should be relieved. The third most important factor was FAR's tactical weakness in that the units at Nam Bac did not patrol ag-gressively in that perimeter. Nor would they attack the enemy in order to clear their perimeter and enhance its security. Lack of patrolling re-sulted in FAR not having accurate, daily updated intelligence. Because FAR did not have accurate intelligence, it was not using its T-28 air strikes to hit pinpointed targets, but was hitting area targets instead. This negated the value of the tactical air support which was given to FAR units at Nam Bac by RLAF T-28s.

The real tragedy of Nam Bac is that it should not have been lost. With any real effort on its part, FAR should have been able to hold Nam Bac. This would have been particularly true if FAR had com-pleted its operation to link up its forces on both sides of the Nam Hou River at Muong Ngoi. General Vang Pao, Commanding General of the Second Military Region of the FAR, succeeded in his move on Muong Ngoi whereas Bounchanh did not because he could never get his troops to move out of the Nam Bac perimeter.

Ted Shackley serving in the U. S. Army in Germany circa 1946-47.

Shackley receives his first CIA Distinguished Intelligence Medal in 1965.

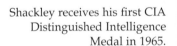

The Morning Market in Vientiane, Laos, during the September 1966 Mekong River flood. Access to the American embassy, located near this site, was by military vehicles, rafts manned by U.S. Marines, and then wading through the courtyard into the embassy.

U.S. Government Photographs

Shackley receives the Order of Million Elephants and White Parasol, Officer, in Laos in August 1968.

Shackley's final visit to Laotian general Vang Pao's headquarters in 1968.

With wife Hazel and daughter Suzanne, at a farewell party in the home of General Rathikoun in Vientiane, 1968.

The U. S. Mission Council, Saigon, 1969. Shackley is standing, second from left. Ambassador Ellsworth Bunker and Gen. Creighton W. Abrams are seated center and second from the right, respectively.

Shackley receiving the National Defense Award from a Vietnamese official in January 1972.

Shackley and Ambassador Ellsworth Bunker in Saigon in 1972.

U.S. officials meet in the MACV briefing center in Saigon in 1971. Shackley is standing, directly below the doorknob at the right.

Receiving a second Distinguished Intelligence Medal in 1974.

Gen. Fred Weyand heads a U.S. presidential fact-finding team meeting with President Nguyen Van Thieu in Saigon in April 1975, days before the city fell to the communists in April 1975. Seated on the far side of the table, clockwise from left: Shackley; George Carver; Maj. Gen. Homer Smith; Eric von Marbod, assistant secretary of defense; General Weyand; Amb. Graham Martin; Thieu; Vice President Tran Van Huong; Prime Minister Tran Van Khiem; and General Cao Van Vien, defense minister and chief of the general staff.

Reporting to President Gerald Ford in Palm Springs, California, immediately after the April 1975 fact-finding trip to Saigon. Clockwise from left: George Carver; Gen. Fred Weyand; Secretary of State Henry Kissinger; President Gerald Ford; Eric von Marbod; Shackley.

A daily 9:00 A.M. briefing of CIA Director George Bush at CIA headquarters in Langley, Virginia, in 1976–77.

Ted and Hazel Shackley with George Carver at farewell reception at CIA head-quarters in 1977, when Shackley left the position of associate deputy director of operations.

Shackley in 1979.

In May 2003, the Lao Veterans of America dedicated their national day ceremony at the Lao Veterans' site in Arlington National Cemetery, Virginia, to the memory of Ted Shackley. His widow, Hazel, represented Shackley.

14

AIRPOWER

BY July 1968 the combined Pathet Lao/North Vietnamese forces in Laos had been expanded to 100,440 men. This was an increase of 28,640 troops over a two-year period. In a third-world theater of war like Laos, where the Vietnamese were tigers in a land dominated by lotus-eaters, that is a significant escalation in troop strength.

The friendly force levels were

FAR	55,000
FAR ADC	5,000
FAN (neutralist armed forces cooperating with FAR)	10,000
CIA paramilitary	40,000
Total	**110,000**

Fundamentally, the equalizer in this equation for the United States was airpower. By combining the skills of the guerrillas with airpower, we did what the policy makers wanted. Vietnamese manpower was tied down and bloodied in Laos. In 1968's second and third quarters, Pathet Lao/North Vietnamese forces in Laos were suffering a monthly average of 920 men killed and wounded, which on an annualized basis was about an 11 percent loss factor. Such attrition is difficult to sustain in a protracted war, which was what Hanoi was pursuing.

In assessing my experiences in Laos, I conclude that the marriage of airpower and guerrillas revolutionized irregular warfare

and put an essentially new weapon into the hands of American policy makers. Airpower, for one thing, gave guerrillas an unprecedented level of mobility. Helicopters and STOL aircraft like the
Pilatus Porter were used in a permissive air environment such as
Laos to move guerrillas into or close to operational areas. These
same aircraft could extract paramilitary teams from operational areas. Both techniques combined to prolong the guerrillas' staying
power in their operational area. In addition, STOL aircraft, C-123s,
or C-130s could air-drop supplies to guerrillas operating deep in
enemy territory, thus keeping them alive and operational even under the most adverse circumstances. Aircraft were also used to provide medical services or to evacuate wounded guerrillas, a fantastic
morale booster for the troops.

Cargo aircraft, when not providing support to guerrillas in operational areas, could be an important adjunct to nation-building programs. For example, at Hmong mountain outposts such as Bouam
Louang or Na Khang, fixed-wing aircraft could be used to deliver
building materials, agricultural supplies, and livestock or to evacuate the sick for treatment. Such actions helped to persuade guerrillas' families that leaders such as Vang Pao were determined not only
to win the war but also to improve the lives of their followers.

Air America and Continental Air Services, under contract and
for a competitive commercial fee, provided excellent support to
guerrilla operations in Laos. Being a CIA proprietary and having
the larger and more versatile fleet of fixed-wing aircraft, Air
America carried the major share of the load. Its admirable performance in Laos was due in part to its success in putting together and
keeping a first-class assortment of deeply committed, professional,
and courageous pilots.

That said, the fact remains that all CIA officers who worked in
Laos came away with at least one or two good stories about flying
in that country. One of mine involves being picked up by an Air
America Porter late in the day at LS-166 on the Bolovens Plateau
with the intention of flying over PS-4, another Bolovens Plateau
camp, and back to Vientiane. The Air America pilot who picked me
up was a new face. I asked him where in Laos he had been flying.
He said this was his first day on the job. That was a surprise, as it
was unprecedented for such a greenhorn to pick up the chief of station. As the flight plan was essentially a milk run in good weather, I

thought, Why fight it? I opened the map that I carried at all times while airborne in Laos, folded it, and laid it on my knee.

We took off, but instead of heading north-northeast for the PS-4 area, we headed south-southeast toward Attopeu and Pathet Lao/North Vietnamese territory. I told the pilot we were off course and were headed into an area containing antiaircraft capable of bringing us down. The pilot argued. I showed him my map. He checked his bearings against the Se Kong River, did a double take, and corrected his flight path.

Landing without further incident at Vientiane, I had the station air operations officer, Charlie Gabler, check on the pilot and his skills and was told he was technically well qualified. When asked to explain himself, the pilot said he had decided to deviate from the expected flight plan in order to see if I would detect the error. That was his idea of a joke, telling the boys at the Hotel Constellation bar in Vientiane that night that the station chief did not know where he was flying while approaching enemy territory.

My response showed a distinct lack of humor. I reminded the Air America station manager that we were fighting a war and that sophomoric stunts of that type would not be tolerated. For the next four months the pilot was assigned exclusively to rice drops and was allowed to carry no live passengers.

The air transport scene in Laos had its share of legendary figures. One was Air America's Fred Walker, who had arrived in Laos around 1959. By the time I appeared on the scene, Walker was Air America's chief pilot. As such he was the ramrod who kept the show on the road. He was well qualified for that task, having flown in dicey air operations for the Civil Air Transport (CAT) in support of French forces under siege at Dien Bien Phu.

Equally a legend in his own time was "Dutch" Brongersma, another pilot who had flown with CAT at Dien Bien Phu. Jim Glerum of the CIA's Special Operations Group introduced us in Washington in 1966, and I listened while he and Brongersma discussed whether the CIA could profitably use Continental Air Services, Inc. (CASI), a newly acquired subsidiary of Continental Airlines, for air transport operations in Laos and Vietnam. After hearing Dutch argue the affirmative, I told him his presentation made a lot of good points that I would like to discuss further with him in Vientiane, once I had a better grasp of operational realities. I spent the rest of the evening enjoying Brongersma's humorous tales of life in China as a former Marine Corps pilot who had joyfully seized the opportunity offered him by General Claire Lee Chennault to join the Flying Tigers and fly combat missions against the Japanese. In time I came to cherish Dutch both as a friend and as a walking reservoir of knowledge on China and Southeast Asia that I needed to tap as I filled my own canteen.

The Lao held Dutch in especially high regard. It was from Vang Pao that I got my first hint of his historic flight over the Plaine des Jarres in February 1961. As I learned later from Dutch himself, he and Bill Bird had started in 1960 to create an airline for service in Laos and Thailand, beginning with one C-45. When before long they added a P2V7 to their fleet, the CIA station chief in Vientiane proposed that they modify their new acquisition to enable it to carry some reconnaissance cameras. Bird and Dutch jumped on the idea, seeing it as the germ of another revenue stream.

Once the cameras were installed, the airline got some additional flight hours, but it was no bonanza, and Dutch was mildly disappointed. Then came the big break. Learning that a big celebration was being planned for the Plaine des Jarres, involving the arrival of Soviet aircraft and high-level visitors from Hanoi, CIA Vientiane contracted with Dutch to fly a photoreconnaissance mission on the target date. By chance Dutch arrived over the Plaine des Jarres just seconds after Prince Souphanouvong, the Pathet Lao leader, landed in a Soviet aircraft.

Dutch made his first pass over the assembly area where VIPs were greeting Souphanouvong and where lots of previously unconfirmed Soviet military equipment was on display. When he made a second pass to finish the day's work, he was met with a barrage of ground fire and took a few hits. Dutch limped back to Vientiane, made a tough emergency landing, and walked away from a badly damaged airplane. The reconnaissance flight, however, had been a smashing success. Souphanouvong was photographed being fêted by the North Vietnamese, the Russians, and the Chinese, and hard intelligence was obtained on the flow of Soviet equipment to the Pathet Lao. Dutch recalled that he got a significant bonus for this successful flight.

For Vang Pao that was a red-letter day, for it persuaded Washington that the Pathet Lao were not a mere indigenous breakaway Lao faction but were supported by Hanoi, Moscow, and Beijing and threatened Laos's stability. Vang Pao and the Royal Lao military therefore felt that Dutch had earned a place of honor in Lao military history. They were right.

USAID and the CIA both eventually contracted with Dutch for some CASI flight hours, and the CIA at least never had cause to regret it. CASI's maintenance performance at times was better than Air America's, particularly with the Porter aircraft. The sound, safe air hours that Dutch's organization provided, mainly in STOL aircraft, added to our operational capabilities as well as our flexibility.

Dutch was also instrumental in seeing to it that as CASI worked itself into an ever-wider niche in the Lao air market, its corporate VIPs like Bob Six, the head of Continental Airlines, got exposed to the nitty gritty of the war. Because of that, Clyde M., Charlie Gabler, and I, plus our families, got well acquainted with the CASI/ Continental Airlines team. That included Bob Six; his charming wife, actress Audrey Meadows; Robert Rousselot, an old CAT and Air America hand; and Pierre Salinger of Kennedy Camelot fame. These were solid, patriotic folks who worked to understand the Lao war. In so doing, they did their best to see that American policy objectives were achieved.

To the mobility that the guerrillas derived from the use of tactical air must be added firepower. The air support that we could provide to our paramilitary forces gave them an unprecedented ability to inflict damage on the enemy. Where else in the history of guerrilla warfare could an irregular force of ten or twenty men engage a superior enemy force with small-arms fire, fix their positions, and then bring in the awesome firepower of 500-pound bombs, rockets, and .50-caliber machine gun fire that could be delivered by T-28s, or the more complicated ordnance mix that could be obtained from A-1s, F-105s, F-4s, or C-130 gunships?

The shift from classical guerrilla tactics to a system marrying the irregular with airpower did not occur overnight. It was an evolutionary process in which a lot of CIA officers, myself included, climbed a learning curve. Before coming to Laos, most of us had had some military training or agency experience in working air-cargo ton-mile logistics problems or handling airdrops and medical evacuations by fixed-wing aircraft or helicopters. Our experience with tactical air operations on the other hand was theoretical at best. Prior to mid-1966, CIA operatives in Laos used tactical air-power only as a defensive mechanism to help irregulars hold fixed sites like Nha Khang.

With the expansion of operations into the Ho Chi Minh Trail during late 1966, airpower started to become an offensive weapon. This is where the school of hard knocks left its indelible impression on Bill Lair, Pat Landry, Tom Fosmire, Dave Morales, and me. Our tutors were many. Colonel Paul "Pappy" Pettigrew, the Air attaché in Vientiane, contributed significantly to my early education in the subject of ordnance suitable for use on strike aircraft.

All of us also profited from the Vietnam combat experiences that Captain Dick Secord brought to the table when he was assigned to the CIA station in Laos in mid-1966 and went to work for Bill Lair and Pat Landry at Udorn. We also benefited from the words of wisdom offered in various ways by Colonel Heinie Aderholt, who was then commanding the 56th Air Commando at Nakhon Phanom, Thailand. Monthly coordination sessions with Colonel Jack Singlaub, commanding officer of MACV SOG, also helped shape our doctrine. Since September–October 1965 MACV SOG had been sending small teams, manned by indigenous personnel from South Vietnam—Bru, Cham, Montagnards, and Khmer—and officered by three Special Forces soldiers, into Laos to a depth of fifteen to twenty-five kilometers. There they carried out reconnaissance de-signed to ascertain the extent and nature of Hanoi's activities in the Laos–South Vietnam border area. In many cases the teams acted more like forward air guides than reconnaissance units, as their members, particularly the American leadership element, were well trained in ground-to-air radio communications and could call strike aircraft onto lucrative targets. In any event they were more aggressive in calling in helicopter gunships and tactical air strikes to support their operations than were the all-indigenous teams we were using in the Lao panhandle.

By the time I arrived in Laos, this MACV program was known under the code name "Prairie Fire." The chief purpose of our monthly coordination meetings was to ensure that the CIA and MACV SOG did not put teams into the same area or create other "wire-crossing" complications. But for me, a secondary purpose was to see what lessons I could learn from MACV SOG's successes. Late in 1966 I noted that the 117 penetrations MACV SOG had made into Laos during the year, or slightly fewer than ten per month, had resulted in 130 helicopter gunship sorties and 405 tactical air strikes, which suggested to me that the teams had been operating effectively in a target-rich environment.

At about the same time I participated with Ambassador Sullivan in a Southeast Asia Coordination (SEACORD) meeting in Udorn at which General William Westmoreland, then still head of MACV, said that air strikes called in by MACV SOG units had produced significant results in terms of disrupting enemy plans in the Laos–South Vietnam border area. That evaluation, even when submitted to the harsh scrutiny resulting from a belief that it was part of a sales pitch designed to expand the depth of the Prairie Fire operating area, still led to the conclusion that MACV SOG teams were doing some things that might be adapted to our two-front war in Laos.

Experience was also a great teacher. Lessons in the offensive use of airpower learned in the Ho Chi Minh Trail area were quickly applied to the war of position and maneuver in North Laos. The converse was also true. As a result, in a relatively few months the leadership team at the Vientiane Station was comfortable with the offensive use of airpower. We therefore started systematically to include its utilization in our monthly planning cycles for road-watch-team deployments, raid-and-ambush operations, offensive salami-slice attacks to gain territory, and in some cases just to use airpower in its naked form to hit Pathet Lao/North Vietnamese supply depots and troop concentrations.

I can't leave the subject of offensive airpower without mentioning the absolutely marvelous project, designed and shepherded to a successful conclusion by Bill Lair, for having Hmong fly T-28s in tactical close-support missions. To appreciate the magnitude of this achievement, consider that it took members of a primitive tribal society in one bound from transport by pack animals to modern sophisticated aircraft.

Lair started this project in 1966 on a shoestring and a prayer when he found a way to train ten or so Hmong to fly a Piper Cub. This was done at a Thai private air school run by a friend of Lair's. After the Hmong had mastered the Piper Cub, Lair had them advance to further private training in a Cessna 180. Finally, when a Waterpump T-28 training class was being scheduled for the Lao in 1967, an effort was made to get two Hmong included in the program.

Vang Pao in his capacity as MR-2 commander pushed for this through the FAR chain of command, Colonel Pettigrew lobbied for it through his channels, and I pushed it with Generals Ouan and Oudone. This combined effort carried the day, and two Hmong entered the program. By January 1968 they were qualified T-28 pilots. Ly Lu, one of the two, became a living legend, having flown more than an estimated five thousand combat missions prior to being shot down by ground fire in July 1969 near San Luan in North Laos.[1] The irony is he never had the time or need to learn how to drive an automobile. After his death, Ly Lu was awarded a Distinguished Flying Cross by the U.S. Air Force.

Other Hmong became competent T-28 pilots. Lair also had visions of the Hmong having their own civil air transport. I supported that endeavor, and it resulted in our helping Vang Pao to set up Xieng Khouang Air Transport with an old DC-3. This airline became operational while I was in Laos.

Not all of our air operations were a success. Project Mud, to take one unhappy example, was born of the constant pressure from policy makers in Washington and the military commands—CINCPAC in Honolulu and MACV in Saigon—for more to be done from Laos against the Ho Chi Minh Trail. CIA headquarters, trying to be helpful and attempting to take some of the heat off of the Vientiane Station, had the Technical Services Division study what could be done with gadgets and wizardry to help inhibit North Vietnamese truck traffic on the trail. In due course steel drums of a powder-like substance arrived in Udorn. Our instructions were to dump this on rain-soaked slopes overlooking roads in the trail area, the idea being that the powder would generate mudslides and make any mud already on the roads more slippery. This in turn, the theory went, would reduce traction and cause trucks to get stuck at critical choke points on the trail. Then, the 7/13th Air Force would have a turkey shoot and knock out the trucks.

Udorn went to work and, using all-source data, particularly aerial photography, picked out a suitable series of targets. The powdery substance, which we had been told by headquarters was not toxic, was packaged in brown paper sacks for air delivery onto the selected target areas. The paper bags were expected to burst on impact, covering the target with the magical powder and creating mudslides. When everything was ready, C-130s hauled the cargo to a target area close to the Mu Gia Pass. They circled, kickers pushed the bags out, and the targets were saturated. Proof of delivery on target was obtained by aerial photography. Folklore has it that one hundred fifty thousand pounds of powder were put on the targets. I can't vouch for that. It was, however, crystal clear that several subsequent photoreconnaissance flights over the area produced not one shred of evidence that the powder had had any effect. Then, as we were doing our postmortem on the operation, we learned that the magic powder was a soap detergent of the Calgon type. That left a bitter taste in our mouths, considering the risk to human life and aircraft that we had taken in getting that job done. We had expected more from the apostles of Merlin back at headquarters.

In the early days of my tour in Laos, only the CIA had any interest in Phu Pha Ti, a steep, fifty-five-hundred-foot ridge located twenty-five kilometers from the border between Laos and North Vietnam, and forty-five kilometers west of Sam Neua, Laos. Two hundred yards or so from the summit, a reasonably level six-hundred-foot-long patch of ground could serve as an airstrip for an exceptionally daring STOL pilot, and we were using this to support the Hmong guerrilla teams that were operating in Sam Neua Province to collect intelligence as well as harass North Vietnamese and Pathet Lao forces. A STOL aircraft or helicopter could airlift a team from Long Tieng to Phu Pha Ti, cutting to an hour or so what would otherwise have been at least a ten-day march through rough mountain terrain and enemy-infested territory. The guerrillas, upon landing at Phu Pha Ti, would then descend the mountain under the cover of night when security conditions in the area were appropriate. They would then move out to their areas of operations. Mission completed, they could radio for transport, and somebody would pick them up again, either at Phu Pha Ti or an emergency LZ. We also used the mountain as a forward storage site for supplies that we could airlift and drop to the guerrillas as needed. Our code word for this facility was "Site 85."

Resemblance between Site 85 and a modern airport ended once we had installed Single Sideband radio and a tactical air navigation system (TACAN) station. There was no lighting, much less a landing-path beacon, and night operations were impossible.

The Air Force joined us on the mountain in mid-1967. Although Laos itself was low on the Air Force's priority list, North Vietnam was as high as it gets, and Phu Pha Ti was just close enough to North Vietnam and had just enough elevation to provide a base for the TSQ-81, a system that directed and controlled jet fighters and bombers attacking targets in North Vietnam.

The Air Force installed its hardware and enciphering devices up above our operating guerrilla base at the summit of Phu Pha Ti and kept roughly sixteen personnel there at all times to operate the equipment. These men, primarily enlisted personnel, had been "sheep-dipped" by the Air Force, which meant that they had ostensibly been discharged from the Air Force and were working as civilian contractors for Lockheed Aircraft Services. But this was only for show, and their service jackets were still in an active file somewhere in the recesses of the Pentagon.

For rotating the men on and off the mountain and for keeping them supplied, the Air Force relied primarily on its own heavy-lift helicopters, but on occasion they would call on Air America's aircraft and pilots and the little STOL airstrip. For defense of the site, the Air Force depended on our Hmong guerrillas and some Thai soldiers. On the southern side of the mountain, up which our access track wound, we had rigged flares and claymore mines to give us early warning of an enemy's approach, and at strategic points along the paths leading to the mountain there were irregular troops waiting to ambush and slow an approaching enemy. This was a typical guerrilla position, one not meant to be held against a strong force of infantry, but to be evacuated when the pressure became irresistible and the North Vietnamese enemy and its Pathet Lao surrogates had paid a price in killed or wounded for attacking one of our base areas.

The northeastern and northwestern sides of the mountain were deemed unscaleable, a mistake that had been made before at places like the Plains of Abraham and will doubtless be made again somewhere.

Nevertheless, we were under no illusions that Site 85 could be held if the North Vietnamese wanted to drive us off of it, and in late 1967 we saw signs that they were becoming increasingly interested in the mountain. Enemy documents captured by our guerrilla patrols revealed that a reconnaissance of some sort had been decided on, and on October 20 two suspects were caught on the summit of Phu Pha Ti. The fact that they had a camera with them reinforced the suspicion that they might have been spying out the land for the North Vietnamese, so we flew them back to Long Tieng for interrogation and a look at what was on their film. As we were unable to refute their claim that they were Buddhist monks, we let them go.

Then, on January 12, 1968, the North Vietnamese carried out an air raid against Phu Pha Ti. To my knowledge, this was the first and only time that Hanoi made offensive use of its air arm against any target anywhere in Indochina during its war with the United States. The strike force consisted of four An-2 Colts, a biplane that the Soviets had built for use in crop dusting or as a short-distance military transport. The North Vietnamese had ingeniously converted these machines to bombers by installing a Rube Goldberg–type tube contraption through which 120mm mortar rounds could be dropped. Two of these aircraft made passes at the summit of Phu Pha Ti, rocketing, strafing, and bombing the site. Two women civilians and two guerrillas were killed, and two guerrillas were wounded.[2]

By chance, two Air America helicopters were in the area at the time. One of the chopper pilots managed to maneuver his aircraft so that it was directly above the Colt, whereupon one of the Air America personnel in the helicopter opened fire on the Colt with a weapon that I remember as being an M-2 carbine with a banana clip. Others, in recounting the story in recent years, claim it was an M-16 that the helicopter pilot carried as an unauthorized personal weapon. Either way, and incredibly, the unorthodox attack downed the Colt. Our Hmong guerrilla forces on the ground opened up on the second Colt as it came in for its bomb run and downed it. The other two enemy aircraft beat a hasty, but prudent, retreat.

The next morning I received a cable from Bill Colby reading, "Congratulations to Snoopy and all you other guys out there who are fighting the Red Baron." Prior to receipt of that message, I could not have imagined Colby as a fan of the *Peanuts* comic strip.

Although the Colby cable was a nice touch, we still weren't kidding ourselves that Site 85 could be held for long. Among other reasons for pessimism, our aerial photography of Phu Pha Ti and the surrounding area showed that the North Vietnamese were building an extension of Route 602 aimed straight at the mountain. We could watch it inching forward week by week and knew the day was approaching when the enemy could bring up artillery, mortars, and major bodies of infantry to sweep our lightly armed guerrilla forces, the Thai infantrymen, the sixteen sheep-dipped airmen, and their TSQ-81 installation off of the mountaintop.[3]

Again this situation was the classic "good news, bad news" scenario. The good news was the TSQ-81 was hurting North Vietnam more than a little; thus, Hanoi was willing to go to extraordinary lengths to get rid of the electronic menace. The bad news was the Air Force would soon have to dispense with the TSQ-81's services. The time-sensitive, critical question was how soon. The Air Force could bow to the inevitable and evacuate its little force of technicians, but to do this would be to reduce the effectiveness of its all-weather air war against North Vietnam's infrastructure. Alternatively, it could opt to delay the inevitable by employing some of its bombers against the road builders, but doing this would ultimately lead to the same undesirable result, evacuation of the site. The key unresolved issue was how much expenditure in aircraft resources would be required to buy the delay, and what this block of time would mean to the effectiveness of the air war against North Vietnam. In recognition of this dilemma and faced with a choice between two unappealing alternatives, the Air Force did what many individuals would do in a similar quandary—they procrastinated.

Ambassador Bill Sullivan, reacting to the steady flow of CIA reporting on the deteriorating situation around Phu Pha Ti, told me on February 25 that something had to be done to concentrate people's minds on this matter. He said that he intended to use State Department channels for a message devoted exclusively to this military problem and that he wanted me to produce an estimate of how long the site could be held. "I know about the estimating process," he told me, "but you've got to come up with a hard date, a date certain."

The estimating process is a little like marksmanship. The better your aim and the better the tools you have to work with, the more likely you are to score a hit in the black. But neither the intelligence estimator nor the target shooter expects to hit the bullseye every time. A good tight cluster, with an occasional round spot-on in the center, is a perfectly respectable score. Bill Sullivan, being the experienced Vietnam War hand that he was, understood this.

As it happened, I hit the bullseye with my estimate of the longevity of Site 85. I looked at OB information about the NVA in

Laos, and I then consulted with our CIA OB specialists in Udorn. I also talked to Bill Lair and Pat Landry and the other experienced guys involved in managing the day-to-day, moment-by-moment war in northern Laos. And I worked out the average rate of speed at which the North Vietnamese were completing their road. I also factored in the average number of air strikes we were getting from the 7/13th Air Force to slow the construction of the Route 602 extension. Then I told Bill Sullivan that the site couldn't be held beyond March 10. He in turn recorded that pearl for posterity in a message sent to appropriate diplomatic and military recipients in Saigon, Udorn, Bangkok, Honolulu, and Washington. The warning bell had been rung. The question was, Who was listening? The alarm gong was rung again on March 9 when I wrote an intelligence report[4] that was forwarded by immediate precedence. (The "immediate" processing indicator guaranteed that the designated recipients would have the report in a matter of minutes after it left Vientiane.) The report clearly stated that the enemy had the capability to move on Phu Pha Ti without further delay. Specifically, I said, "In view of this it must be recognized that the integrity of Site 85 as a functioning TACAN and navigational site is in grave jeopardy and it can no longer be considered that friendly ground force dispositions are such that they can assure the integrity of the site because they are outnumbered and outgunned." The record shows that appropriate decision makers at MACV, the Seventh Air Force, CINCPAC, the Joint Chiefs of Staff, the State Department, and the White House had virtually instant access to this report.

When I left my embassy office on the evening of March 9 at about 7:00 P.M., it was my view that intelligence had done all it could for the Air Force position on Phu Pha Ti. The enemy buildup had been detected and reported on in depth and in a timely manner. The CIA's Hmong irregulars under Vang Pao's leadership had mounted ground harassment operations against the North Vietnamese forces in the area. This not only inflicted casualties on Hanoi's troops and slowed their advance, but also provided data for enhancing the quality of the American air strikes then being put on the advancing North Vietnamese. In this context it was my gut feeling—one shared by Ambassador Sullivan—that it was time for the Air Force to pull back from Phu Pha Ti. The decision to do so in an orderly manner was obviously a judgment call related to the strategy of how to fight the Vietnam War. As a result, it was clearly going to be made at the top echelon of the Washington power pyramid and not by anyone in Vientiane.

We had two men at our Phu Pha Ti STOL site on March 10, Howie Freeman and John "Woody" Spence, a former Montana smoke jumper under contract to the agency on a paramilitary assignment. We were keeping them there in the face of the increasing enemy threat in order to improve the odds for an orderly evacuation of American, Thai, and Hmong forces from Phu Pha Ti, should that become necessary. Howie and Woody were in communication with us by Single Sideband radio via Pat Landry and Major Richard Secord in Udorn. They also had a backup channel to Jon R., our man at Vang Pao's headquarters at Long Tieng. Secord had been trying to cajole more air strikes out of the 7/13th Air Force for weeks in order to prolong the viability of Site 85. His efforts had unfortunately been only moderately successful. In its wisdom, the 7/13th Air Force had decided it could not spare additional resources to defend the site.

On the night of March 10, Howie told Udorn that North Vietnamese artillery rounds had begun striking the summit of Phu Pha Ti, about two hundred yards or so above the STOL site, and Udorn notified me. It wasn't clear at first that the shelling constituted the sort of emergency for which our evacuation plan had been made, but in any case the plan couldn't be implemented at night. All I could do was put a helicopter crew on standby, stay by the telephone, and have the Single Sideband circuit monitored in Vientiane on the off chance we might hear something Udorn missed due to frequency disturbances.

Howie continued to report as the night wore on, and at one point he said he had heard the sounds of small-arms fire on the mountaintop. That was a very alarming report. It suggested an enemy unit had penetrated our defenses. The pressing question was how. At first light on March 11, therefore, we dispatched the evacuation helicopter and ordered Freeman to reconnoiter the summit.

Taking a shotgun, a handheld radio, and two Hmong guerrillas, Freeman started up the path to the summit, followed at a prudent distance by Woody, who provided him with a communications link back to the STOL site where a sergeant was keeping us informed by a Single Sideband radio link to Udorn.

The reconnaissance quickly turned into a skirmish. The full details escape me now, but in overview I recall that Howie and his Hmong guerrillas exchanged fire at least twice with groups of North Vietnamese soldiers. The first encounter ended with three or four Vietnamese dead. In the second firefight, the highlights were that Howie's weapon jammed and he took an enemy round in the leg. Woody helped get him back to a site where a helicopter picked Howie up and evacuated him. Woody was subsequently taken out by another helicopter. In the chaos of battle, a daring helicopter pilot evacuated five airmen, one of whom was wounded when the North Vietnamese opened fire on the aircraft as it was taking off. When this man was brought to a transfer point in Laos, he was given medical attention, placed in a fixed-wing aircraft, and moved to Thailand. We heard that he died en route.

We never learned to our complete satisfaction what happened that night on the top of Phu Pha Ti. Our best guess in the weeks that followed was that the North Vietnamese mortar and artillery barrage, by forcing the sixteen Air Force personnel to take cover, had enabled a squad of between ten and twenty North Vietnamese infantrymen to clamber noisily up the northern face of the mountain, possibly using natural footholds and those created by the exploding shells.[5] At least part of the answer to what happened after the firefights began was given the next day by our aerial photoreconnaissance which showed eight dead bodies on an outcropping about two hundred feet below the summit.[6]

The photos also showed some strange shadows on the cliff wall. As these shadows did not appear on earlier photos of the same area, we asked the four surviving airmen if they knew what the shadows signified. They did—all too well. According to what they told us, the rocky outcropping was concealed from viewers at the summit by another flat piece of karst that jutted out from the cliff wall. This fact gave rise to an emergency plan worked out and agreed to among themselves by the sixteen operators of the TSQ-81. The idea was that they would attach webbed straps or slings to the cliff wall and, in case of extremity, lower themselves by this means to the ledge below. It would appear that some of them had tried to implement the plan but had been overtaken and killed by the North Vietnamese soldiers.

On March 12, once we knew that the Vietnamese were on the

mountain to stay, we bombed the hell out of Site 85 in order to deprive the North Vietnamese of the heavy technical equipment installed there, and we believe we succeeded. It is probable, however, that the lighter encryption devices and related material had already been removed on March 11.

I put Howie Freeman in for the CIA's highest medal for valor, the Intelligence Star. In due course it was awarded him. Woody also received special recognition for his dedication to duty. When honors were distributed up in Hanoi, I hope that General Vo Nguyen Giap remembered the gutsy performance of his own soldiers who scaled a mountain cliff that seemed inaccessible except to professional mountain climbers of a quality that were not known to be in the NVA.

Site 85 could not have been held, but it should not have been necessary to lose three quarters of its complement. What makes such a loss especially painful is the uncertainty surrounding it. That some of the airmen were killed on the spot goes without saying, but which ones were they, and, more basically, how many were killed? We saw eight bodies in the March 1968 photographs, but could some of them have been the bodies of North Vietnamese soldiers? Equally puzzling, could there have been American bodies that the pictures did not show?

In our initial postmortem of the fall of Phu Pha Ti, we started from the fact that there were sixteen airmen on the site in the afternoon of March 10, that five had been evacuated on the morning of the March 11, and that the number presumed to have been killed on the mountain was probably eight. That left three airmen unaccounted for who might conceivably have survived. Since we were unable to recover the bodies of the eight, we did not know who had been killed. As a result, the early afternoon reports showed a lack of precision about the three who were unaccounted for. This created a lot of uncertainty for eleven families. My understanding is that, with the help of the survivors, the Air Force was able in time to obtain a more accurate appraisal of what happened to each man. I have not seen a copy of that report.

15

TECHNICAL OPERATIONS

IN the context of a two-front war, China posed a special problem. The central question was always, What were China's intentions? Did it plan to intervene from its stronghold in Yunnan Province and play a decisive military role in Laos at some critical juncture? Or did it plan to use Laos simply as a thoroughfare for supporting an insurgency in northeast Thailand? No ready answers were available to these very legitimate policy concerns.

When we talked with the Lao, whether at the senior political or military levels, the response was always the same. On one occasion Sisouk na Champassak, the minister of finance, told me in the presence of General Oudone Sananikone that the Chinese had been given a mandate by the Lao in 1962 to build a "friendship" road from Mengla in China's Yunnan Province to Phong Saly in the northern portion of MR-1. With the passage of time, Beijing had interpreted its mandate to include building roads from Meng Mang in Yunnan southward to Moung Sing, Laos, and beyond. Somewhat caustically Sisouk said, "We Lao are grateful for the capital investment. It is an offer we cannot refuse."

The Lao ability to shrug off the multiple implications of the Chinese road-building activities was not something we in the CIA could mimic, particularly since the Chinese seemed to be steadily increasing the size of their engineer and coolie labor force in Laos dedicated to road building. By late 1966 this force was in excess of twelve thousand men. This number posed a related question: When might a coolie become a soldier, and when might an engineer become an officer? How long would it take their workforce to become a People's Liberation Army (PLA) unit?

As a result, the Vientiane Station during my tenure had a program for attempting to find answers to key questions related to China's intentions towards Laos. This involved sending paramilitary teams into China's Yunnan Province with a threefold mission. Our objectives were as follows:

1. To collect tactical and strategic intelligence providing insight into the strengths, weaknesses, and intentions of those Chinese forces operating in, from, or through Yunnan Province.
2. To obtain early warning intelligence on any major Chinese intent to move into northwest Laos, Burma, or Thailand.
3. To recruit resident agents in the Lao/China border area who could be developed into long-term sources of positive intelligence.

We used two separate sources of manpower for these operations. Initially, the Wa of Burma were used for probes into Yunnan because an officer at Udorn, Bill Young of the legendary missionary family, had excellent contacts among this group. These operations progressed slowly because of the need to meet these people in Ban Houai Sai in southern MR-1 and because it took months for them to reach there from the points in Burma which they used to go in and out of Yunnan, China. This made their intelligence obtained via observation of roads and PLA camps quite out-of-date when we received it. The same evaluation applied to data they collected from fellow tribesmen living in China. The marginal aspects of this intelligence, its lack of timeliness, and the increased political risks inherent in running such teams through Burma caused us to abandon the project in 1967.

Our second sources of manpower were the Yao and Lu, and Nam Yu became the center of operations using these tribal groupings. Tony Poe, the Nam Yu unit chief, formed his teams from personnel nominated by tribal leaders Chao Ma and Chao La.

Profiting from our experiences with the Wa teams, we decided to see if we could improve the quality of our intelligence by putting taps on the telephone lines in China around Meng Mang. Route 411 ran southward from Meng Mang toward Moung Sing, Laos, so we assumed the telephone line that paralleled Route 411 would be used by the PLA in any movement of troops toward Laos.

Using the technique of lifting a team by helicopter from Nam Yu up to an area south of Moung Sing, we sent the first telephone-tap team into China in late 1966. The team found the line we had targeted for them, put a tap on it, ran a wire from the line to a concealed tape recorder, and operated the device for thirty days. With their bounty of tapes, the team exited China and walked to an LZ west of Moung Sing, where they were picked up by helicopter for a return to Nam Yu.

Technically, the operation was a success, so we sent the tapes to Washington for analysis. While the latter task was in progress, a second team was readied for dispatch to China. This team was in China by November–December 1966. It set up its tap and started recording. Then, our luck turned bad. A PLA unit routinely patrolling the telephone line spotted the wire leading from the tap at the telephone pole crossarm and followed it back to the recorder. This caused the PLA to mount a sweep of the area, and that in turn drove the team back into Laos. As the team fled, there was a firefight. One team member was wounded but made it back to Laos. Another member was unaccounted for, so we assumed he was dead as we could find no subsequent Chinese reporting on the capture and trial of any "bandit elements."

Persuaded that this incident had heated up the area, we shifted our tactics. In looking at lessons learned from the previous operations, we decided we had to have a way of transmitting the product of the tap to a location without the use of a wire. The Technical Services people designed a transmitter that could be concealed in the insulators on the telephone poles through which the lines ran. With that equipment in hand, a new team was selected and trained. In mid-1967, probably in July, the team was in China. They found a line on Route 412 between Shang Young, China, and Batene, Laos, put the tap in place, and obtained several weeks' worth of product. With that in hand they exfiltrated. The work product was sent to Washington for analysis.

Subsequently, about three additional missions were run into China out of Nam Yu. Each was a technical success in that lines were tapped, product was obtained, and after three to four weeks on target, the teams were exfiltrated. In each case tapes were sent to Washington for review. Unfortunately, we were getting no feedback on the value of the product. Clyde M., a Bucknell graduate and experienced Asian hand fluent in Japanese who had replaced Jim Lilley as my deputy, kept pressing headquarters for an evaluation of the product. Clyde had played a key role in getting equipment for the latest series of operations into China. Finally, we learned that the hangup was at NSA, the agency that was doing the technical and substantive evaluation of the product.

In early 1968 we told CIA headquarters that the current state of play made no sense. Men were risking their lives to obtain data that we could not get evaluated. So we proposed to shut down the program. This elicited the response that NSA had concluded that we were not able to sustain sufficient continuity of coverage on the tapped lines to make the operation worthwhile. In view of that, in early 1968 we brought this effort to a close.

After that we limited ourselves to monitoring the Chinese road building within Laos. This was designed to prevent our being surprised by the sudden appearance of a new enemy combat force in an area that we were already contesting through force of arms against the Pathet Lao/North Vietnamese.

On balance, however, it did not seem likely by early 1968 that China would want to become a combatant in Laos. Instead, it appeared that Beijing's policy at that juncture was centered on maintaining a degree of leverage in Laos that would permit it to blunt American, Soviet, and Vietnamese influences in the country. In pursuit of that objective, China used a two-pronged approach. One of these permitted Beijing to make modest contributions of war matériel to the Pathet Lao. Under that aspect of their policy, in 1966 China assigned a party liaison team headed by General Tuan Suchan to work with the Pathet Lao at their Sam Neua Province headquarters. This move irritated Hanoi.

Paralleling that action, Beijing hedged its bets and continued to maintain a diplomatic mission in Vientiane, which was accredited to the RLG. Our monitoring of this embassy indicated it was focused on issues that would make it a voice, albeit a muted one, in the ongoing multiparty struggle for dominance in Indochina. On that issue Chinese concerns seemed to be driven by a desire to see that their borders remained secure at all times. In that context a neutral Laos did not appear to be something Beijing would want to destroy.

As the scope of Chinese road building expanded, we became convinced that this was part of China's contingency planning for future conflict, perhaps in Laos or Thailand. Henry Kissinger in his memoirs indicates that he did not accept this explanation and was perplexed about what this road construction reflected in terms of China's intentions toward the Indochinese peninsula.[1]

Perplexities were frequent during my tour in Laos. One of these began with a cabled message from Dick Helms, the DCI, asking that I meet with Lieutenant General Alfred Starbird while the latter was in Thailand. Helms also asked that we extend to Starbird's mission all possible assistance. At my first meeting with Starbird in 1967 in Udorn, it quickly became clear that Starbird and his team wanted to brief me and my senior associates on what came to be called, in popular jargon, the McNamara Line. In the briefing that was subsequently laid on, the CIA beneficiaries were Bill Lair, Pat Landry, Dick Secord, and myself.

In simplified terms, Starbird had been charged to design an electronic barrier to be laid across the Ho Chi Minh Trail. In essence, the electronics would identify targets such as trucks, and airpower would eliminate them. If such a system were to work, Starbird needed in-depth samples of the natural sounds that existed in the terrain of the Ho Chi Minh Trail. This meant putting recorders in selected jungle spots and then recovering them for analysis.

Starbird wanted our road-watch teams to do the work, using ultrasensitive recorders that he would provide. Having had past experience with the dangers of retrieving equipment from hot spots like the trail, I was less than eager to ratchet up the risks to which our indigenous personnel were already exposed. Starbird was asked if what he wanted could be obtained in any other way, such as debriefing our experienced road-watch teams on sounds they routinely heard in the trail area. "No!" was the curt response.

As Lair, Landry, and Secord pitched various questions at him, it became evident that Starbird wanted the exact decibel level of the various jungle sounds in the trail area. Collectively, we tried to shoot down the idea, for identifying targets on the Ho Chi Minh Trail was not the problem. The issue was how to destroy the trucks and manpower that our intelligence was already identifying. Our view that we needed more effective air strikes fell on deaf ears. This provoked some sharp comments from Secord, particularly when Starbird said his job was simply to develop the system. Its deployment, said Starbird, was a judgment that he had to leave to others—suggesting that "others" meant Secretary of Defense Robert McNamara.

Realizing we were at a dead end, I told Starbird we would deploy the recorders with the next cycle of road-watch teams. I was convinced, however, we would get no unique sounds. In fact, I told Starbird we could probably get the same sounds on the Bolovens Plateau or a few kilometers due east of Savannakhet. Then, I said somewhat impertinently that it was likely the most dominant sound we would get would be monkey screams. On that point our meeting adjourned, with Starbird making it clear he expected early results.

A few weeks later Starbird was back in the area wanting to know when he could expect to get some tapes. He was told the recorders had been deployed but not retrieved. I assured him we would forward the tapes promptly once we had them in hand. It then emerged that MACV SOG had already gotten some tapes in the Prairie Fire area, and Starbird was keen to do some information comparison testing. He therefore wanted our tapes sooner rather than later.

A few more weeks passed, and Udorn advised me by cable that a Savannakhet road-watch team had recovered the recorder they had placed in the trail area. Did I want to participate in reviewing the tape? My answer was yes. Having a full agenda of items to discuss in Udorn, I flew there the next day.

A tape-listening session was set up. Bill Lair, Pat Landry, Tom Fosmire, and a few others were there. The tape was turned on. The first audible sound on the tape was a monkey's scream. I burst into laughter as did Lair and Landry.

"Okay," I said, "who doctored the tape? This is a great in-house joke for us, but we can't send Washington anything that isn't authentic."

Fosmire looked puzzled. Landry told him about my comment to Starbird about getting a recording of a monkey scream. Then, Fosmire joined in the mirth but quickly recovered his composure and said the tape was authentic. We subsequently forwarded it and a few others to Washington for passage to Starbird.

Fortunately, in early January 1968 the RLG rejected the idea of the electronic fence intruding into its territory. The project as originally envisioned died, although various air-dropped sensors were used in the trail area by MACV and the 7/13th Air Force in hopes of increasing their truck kills while also permitting more effective air strikes on infiltrating North Vietnamese troops.

Some of our other technical ventures were quite successful. One in particular stands out. It was our plunge into low-level tactical voice intercept operations against North Vietnamese and Pathet Lao radio communications. The enemy used radios extensively to control its combat units. Our ability to intercept this traffic without the enemy's knowledge produced a fountain of useful intelligence. The information that we obtained was used to plan our operations, defensive and offensive, against the North Vietnamese and Pathet Lao. It also helped us to better understand the enemy's OB, thus improving the quality of intelligence reporting.

The decision to tap this SIGINT gold mine evolved from my experiences in operations against Cuba and from the lessons that were emerging from American combat operations in South Vietnam. My push into this arena was facilitated by the enthusiastic support of people like Carlton Swift, the head of Staff D at CIA headquarters, Lou Tordella at NSA, and a variety of other experts from the SIGINT world, both civilian and military. They made it possible for the Vientiane Station to get the required training and equipment to start the program.

It was Vang Pao, however, who made manpower available for our pilot effort. As it achieved success in his area, we grafted this technique relatively easily onto the operational programs that the CIA was managing in the other military regions. The benefits were huge when we had this effort in full bloom in all of our operational areas. On more than one occasion, this technique enabled us to detect a planned North Vietnamese attack and crush it.

16

GOLDEN TRIANGLE

EXCEPT for veteran case officers who had worked in Bangkok in the early 1950s, it is doubtful that anyone in the CIA ten years later was really aware of the scope and pace of the narcotics trafficking in the Burma–Lao–Thai border region known as the Golden Triangle. Certainly no one in the CIA was aggressively collecting narcotics intelligence anywhere in the world for the simple reason that narcotics intelligence was not wanted. The wise old men who met at least annually to codify American national security interests in a mission and functions statement for the CIA had not yet thought of the drug traffic as a threat, so none of the field stations had it as a target.

By 1966 the dimensions of the opium problem in Southeast Asia were widely known. The files that I read before going to Vientiane, my discussions with officers who had served there, and a review of the open-source literature all brought the issue home to me. In brief, Laos was not going to be at all like Florida. In Miami the dragon was outside the wall, and my task had been to keep him there. In Laos, on the other hand, he was already inside the perimeter, and I was going to have coexist with him without being seared by his breath.

I can already hear the howls of outrage: "Coexist with narcotics traffickers! Just as we always thought! He should have been wiping them out."

Well, only rogue elephants charge at everything in their path, and the CIA was never such an animal. The critics' point of view is a respectable one, perhaps even reasonable, if you leave out of consideration the fact that the CIA takes its orders from higher authority and that nowhere in these orders at the time under discussion—now a generation ago—was there any mention of narcotics. The mission that had been handed me was to fight a war in northern Laos against the Pathet Lao and the NVA and to interdict, along the Laotian part of the Ho Chi Minh Trail, the flow of military manpower and matériel from North Vietnam to the battlefields of South Vietnam. My plate was full.

In addition to this, the cultivation of poppy and the medicinal use of opium formed part of the economic and social fabric of the area I would be working in. The CIA inspector general, reporting in September 1972 on the drug situation in Southeast Asia, said that when the United States arrived in the region, "Opium was as much a part of the agricultural infrastructure of this area as was rice, one suitable for the hills, the other for the valleys."[1]

This generalization was as true for Laos as it was for the rest of Southeast Asia, but it tends to obscure the fact that this common agricultural infrastructure supported and was supported by a multiethnic society. Among the Laotian hill tribes alone there were the Hmong, the Yao, the Lao Thung, and the Lu, just to identify a few, and the Hmong were further subdivided into the Red Hmong, the Striped Hmong, and the Black Hmong. These tribes and subtribes all shared a common culture in which the cultivation and use of opium played a part, but each had put its own individual twist on it. Subjecting all these groupings to a standard set of mores is a job I would not wish on any social engineer.

I did have to ensure that the guerrilla units we were supporting were not trading or using opium and to minimize the prospects that Air America or Continental Air Services aircraft were being used for opium-smuggling tasks while under contract to us.

It is not generally realized, I think, that these carriers were not exclusively at the beck and call of the CIA. USAID also had regular use of them, and on occasion so did the military attachés. It was not unusual for a given aircraft to work for more than one agency on the same day. An aircraft might leave Vientiane, for instance, early in the morning for a flight on our behalf to Site 32 and then fly empty ("deadhead") to Sam Tong to pick something up for USAID.

Another question was how to organize the Vientiane Station so that our connection with the RLG did not expose us to the pitfalls inherent in being in regular dialog with those in the Royal Lao Army and police who were allegedly involved in opium or heroin trafficking in or through Laos. Of particular concern were the allegations that General Ouan Rattikone, the commander in chief of the Royal Lao Army, and General Kouprasith Abhay, the MR-5 commander who controlled Vientiane, were important figures in the opium trade.

Upon arriving in Vientiane in July 1966, I reviewed this series of interrelated questions with Jim Lilley, my deputy, and Bill Lair and Pat Landry, the chief and deputy chief of Udorn Base, from which we managed the station's paramilitary operations. Soundings were also taken in Udorn with Thai Colonel Dhep. Agreeing that we could not fight a war and simultaneously try to eradicate a centuries-old tribal habit of opium use, barter, or sale, we settled on a package of defensive measures that we hoped would insulate our activities from direct or indirect involvement in opium trafficking. In my initial get-acquainted visits to our key Laotian counterparts—General Vang Pao in MR-2 and General Phasouk in MR-4—I made it clear we could not tolerate opium use or trafficking by those forces supported by us. These officers accepted my position without demur. They both pointed out, however, that I would have to obtain General Ouan's support for this policy. Without this, General Vang Pao felt his arch rival, General Kouprasith, would make trouble for him within the Royal Lao Army. According to Vang Pao, Kouprasith objected to certain aspects of Vang Pao and Phasouk's cooperation with the Americans on the grounds that they were not of prime concern to the Royal Lao Army (i.e., search-and-rescue missions to pick up downed American pilots, attacks on North Vietnamese forces in the Lao panhandle as they moved into South Vietnam, and nation-building techniques designed to integrate the non-Lao ethnic groupings into a multicultural Lao nation). I assured both military region commanders that they would get from Ouan the political backing that they required.

The system of spot checks that I had found effective in Miami was applied to Laos. CIA officers at the various up-country sites stepped up their vigilance, and as we got more operations officers in Laos to work on expanding our paramilitary capabilities—both in the north and in the southern panhandle—we could pay more attention to the quality of our indigenous personnel. This led to the occasional identification of an opium user who was then dropped from our rolls.

Once, when General Vang Pao and I were on an inspection trip to a field unit in MR-2, we had occasion to enter one of the barracks. The occupants all stood to attention, but the military manner of one of them left something to be desired, and I took a second look at him. He seemed to me to be under the influence of something, presumably opium, and I said so to General Vang Pao, who then questioned the man in Hmong. The man admitted he had been smoking opium obtained from some Hmong village on a patrol the day before. Vang Pao and the CIA officers responsible for this sector took immediate action to separate the man from our guerrilla service and to return him to the Royal Lao Army.

I am aware that we did not, in this one stroke, eliminate a Laotian social problem. By taking this individual soldier off our rolls, we reduced his pay and quality of life, but by no means did we cure him of his taste for opium. Once back in a Royal Lao Army unit, he could continue using it if he could afford to buy it. All we did was improve the quality of one of our fighting units. As that was job number one at that moment, I offer no excuse for being preoccupied with the mission at hand.

Not all of the CIA personnel working in Laos shared my willingness to coexist with the narcotics dragon, but as far as I know, none of them tried to play St. George during my tour of duty there. An incident that took place after my reassignment is more illustrative, I think, of the aversion that our people all felt towards the poppy and its derivatives than of a lack of discipline. In the words of the inspector general's report,

> One young officer even let his zeal get the better of his judgment and destroyed a refinery in northwest Laos in 1971 before the anti-narcotics law was passed, thus risking being charged with destruction of private property.[2]

Spot checks were also applied to Air America and Continental Air Services flights that were used by the station. I had no jurisdiction over the security of USAID's contract. Nor did I have any right to interfere with the movements of deadheading aircraft, although in practice I did see to it that any deviation from their proper course was instantly noted and reported. My main concern was that something illicit not be loaded onto an airplane while it was under our control.

After this system was put into effect, it produced results. Around May 1967, a footlocker was detected as it was transferred from a Royal Lao aircraft to an Air America C-123 being prepared for a cargo flight to Saigon. An Air America security officer at Vientiane's Wattay Airport intercepted it because of the unusual nature of the transfer and brought the footlocker to our air operations staff.

We examined the box and found that it contained blocks of opium base wrapped in cellophane. On the right-hand corner of each block was a crudely drawn animal figure probably intended to represent a dragon.

We were holding the proverbial hot potato. None of the American agencies in Vientiane wanted to take possession of the seizure as procedures were nonexistent at that time for disposing of such hauls. And the Bureau of Narcotics and Dangerous Drugs (BNDD) unit in Bangkok, to whom we had promptly reported the find, contended they had no jurisdiction for actions in Laos.

After a short interval, perhaps of a day or two, Ambassador Sullivan urged me to have the seizure destroyed. I told him I would have it burned, with a certificate of destruction signed by the responsible officers, and that I would use the incident to impress my own people, Air America, Continental Air Services, and the Laotians with the need for enhanced vigilance.

My talks with station personnel and with representatives of the two air carriers are not worth describing in detail. Our discussions proceeded along normal managerial lines and resulted in tightened procedures at Wattay Airport for the handling of all cargo moved for anyone by Air America and Continental Air Services.

Dealing with the Lao, however, was another matter entirely. Readers in my age bracket who remember the Milton Caniff comic strip *Terry and the Pirates* may recognize some of its characters among the people I now had to deal with.

I went to General Ouan's office at the general staff headquarters and told him I was having communications problems. Could he help me?

With a benevolent smile, Ouan said that he would see what he could do. He sent for his chief of staff, General Oudone Sananikone, and a uniformed servant brought us tea.

"General," I began, "you may recall our previous discussions about American attitudes toward opium and how I wanted to isolate our paramilitary operations and aircraft from the traffic."

Ouan's smile became even broader, but his body language betrayed restlessness. The topic that I had introduced was evidently something he intended to delegate as quickly as possible to General Oudone. "Yes," he agreed, "I recall that."

"Well," I continued, "the policy of checks and security that I instituted at the training camps and operational sites and on aircraft movements seems to be respected by my officers, guerrilla troops, tribal leaders, and Royal Lao Army personnel. This is most gratifying. On the other hand, a recent incident has convinced me the Chinese community hasn't yet heard my message, or—having taken note of it—is testing my resolve. This suggests I have a communications problem that needs prompt attention."

Ouan stopped fidgeting with the items on his desk. I now had his undivided attention.

Pressing on, I told Ouan that we had intercepted an opium shipment. I then reached into my briefcase and gave him a facsimile of the dragon chop that had adorned each opium block.

Ouan's face remained impassive, but his eyes widened.

"None of my officers is familiar with this chop," I said, "but we assume it's Chinese. If that turns out to be the case, what can I do to make it clear to those Chinese entrepreneurs in Vientiane who organize opium shipments as a venture capital enterprise that we are serious about not getting sucked into these illegal activities?"

Ouan stared speechlessly at the chop. To fill the conversational gap, I said jokingly that one could not help noticing there was no shortage of old C-47s in Laos and Thailand, nor of qualified pilots in Vientiane. My reference was to the so-called air opium operation that local rumor associated with the Corsicans to be seen in the two or three Vientiane restaurants frequented by Westerners.

Ouan found his voice. He considered that our suspicion was correct, he said, and that the chop betrayed a Chinese hand in the deal. He again lapsed into silence, and now General Oudone Sananikone too showed signs of nervousness.

I sat back, sipped my tea, and waited for Ouan to speak. Finally, the silence was broken. Ouan said he was well acquainted with the elders of the Chinese community and would take steps to identify who was behind this chop. Action would then be taken to have the police put him out of business. Word would be leaked to the Chinese community that the flaw in the operation had been the culprit's use of Air America aircraft, and this would cause traffickers to use other means of transportation because they were in these ventures for the sole purpose of making money.

I agreed that this was an excellent idea. Then, to head off any attempt by Ouan to obtain custody of the evidence, I said that Ambassador Sullivan had instructed me to have the opium destroyed. In order to meet all of our American internal requirements, I had arranged for a couple of my officers to burn the opium on the next Sunday at 11:00 A.M. at the That Luang, a large open area and occasional fairground in front of Vientiane's most famous Buddhist pagoda.

"If you find you need a way to emphasize America's seriousness about this business," I said, "you might wish to pass the word to the Chinese community. Then, their people can see us destroying the opium blocks with their own eyes."

Ouan by now had become totally mute. With a wry smile on his face, General Oudone said this had been a productive meeting, and with that we adjourned.

As scheduled on the following Sunday, Ed Connor, a senior air operations officer, and Bill Finch, our security chief, accompanied by a few others, burned the opium at the That Luang fairgrounds. This event aroused the interest of various locals who observed it from a respectful distance.

At lunch at my house in Vientiane about two weeks later, General Oudone Sananikone told me General Ouan had been impressed with my use of Asian-style diplomacy in dealing with this opium problem. Oudone also said General Ouan knew, without making any inquiries, which syndicate was behind the shipment. In view of that, it was Oudone's opinion that we would not be troubled by that group again.

Translated from the Asian-diplomatic, the general had just said, "Your message was received and understood. It won't happen again." I think it probably didn't happen again, if only because the unscheduled nature of Air America flights made them an imperfect vehicle for large-scale smuggling operations and because of the availability in Laos of alternative carriers including Royal Air Lao, Lao Air Development, and Air Laos, not to mention the Royal Lao Air Force, or the "old C-47s" that had figured in my conversation with General Ouan. In the dry language of the inspector general's report, "It is highly problematical whether these airlines have a full platter of legitimate business."[3]

The fantasy that the CIA was smuggling opium for its own profit has been examined and dismissed as the nonsense it is by a select committee of the United States Senate. The committee's conclusion reads as follows:

> Persistent questions have been raised whether Agency policy has included using proprietaries to engage in illegal activities or to make profits which could be used to fund operations. Most notably, these charges included allegations that the CIA used air proprietaries to engage in drug trafficking. The Committee investigated this area to determine whether there is any evidence to substantiate these charges. On the basis of its examination, the Committee has concluded that the CIA air proprietaries did not participate in illicit drug trafficking.[4]

The BNDD organization in Bangkok subsequently sent more people to Vientiane to see what could be done about the opium trafficking from the Golden Triangle, and we arranged for them to meet Lao law enforcement and intelligence people, in particular Colonel Vattha Phanekham, head of the Special Branch of the police, and Colonel Etam Singvongsa, G-2 of the Royal Lao Army. Doug Beed, our liaison with these organizations, was the officer responsible for negotiating the details. But, to ensure that the meetings actually took place, I would have to take the first possible opportunity to have a private word with General Ouan. Given the peculiarities of the covert war in Laos, which gave Vientiane something of the atmosphere that permeated Lisbon in World War II, I often found my best chance for a discreet chat with Ouan was at a diplomatic reception or a social function in the home of a mutual acquaintance where I could talk with him without drawing the attention of the French, South Vietnamese, Indonesian, Indian, Canadian, and Polish military personnel who were constantly hovering around his office or residential compound.

When the BNDD eventually called on us for intelligence on traffic in the Golden Triangle, we had to tell them we were without significant resources in that key opium-trading area. Our assets, we said, were all located north of Ban Houei Sai in the Nam Yu area. We would certainly task them to report on opium trafficking in the sector where they had access, and that might sometimes include parts of China's Yunnan Province. We also agreed that when targets of opportunity appeared and credible intelligence on opium trafficking was obtained, we would put it into intelligence channels.

This dialog, although professional and friendly, created tensions because the two agencies had different priorities. The agency with the law enforcement mission justifiably wanted seizures, arrests, and convictions. The one with the intelligence mission lacked any police charter and had to decline to allow its staff or agent personnel to appear in court cases if it was to comply with its obligation to protect sources and methods. These fundamental differences were not unique to Laos. In fact, they took years to resolve on a worldwide basis, and our talks in Vientiane with the BNDD were part of the learning curve.

On trips back to Washington from Laos in late 1966 and early 1967, I saw that the narcotics question was receiving more policy-level attention. Des FitzGerald, the deputy director for plans, had even created a special assistant job for narcotics and put Seymour Bolten in that slot.

Seymour, who had entered the agency via postwar military government service in Germany in the 1950s, was a political action specialist. At one time he was an expert on the West German political scene, but as his career progressed he moved from one political priority to another. In the Cuban missile period, he had served in Task Force W under Harvey and FitzGerald. Later, he went to the Senior Seminar on Foreign Policy, an in-house State Department training course similar to the National War College and one in which the CIA routinely placed one or two officers. While there, Seymour became interested in the growing narcotics issue in America and wrote his required dissertation on this topic. Upon returning to the CIA from the seminar, Seymour became the main advocate, under FitzGerald's protective wing, of a more activist role in narcotics intelligence collection.

Seymour, who had been a friend of mine for years, lobbied me heavily on one of my trips to Washington. Although the collection of intelligence on drug trafficking was not yet in the CIA's missions-and-functions statement, he said, it was inevitable that it would be soon. To the extent that it could do so without compromising its number-one task, he urged me to have the Vientiane Station pay some attention to the movement of opium and heroin out of the Golden Triangle.

I said we would do what we could, stressing that we could only be expected to produce intelligence on narcotics trafficking as a by-product of our other activities. Seymour said he understood.

With this conversation in mind, upon returning to Vientiane I briefed my key associates on the new trend in Washington. Each senior officer was asked to be alert for targets of opportunity that would enable us to collect and report intelligence on opium and heroin trafficking.

Bill Lair, Tony Poe, who was then our unit chief at Nam Yu, and other old Lao/Thai hands, passed the new requirement to their staffs, who in turn briefed their agents, informants, and casual contacts, and fragmentary reports began trickling in. I especially remember three prolific contributors—the Yao paramilitary leaders Chao Ma and his brother Chao La and Bill Young. Bill was stationed in Udorn and specialized in the recruitment of Lahu and Wa tribal groups, who would come into the Ban Houei Sai area from Burma. Although these people were being trained primarily to collect OB information in China, they also had contacts in Burma, and reports of doings in the Golden Triangle began arriving from this quarter.

Eventually, OB analysts in Udorn pieced together a series of reports from a variety of sources to the effect that a caravan of horses and mules would be moving from Burma through Laos to Ban Houei Sai in June 1967. As was typical with reports from untrained sources, we were told only that the caravan was an unusually large one, and we were left to make our own guess as to its size. Caravans could run from fifty to six hundred mules, and our guesses veered toward the larger figure. In any case, an enormous amount of unrefined opium was involved. Estimates vary, but one pack animal can carry between forty and fifty kilograms (about 88 to 110 pounds).

If we were ever told who was funding this caravan, I no longer remember. It does stick in mind that security for the caravan was being provided by Shan guerrillas loyal to Chan Shee Fu, or Chang Chi-Fu, as some agents called him. We already had some knowledge about this upstart warlord and would soon acquire more, for he was already expanding his private army and therefore his influence in Burma's Wa and Shan states. He later went by the war name of "Khun Sa" and was believed to be responsible for an average annual export of three hundred metric tons of opium. Newspaper headlines identified him as the "Prince of Death."

We were also left to guess the strength of the caravan's escort. Considering the probable size of the pack train, together with the fact that the narrowness of the region's tracks would oblige the caravan to proceed in single file, we felt that nothing smaller than battalion size could be very effective. As escorts were typically armed with M-16s and mortars and occasionally with old .50-caliber machine guns, we were looking at a potentially formidable force.

Our intelligence on this caravan was distributed in U.S. channels to all interested parties. If anything was to be done about the situation, it would have to be done by Lao or Thai armed forces, so I obtained Ambassador Sullivan's approval to include these two governments in the dissemination. I don't remember the Thai taking any action at all. General Ouan, on the other hand, told me casually at a social gathering that he was carefully monitoring the opium-caravan situation in northwest Laos in MR-1.

That statement proved to be quite true, for in late July 1967 a battle took place at Ban Khwan, Laos, located on the Mekong River. Some *Kuomintang* (KMT)[5] units and some Shan were involved, and so eventually were the Royal Lao Armed Forces. In their tangle with the Shan and KMT forces, the Lao used a paratroop battalion supported by gunboats on the Mekong and unleashed T-28 air strikes, making this the best combined-arms operation to be mounted by Lao conventional forces during my tour in Laos.

The Lao, under General Ouan's command, won the battle, and the Shan retreated by small boats along the Mekong into Burma. The KMT retreated northward, were blocked by the deployment of additional Lao troops, and finally negotiated a settlement with the Lao that permitted them to enter Thailand by mid-August 1967.

This battle was another scene out of the *Terry and the Pirates* comic strip. What happened to get these different elements into a two- or three-way firefight that resulted in a reported 150 to 160 dead, a loss of precious equipment for the Shan and the KMT, and, more importantly, the disappearance of around fifteen to twenty tons of opium? We never found out.

Some in the media claimed that this was a classic turf battle. According to this version, Chan Shee Fu had organized the caravan, and the KMT's Third and Fifth Armies had tried to block him so that he would not cut into their own lucrative opium trade. General Ouan, who owned a sawmill at Ban Khwan, had supposedly contracted with Chan Shee Fu to buy this opium, and when the transaction went off the tracks in Laos, Ouan's own turf, he moved in with the approval of Prime Minister Souvanna Phouma under the guise of protecting Lao sovereignty. His victory, said these analysts, gave Ouan control not only of the battlefield but of the opium, which somehow disappeared in the heat of battle.

I never saw any hard intelligence to confirm the media's version, but it is a plausible explanation. From our point of view as collectors of intelligence on narcotics trafficking, this incident raised more questions than it answered. Yet, it was part of the process of learning how to collect this type of information, how to authenticate it, to whom to disseminate it, and what results to expect of it.

Our handful of reports on the opium convoy probably did little more than convey a warning to Ouan and any others who may have been involved that their security needed tightening. I don't think that our reporting triggered the battle of Ban Khwan. Chan Shee Fu, however, may well have thought so. If one wishes to survive as a senior bandit chief, he must have a well-developed appreciation of counterintelligence, and Chan Shee Fu had shown himself to be a survivor. Given the number of untrained people who were asking questions on our behalf in the Shan and Wa tribal areas, I consider it highly probable that at least one of them had been brought to Chan Shee Fu's attention and that his own enemy OB estimates thus included American intelligence units in Udorn and Vientiane.

17

PUBLIC RELATIONS

MY Lao assignment had something to teach me about public relations. Our so-called secret war attracted a steady flow of VIPs to whom, either at the request of CIA headquarters or Ambassador Sullivan, I was to give an overview of the tactical and political situation on the ground. These briefings were as factual and timely as we could make them. Among the many notable recipients of these presentations were Senator Charles Percy, Senator John Tower, Ambassador Chester Bowles, General Creighton Abrams, Joe Alsop, and Senator Stuart Symington.

The distinguished senator from Missouri, Symington, proved to be an enigma wrapped in a dilemma. My initial encounter with Senator Symington was at Udorn in the fall of 1966. Symington was on a trip to Southeast Asia in his role as a senior member of the Senate Armed Services Committee. For some reason, he and Ambassador Sullivan could not agree on an appropriate schedule for Symington to visit Vientiane. The compromise that emerged from a flurry of traffic in State and CIA channels between Washington, Vientiane, and Bangkok was that Symington would be met in Udorn, taken to CIA offices, and briefed on the war in Laos. I remember this session well, for it was my first congressional briefing after arriving in Vientiane.

Symington, who had been a successful businessman and secretary of the Air Force and was now a distinguished senator, projected an aura of charm and intelligence when we met him. He asked excellent questions and was keenly interested in what we were doing and going to do against the Ho Chi Minh Trail. At the end of our session he told Bill Lair, Pat Landry, and me that the CIA show in Laos was first-rate. Symington then said the American show in Laos probably cost $200 million a year, whereas in Vietnam the United States spent that much in a week. According to Symington, America should take the Lao effort as its model when fighting wars in Asia. He told me he was going to arrange with DCI Dick Helms for me to give a briefing on the Lao operation to a closed session of the Senate Armed Services Committee, an event that took place in Washington on October 5, 1967, with Senator John Stennis presiding. The meeting went well from the CIA point of view, and at its conclusion Stennis and Symington were both laudatory about our program in Laos.

Symington made at least one additional trip to Laos while I was the station chief. On that occasion he was the guest of honor at a dinner party at my home where he met numerous CIA officers and a handful of Lao military officers who were working closely with us on a variety of paramilitary and intelligence programs. In addition, he traveled with me to Long Tieng where he was given a briefing by Vang Pao, saw Air America airplanes unloading rice and ammunition, and watched with interest as helicopters and T-28s operated in and out of the Long Tieng airfield. After that he was a dinner guest at Ambassador Sullivan's residence. At that event he sat next to Hazel and spoke glowingly of his up-country travel and what good work the CIA was doing in Laos.

Consequently, I was shocked, to say the least, to read in accounts of the October 20, 1969, Senate hearings and others held in early 1970, that Symington was saying he was surprised or angered or both to learn about the CIA's secret war in Laos. The question that boiled up from the pit of my stomach was, The war in Laos was a secret to whom? Perhaps to the average citizen in St. Louis, but by no means was it a secret to the distinguished gentleman from Missouri or to a significant number of other senators.[1]

It was always a mystery to me why Symington acted in what, by the value judgments that I could apply to the situation, was a grossly dishonest manner. Some of my Washington friends from the media explained it as a sea change dictated by the imperatives of wanting to get reelected at a time when national disillusionment with the Vietnam War was peaking. I was never comfortable with that rationale. Symington had always appeared in his dealings with us in the field to be a man of greater principle. Unfortunately, none of the other theories was any more palatable to me than the first. I could only conclude therefore that even among the major figures of contemporary politics, there were those who had feet of clay.[2]

From our Thai allies I acquired grounding in the Southeast Asian power equation as seen from Bangkok. Colonel Dhep and his senior staff at Headquarters 333 took every opportunity to remind me of their concern over the estimated sixty thousand Vietnamese living in the five northeastern provinces of Thailand. They saw this ethnic minority as a reservoir of manpower and area knowledge through which Hanoi, acting on its own or as a surrogate for Moscow, could pursue the goal of dominating Southeast Asia.

These concerns were valid, for Hanoi was already active in northeastern Thailand, running intelligence-collection operations against targets such as the airfields at Udorn, Nakhon Phanom, and Takhli and recruiting and training potential insurgents. The extent of that effort became clear in 1967 when two Thais were captured in the northeast and interrogated. Presented at a Bangkok press conference, they confirmed the location of a guerrilla warfare school at Hoa Binh north of Hanoi where Thai trainees received at least six months of indoctrination in people's war techniques. Phya Chakkapak, the senior Thai DCI officer at Headquarters 333, said it was estimated that between 1962 and 1967 from seven to eight hundred Thai insurgents had been trained at Hoa Binh. In this context Dhep reminded me that Ho Chi Minh, using the cover of a Buddhist monk, had operated in Udorn province in the 1920s and knew Thailand. In essence the Vietnamese threat was real.

The Thai were also concerned about China's role in controlling the Communist Party of Thailand, a party whose ethnic makeup was heavily Sino-Thai. There was a considerable traffic of communist cadres between China and Thailand, both as clandestine infiltration through Laos and China's Yunnan Province and as legal travel via Hong Kong. As cooperation between the Vientiane Station and Headquarters 333 improved and increased, Dhep worked to expand the level of dialog between the Vientiane Station and key Thai policy makers. Lair and I felt there was merit in such an enhanced exchange. For my part I saw that both parties would benefit, not only in terms of operations in Laos but in pursuit of American policy objectives in Vietnam. Based on that decision we used Lair's excellent Thai contacts to open the door for me to brief Thai Prime Minister Marshall Thanom Kittikachorn and General Prapat Charusathian, who was then holding the portfolios of deputy prime minister, commander in chief of the Army, and minister of interior. Dhep was included in all such sessions, and as they became more frequent, he usually coordinated the timing of these meetings and set their agendas.

Using either Dhep's or Lair's door-opening ability, we held regular sessions with Chief of Staff of the Army General Sirikit Mayalarp and generals such as Serm Nanakorn, then head of logistics, and Saiyud Kerdphol, an expert on counterinsurgency. We also had sessions with the key staff members of the Thai NSC, such as Air Vice Marshall Siddhi Sawetsia and Prasong Sunsiri. This effort paid significant dividends, for the Thai were constantly supportive of CIA efforts in Laos as well as Washington's broader goals in Vietnam.

The Thai, doubtless at the nudging of Colonel Dhep, invited Bill Lair, Pat Landry, Tony Poe, Dick Secord, one or two others, and me to have lunch in Bangkok with Thai prime minister Thanom Kittikachorn, Deputy Prime Minister Prapat Charusathian, and Chief of Staff of the Army General Sirikit Mayalarp. Of course we accepted. On July 27, 1968, Prapat in his capacity as commander in chief of the Royal Thai Army awarded us individually the Order of the White Elephant. Within that order there are grades, and mine and Bill Lair's was commander.

Dhep and I had a brief three-way conversation with Prapat at this affair. Prapat expressed confidence that the barbarians (Hanoi) could be kept outside Thailand's borders for the foreseeable future as a result of America's involvement in Vietnam and Laos, but Thailand could never enjoy real prosperity, he added, until a durable peace prevailed in Indochina. "When might that be?" he wondered. Neither Dhep nor I could provide a meaningful answer despite the depth of intelligence data on Hanoi's near-term plans and intentions that was available to both of us.

Inspired by the Thais' example, Vang Pao arranged a major affair at Long Tieng on August 26, 1968, to be presided over by King Savang Vattana and observed by Prime Minister Souvanna Phouma. On that occasion the Order of Million Elephants and White Parasol was awarded to a number of USAID and CIA officers: "Doc" Weldon was the one USAID official to receive the award whom I can recall with certainty; the CIA personnel included Bill Lair, Pat Landry, Jonathan R., Jerry D., Howie Freeman, and myself.

An interesting exchange took place at this event. Prime Minister Souvanna Phouma, who spoke fluent French and halting English but had a flair for getting off penetrating comments in appropriate social situations, walked up to me after the king had pinned the medals on our suitcoats. Souvanna jokingly said in French, which someone translated for me, "We have come a long way from the early days of your service in Laos. At that time Ambassador Sullivan had wanted to keep you in the shadows. I remember how difficult it was to get you to come to my office to brief me and our key generals on the logistics support that would be provided by your organization to a joint FAR and Armée Clandestine operation. We resolved that matter by my calling the ambassador."

"Yes," I replied, "We have come a long way since those early days."

"We still have much to do in our common cause," Souvanna said, tapping me with his champagne glass.

As Souvanna walked away, I had one of those flashbacks that one experiences when recalling a particularly memorable incident. The Souvanna story had its origins in Ambassador Sullivan's early cautionary advice to me to regard the American dialog with Souvanna as the sole responsibility of the ambassador. That posed no problem until Hazel began meeting a "very charming lady" at Vientiane's only fashionable hairdresser. Once I realized that the lady was Souvanna Phouma's wife, I told Hazel that we had to stay at arm's length in our relations with the prime minister and his family.

Hazel's encounters with the lady led in time to occasional invitations to small gatherings being hosted by the prime minister. We always found a way to bow graciously out of them, only accepting invitations to massive ceremonial occasions such as National Day or the king's birthday.

This state of affairs lasted until the FAR general staff had to brief Souvanna on a series of planned operations, one of which included a joint effort by MR-2 and MR-5 forces. General Vang Pao, the MR-2 commander, and General Kouprasith, the MR-5 commander, were therefore in attendance, along with General Ouan and others.

When Souvanna asked about some logistics aspects of the operation and raised some issues on the use of airpower, Vang Pao and Kouprasith said the Americans were handling that.

"Which Americans?" asked Souvanna.

"Mr. Ted," replied Vang Pao.

According to what General Ouan and Vang Pao told me later, Souvanna paused, puffed on his pipe, and said, "Ask Mr. Ted to join us."

Vang Pao had a call placed to me at the embassy. When he outlined the problem, I told him it was not possible for me to come as the ambassador had made it clear that he was the only embassy channel to Souvanna. Vang Pao reported my position to Souvanna, who became visibly agitated.

Phoning Ambassador Sullivan, Souvanna expressed his displeasure that an embassy officer and his family were reluctant to socialize with the prime minister and his family. Added to that was the officer's polite but firm refusal to brief the prime minister, saying that that was the ambassador's job. Sullivan told Souvanna that if I were then in the embassy, he would have me join the meeting immediately.

Responding to Sullivan's urgent summons, I entered his office. "What," he asked, "has set off this hornet's nest at the prime minister's office?"

I reminded him of our very first meeting when he had instructed me to stay away from the prime minister. I had done just that, I said.

"Most CIA types," Sullivan laughed, "ignore ambassadorial guidance and create problems. The cross I have to bear is that I am working with a CIA officer who honors instructions and creates problems. Hurry over to the prime minister's office and get them sorted out. Also, forget the code of conduct you developed in Germany. In Asia one bends like the bamboo."

I followed both sets of instructions. My briefing of Souvanna and the assembled generals was in English. General Oudone Sananikone then translated the information into Lao. Souvanna had a few questions, and when these were dealt with, he approved the operation.

After that experience, my dealings with the prime minister were more frequent and less structured. This in no way, however, did anything to alter the reality that Ambassador Sullivan was the prime point of contact between the United States and the prime minister. It was interesting that Souvanna recalled the incident many months later, even as he was talking about what still had to come.

The congruity of Lao and American interests had begun to weaken by mid-1966, and Ambassador Sullivan occasionally had to smooth ruffled Laotian feathers. In early January 1967 I had an urgent call from his office. Arriving there promptly, I found the ambassador completing a telephone call in French.

Hanging up, the ambassador turned to me and said, "What's going on east of Thakhek? The prime minister's office has reports that people are fleeing east to west along Route 12 headed for Thakhek from the Mahaxay area as a result of some battlefield developments. FAR says they know nothing. By elimination that leaves your paramilitary troops as the culprits. What gives?"

"We're running no planned operation in the Route 12 area around Mahaxay at this time," I told him. "We'll check to see if some target of opportunity has caused a firefight somewhere along Route 12 and panicked some of the local population."

Sullivan said, "Okay, but get back to me as soon as you can. This situation, whatever it is, has made the Lao nervous."

Upon returning to my office, I contacted Udorn. When queried, Pat Landry said that Tom Fosmire had a confused, but fluid, tactical situation on his hands. It had started with our getting our hands on a Lao who had recently been at a POW camp near Mahaxay. This man had been debriefed in Savannakhet and provided a lot of exploitable tactical intelligence on the POW camp. This intelligence compared favorably with our file holdings on this area. Fosmire had opted to exploit this target of opportunity to mount a raid on the prison complex. As the operation progressed, both Walt Floyd, the case officer running it, and Fosmire had begun calling for backup helicopter and strike-aircraft assistance; Udorn was now breaking its back to provide that support.

As I listened, Landry said there was no mass exodus of people along Route 12. He did say, however, that about eighty people might have been released from the prison camp. Some had immediately taken to the bush. Others were being aided in their escape by the Savannakhet team that had conducted the raid. Perhaps those who had fled on their own were now strung out along Route 12.

When Landry finished his report my comment was, "Operations like this make heroes or goats. I trust that when the day is done we will have more live heroes than dead goats."

Additionally, I said it was disappointing to learn about such tactical activity via an ambassadorial query. Thus, while I would report to Sullivan in good faith what Landry was telling me, it would be most interesting in our postmortem of this operation to look at the timelines that had led up to a decision to launch this operation.

An extended silence at the other end of the line convinced me that the full story on this caper was not yet in hand. Landry finally found his voice and said he was confident that all would end well.

Not being as sanguine as Landry, I put in a call to Fosmire. My question was simple. Did he need anything he could not get from Udorn that we might supply from Vientiane? Fosmire said the situation was still fluid, but he was getting the tactical air support from T-28s, A-1Es, and F-4s that he needed. Helicopters were being marshaled for pickups of the released prisoners, and he felt it would all turn out all right.

"Good luck" was my only other comment.

Armed with the information provided by Landry and Fosmire and having done a quick check of SIGINT sources to confirm that no big firefight was in progress, I returned to Sullivan's office and told him in full detail what I knew then about the operation. I emphasized the target-of-opportunity nature of the event but admitted to doubts that we had the full story. That could not be remedied now, I said, but in due course all the facts would become known. My immediate concern, I told him, was to make certain that what appeared to be a success did not turn into a disaster. Sullivan, ever the realist, agreed.

All's well that ends well. By day's end some thirty former prisoners had been rescued by daring Air America helicopter operations supported by tactical air strikes and brought to Savannakhet. The Savannakhet raiding party was also recovered without loss.

In the days that followed, I pieced this story together. Here is what I now recall. The time sequence Landry had originally given me was off by at least twenty-four hours. This meant that everything had happened twenty-four hours earlier than originally reported. The Lao source had been picked up on one day, brought to Savannakhet for debriefing and found to be bona fide. The data he supplied fit our previous holdings on the POW camp. Fosmire and Landry then decided to mount an operation.[3] A twelve-man raiding party was put together and helicoptered that same day into the operational area. The next morning between 3:00 A.M. and 4:00 A.M., they hit the prison. In a brief firefight the guards on duty were killed, and the backup guards were either killed or routed by an M-79 grenade attack on the quarters where they had been sleeping.

With the camp in friendly hands, prisoners were promptly released from the caves where they had been held. This revealed that the site had some fifty prisoners. They were a strange mix of humanity who had been incarcerated for a wide range of different reasons. One man was an Air America employee of Thai origin who had been shot down in September 1963 with the American Eugene Debruin. Others were members of a Savannakhet road-watch team that had been captured in the Mu Gia Pass area around Route 12. Some when released melted into the bush on their own. The others, sick and disoriented or pleased to be with their rescuers, stuck together and made their way under the raiding team's protection to a randomly selected LZ where the Air America helicopters picked them up.

The debriefing of the Thai, Phisit Intharathat, who had worked as a cargo handler provided information about Debruin, who had escaped from a POW camp in June 1966 never to be heard from again. He reported bits about Navy pilot Dieter Dengler's captivity and escape at the same time as Debruin's. He also furnished information on Air Force Lieutenant Duane Martin, who had been in the June 1966 escape from a POW camp but had been killed before he and Dengler could be rescued.

When all of the smoke cleared, one and all declared the operation a success. Commendations were given to Walt Floyd, Tom Fosmire, and Pat Landry for a job well done. Privately, however, I told Fosmire and Landry that in future target-of-opportunity exercises, I expected them to find a way to keep me informed on a timelier basis. They both agreed. More importantly, they honored their commitment.

18

CULTURAL EXCHANGE

W E were happy with the progress that Vang Pao was making in integrating himself into the Lao power structure. As of mid-1966, Vang Pao had virtually never come to Vientiane, and as he was a guerrilla leader, there was no reason why he should have. But the irregular war was not the only task on my plate. Nation building was another, and Vang Pao was the political leader of a minority tribal group as well as the RLG's military commander in MR-2. After some discussion about the varied and possibly conflicting roles that Vang Pao could be called upon to play, I succeeded in convincing Lair that we had to find a way to work Vang Pao more into the Vientiane political scene.

The first step was to invite Vang Pao to a luncheon at my house. He accepted with some reluctance, fearing an unpleasant incident if he were on General Kouprasith Abhay's home turf, and said that his appearance would be his first visit to Vientiane in two years.

When the date for the luncheon arrived, I made arrangements for extra security around my residence, including putting a guard in the water tower. Vang Pao and his entourage of twenty arrived at the appointed time, with all but Vang Pao armed to the teeth. They knew that my residence compound was safe, but who could say what dangers lurked outside of it?

Vang Pao was greeted by Jim Lilley and Hazel, I being caught in an air-traffic jam at Udorn. Arriving home about fifteen minutes late, I observed that Vang Pao had his own flank security force out in front of my compound. In addition, inside my fence area, in a jeep in the driveway just in front of my door, an armed Hmong cradled an

M-79 grenade launcher in his lap. And there was Suzanne, obviously fascinated by the grenades on his webbing, and trying to draw him into conversation by offering him a doll. I called to Suzanne, scooped her up, and took her inside. There in my living room was a pile about two feet high and five feet wide of pistol belts and webbing, M-16s, M-2 carbines, and related gear. Obviously, Vang Pao had had his men stack arms before heading for the patio area where drinks were being served. I passed Suzanne off to Hazel with the statement that it was nap time. Suzanne went off with Mommy, but a nap was clearly not on her mind, given all the interesting things that were going on.

Recognizing that Vang Pao wanted to get the show on the road, I moved the party to a screened patio area. Vang Pao was given the place of honor at a long table seating fourteen. The Americans were dispersed both there and at round six-man tables, spaced so that there would be a French speaker for every four Hmong. The tables were set with white tablecloths, white linen napkins, and simple silverware—one knife, one fork, and one spoon. Water glasses were filled, and the guests were offered their choice of wine or beer.

We had briefed Vang Pao that it was our intent to serve Western style. He had said, "Okay, my people need to learn."

I enjoyed watching Vang Pao provide cultural leadership. After he sat down he picked up his napkin with a flourish, making a great show of unfolding it and placing it in his lap. Having followed Vang Pao's moves out of the corners of their eyes, his men now knew the drill, and all napkins were quickly and properly deployed.

The meal had several composite parts—roast beef, ham, rice and vegetables—which Wantana, our Thai housekeeper, had prepared under Hazel's supervision. As the food was served, the Hmong studied how Vang Pao and the Americans handled each item. No social errors were committed by anyone, but this was clearly a tense learning experience for the troops. The hit of the meal was the ice cream and the fruit.

As the luncheon finished and it was time for everyone to pick up his battle gear, Suzanne reappeared with Hazel to say good-bye to her newfound friends. She was fascinated with their toys, particularly the hand grenades. They, in turn, being family oriented, were curious to see how Americans related to their children.

We had calculated that Vang Pao's arrival and departure at

Wattay Airport would be noted and that the servants' grapevine would soon let it be known that Vang Pao had been at my residence. That was our objective, for we wanted to create the impression that Vang Pao had no reason not to come to Vientiane, even if only for a luncheon.

Our ploy worked. That same evening General Oudone Sananikone stopped at my residence around 6:15. He said he had been working late at FAR headquarters at Phone Kheng and on his way home had decided to stop to see if all was well with me. He had been concerned, he said, for earlier in the day while passing my residence he had noted an unusual display of security around my compound. He jokingly said he had recently noticed Suzanne and another Caucasian child riding a water buffalo in the field across from our house. Perhaps, thought Oudone, the children had adopted the beast, and we were now having problems with its Lao owner.

I told Oudone that all was tranquil at the Shackley residence and then mentioned casually that we had had Vang Pao and a few of his senior commanders in for lunch in order to reciprocate for past social courtesies extended to me and my associates by the Hmong.

Oudone, who had a good sense of humor, said, "The next feast will hopefully include me. I know you have an excellent Thai cook."

"Of course," was my response.

After that ice-breaking visit, Vang Pao started to come regularly to Vientiane. We encouraged the FAR general staff to include him in their planning sessions, and in time they did. Vang Pao started visiting in Vientiane with members of the National Assembly and developed easy access to Prime Minister Souvanna Phouma. This, coupled with his relationship with the king at Luang Prabang, fully integrated him into the Lao power structure in less than two years. He was now a political, as well as a military, factor.

Cultural exchange had many aspects, and on various occasions it was I who did the learning. One such event came about early in 1967 when a training school run by the Pakse unit graduated one of our early Kha road-watch teams. Dave Morales, the unit chief, felt it important for his liaison with the Kha and General Phasouk, the MR-4 region commander, that I be present at the graduation.

Accordingly, I flew to Pakse from Vientiane and was escorted to the training site. After a nice military ceremony, we proceeded to a formal lunch where a water buffalo was slaughtered. The hot buffalo blood was drained into a container, and a few minutes later a rather large, brown, clay-type jar, showing signs of having recently been dug out of the ground, was brought to the area. I was told by one of the Thai Headquarters 333 officers at the camp that the jug contained fermented rice wine.

I watched with detached interest as some of the water buffalo blood was poured into the container and mixed with the rice wine. Shortly thereafter, the large container of witch's brew was placed on a straw mat and two large bamboo-type straws were placed in it. Suddenly I found myself being eased over to the jug and introduced as the senior American present to a wizened old man with gray hair and sparkling eyes and clad only in a loincloth. He, the great chief of the Kha in the Attopeu area from which we had recruited the road-watch team, was inviting me to a ceremonial drink.

Seeing no gracious way to refuse, I accepted. We each moved to the straw mat. The chief sat down and motioned for me to join him on the other side of the jug, and I realized with alarm that we were to drink simultaneously through the bamboo straws from the jug. Not being keen on partaking of the concoction, I figured that while the chief sucked up through his straw I could blow down on mine and pass the ceremonial requirements with dignity.

It was not to be. As we sat down and positioned ourselves properly with regard to the straws, the interpreter signaled that we were to start. The chief sucked legitimately on his straw, while I tried to fake it by blowing down through mine. At first it seemed that my ruse had succeeded, but suddenly I saw it had not. The old chief said nothing, only looking at me with his piercing dark eyes and solemn face and waving an index finger in the universally understood motion of "no, no." Realizing there was no alternative, I sucked on my straw and found a gooey sweet substance passing my lips. I swallowed reluctantly, the chief's face broke into a toothless smile, and I quickly covered the rice wine with a bottle of cold Thai Singha beer.

This experience taught me that primitive cultures were not to be fooled in matters involving basic body functions like drinking. Obviously, others had tried like circumventions on previous occasions.

Other cultural lessons had to do with marriage, a complex issue among the Hmong with whom polygamy is quite common. As one

Hmong elder explained to me, "One wife is not enough to run a home and bear the right number of children. Two wives always cause trouble because they compete constantly with each other. Four or five wives are luxuries that can only be afforded by the rich or by politicians needing to strengthen their clan. Three wives are just right because while the husband is making love with one wife, the other two can console each other."

The Hmong New Year always included a marriage fair. One of its features was a simple ball-throwing game in which boys and girls formed two lines arranged in such a way that the girls faced boys from other clans. While a small ball was tossed back and forth, songs were sung, couples flirted, and meetings were sometimes agreed to.

The Shackleys were privileged to attend the July 1967 wedding at Sam Thong of Touby Lyfoung's son and Vang Pao's daughter. This was no brokered match but a modern marriage based on love. Nonetheless, it had the hearty approval of both clans. The marriage also had political implications for the Xieng Khouang Hmong, for it represented a symbolic peace treaty between the Ly and Vang clans, which had been fighting each other for power for years.

The origins of the feud lay in Touby Lyfoung's having been the acknowledged king of the Hmong before 1961. As Vang Pao's star brightened, Touby's went into eclipse. The older man found that hard to take, particularly given his past close association with the French in their struggle against both the Japanese in World War II and the North Vietnamese in the postwar period.

Touby found some modicum of solace, however, in his appointment to the largely ceremonial, but prestigious, King's Council. This permitted him the face-saving luxury of spending his time in Vientiane allegedly monitoring political developments in the National Assembly and among the various Lao interest groups on behalf of His Majesty. In reality, however, Touby was a spent force, and he knew it. As such, he was of no interest to the CIA, although he was on good terms with Mark Pratt, a Foreign Service officer who mixed well with all of the permanent features of the Vientiane diplomatic landscape.

Being both shrewd and opportunistic, Touby attempted to regain his position of moral authority among the Hmong when he tried to mount a political coup shortly after Vang Pao had been wounded in 1966. Vang Pao made a radio broadcast from his hospital bed, and the coup collapsed. Touby and Vang Pao subsequently patched over their differences, but there was no love lost between them. The de facto political ceasefire between Touby and Vang Pao made it possible for Touby's son, a mathematical genius who had a scholarship to study physics in France, to woo and win the hand of Vang Pao's daughter.

The wedding was the Lao social event of the year. The diplomatic community saw it as their one chance to visit Sam Thong and get a feel for the war in North Laos, so virtually everyone who was invited attended. Airplanes shuttled the people from Vientiane to Sam Thong with military precision. Hazel flew up in a CASI Dornier with Dutch Brongersma and his wife. My own trip was made in a C-123 with other American embassy personnel, for in Laos Hazel and I made it a rule never to be on the same flight for in-country trips because of the danger.

Ambassador Sullivan and his wife were also present, so those of us from the CIA who attended had to preserve cover and stay in the background. Clan leaders, who were more comfortable with their CIA friends than with representatives of Vientiane's diplomatic community, heeded the urgings of the CIA officers and Vang Pao to circulate with the "guests" and postpone their chats with the "sky people"[1] until another day.

The event would have made any ethnic leader proud, whether from Ireland, Italy, or Poland. The food was plentiful and good. Beer and whiskey flowed, and Hmong culture in terms of dances, costumes, and rituals was in full bloom.

As the festivities progressed, I noticed changes taking place in those members of the security forces who had been participating in the affair and wondered how effective they would be when they got out on sentry duty. Fortunately, it didn't occur to the North Vietnamese to attack Sam Thong or Long Tieng at this time.

Given the constant uncertainty of weather around Sam Thong, where clouds could suddenly make flying in the mountains quite hazardous, I arranged for Hazel and myself to be on two of the first flights out. As I learned later, bad weather was not the only hazard we escaped. Had we stayed I undoubtedly would have been maneuvered by our Hmong hosts into joining one of the traditional drinking bouts with which the festivities were concluded.

The dark side of cultural exchange was the deleterious effect it was having on the Hmong people. "Pop" Buell, the colorful USAID representative at Sam Thong, had been saying for some time that Hmong combat losses were bleeding Vang Pao's people to death. I knew he was right.

Buell was also claiming that boys hardly old enough to know what war was all about or strong enough to handle an M-16 were being dragooned into the CIA's guerrilla forces. I knew of no forced recruitment of Hmong into our paramilitary forces. We had noted, however, that male recruits in some areas seemed to be younger than sixteen, and this had us concerned. Bill Lair, Pat Landry, and their unit chiefs at sites like Long Tieng and Bouam Long (Site 32) were therefore instituting controls designed to ensure that all recruits were over sixteen years old. We used that as a cutoff age because in the Hmong culture a male at sixteen was a man. But basically, we did not want sixteen-year-old recruits. Our goal was to recruit older manpower, but we had no assurance that in some units underage males were not in the guerrilla force.

Buell was right, though. A protracted war would threaten the survival of the Hmong as a people. For them, everything hinged on an early end to the Vietnam War. As I saw it in the still optimistic days of 1968, prosperity and progress could be foreseen for the Hmong of Xieng Khouang if America won the war. Should the Vietnam War end in a Korean-type solution and a neutral Laos, the Hmong were also destined to do well. An American defeat in Vietnam was unthinkable.

Of course, the unthinkable happened, and the Hmong, who had done so much to delay North Vietnam's victory in Indochina, had to pay the price. Prodded by the lobbying of Dr. Jane Hamilton-Merritt and Philip Smith and by what phone calls I was able to make to contacts on Capitol Hill, a not ungrateful U.S. government has intervened to oppose the forced return of Hmong refugees from Thailand to Laos and has eased their resettlement in the United States. In May 1997 I was privileged to stand before six to seven thousand uniformed Hmong veterans at the Vietnam War Memorial in Washington, D.C., and tell them, "I salute the Sky soldiers."

19

FINAL CEREMONIES

MY time in Laos was fast drawing to a close. Headquarters had notified me late in the summer that my next assignment would be chief of station, Vietnam, and that I was expected to report to Saigon for duty in December 1968.

Now the critical question was where to park my family, for in those days dependents were not allowed in Vietnam. Hazel and I quickly decided we would try to find an overseas safe haven rather than try to transplant the family to the United States. Our choices were limited, however, our initial soundings having revealed that there were no safe-haven slots available in Taiwan or the Philippines. This left the possibility of Bangkok or Hong Kong.

"Why don't I just stay in Laos?" Hazel wondered. "We are settled here. There are friends here for Suzanne. And we have a good servant staff. We'd have to move to a smaller house, but so what?"

When I raised the issue with Ambassador Sullivan, he said, "Ted, please don't push that one. If you do, the hardship allowance for serving here will go up in smoke."

Understanding that bureaucratic reality, I told Hazel her choices were really Bangkok or Hong Kong. After much consideration, Hazel opted for Hong Kong. She wanted the change of seasons that it offered. Additionally, at that time we had a greater number of American friends in Hong Kong who could be a safety net for her and Suzanne in times of emergency. It was thus decided we would rent an apartment in Hong Kong.

My replacement was Larry Devlin. We were acquainted but knew of each other primarily by reputation as we had never served in the same geographic area. Larry had seen service in the Congo during its most tumultuous days and was said to have been the man who put Mobutu Sese Seko in power in what became Zaire. He was a fluent French speaker and was credited with skill in all the requisite intelligence arts—collection, covert action, and counterintelligence. Once Devlin arrived in Laos on a permanent basis, we had a good solid overlap. I did all that could be done to make the transition a smooth one.

My farewell *baci* at Long Tieng was an event not to be forgotten. This traditional ceremony, practiced by both the Lao and Hmong in slightly different forms, is designed to speed the traveler safely on his way and bring him good fortune. It typically features floral arrays in a large *baci* bowl, the burning of incense, and incantations by a shaman. As the ceremony progresses, the shaman loosely fastens white cotton strings around the wrist of the traveler, symbolically tying him to the spirits who are to protect him on his journey. Then, the assembled friends come before the traveler one by one, each tying additional strings around the wrist of the one destined to make the journey. Finally, in a bowl placed in front of the traveler, the well-wishers lay offerings for the journey; hardboiled eggs and bananas are traditional. In some ceremonies it is also appropriate to toast and drink with the traveler. The traditional drink is lao-lao or Mekong, both of which are a local, harsh rice whiskey.

I felt that Devlin could have no better introduction to the Hmong culture than to journey with me to Long Tieng for the farewell *baci*. Vang Pao met us at the airfield, I introduced Devlin to him, and we went off by jeep to Vang Pao's house where we talked for a few minutes on the porch. It was agreed that Devlin and I would spend the next hour or so at the Sky team's office area and then regroup for a two-part evening of festivities. Part one would be the *baci*. Once that was finished there would be a break for an hour or so before we regrouped at the Long Tieng communal long house for a traditional Hmong dinner feast, *lamvong* dancing, and serious exchanges of war stories. At the evening's end Devlin and I were to bed down at the king's house on a hill above the Long Tieng valley.

It all sounded great, so Devlin, Pat Landry, Jonathan R., and I took our leave of Vang Pao and headed for the Sky office area. There the troops briefed Devlin on life at Long Tieng, enemy and friendly OB in the area, and operations then in progress.

While that was going on, Pat Landry and Jonathan R. pulled me aside. They wanted to give me a heads-up alert notice that a large number of SGU unit commanders and road-watch team leaders were in Long Tieng or expected to come in by *baci* time. The word had gone out that my destination was Vietnam, the land of the big-unit war. The troops therefore felt that I would need all the good-spirit protection that I could get and were coming in to do what they could to help me with the spirit world. Landry said that would mean heavy drinking at the *baci*, and he hoped my stomach was up to the task. That concern was quite appropriate. All of us who served in Laos suffered from periodic bouts of intestinal disquiet.

I told Pat it was my goal to walk out of the *baci* on my own power. Once I was outside the long house, there had to be a jeep ready to transport me quickly to the Sky office area. There I planned to void the contents of my stomach as quickly as possible. Pat said he would have the jeep ready.

As the sun was setting, the *baci* started. The guests of honor—Pat Landry and Larry Devlin and I—were seated on the floor on straw mats at one end of the long house with our backs leaning against a solid rough-hewn plank wall. The shaman was in exceptionally good voice and most expressive. When he finished he kneeled in front of me and tied the appropriate strings on my wrists. Vang Pao followed and left the symbolic egg and banana in my bowl. He also opened the floodgates of mutual toasting with Scotch. Other well-wishers streamed by—clan leaders, SGU unit commanders, and road-watch team leaders. Many of these I knew, but some were strangers. Each did his ceremonial task. One of the Hmong ladies kept my bowl empty so that the follow-on offerings could be graciously received. The occasional break in what passed for a reception line gave me a chance to nibble on an egg, some sticky rice or crackers to help dilute the alcohol flow. After ten or so exchanges of toasts, Pat Landry was able to ease out of his guest of honor slot. Devlin and I hung in there. Then, I noticed I was alone; Larry had also managed to slip away. No accurate count was possible, but it was my guess I had shared a toast with about thirty-five people before the *baci* phase was over.

Operating under my own power, I walked with dignity out of the communal hall. True to his word Pat had a jeep waiting for me. We wasted no time covering the short distance to the Sky office.

There in the privacy of the open outdoors, I purged my stomach. After that, Coca-Cola, two aspirin, and a catnap on a bed in the office put me in shape for the evening's events.

The dinner featured roast suckling pig, chicken, carp, beef and ginger, sticky rice, and assorted hot sauces washed down with cold Thai beer and hot tea. Vang Pao made a short speech and a toast. He then presented me with a Hmong musket and necklace. My response was also brief. One and all enjoyed the dinner.

Then, we had *lamvong* dancing, the national Lao dance, which involves a slow revolving circle with parallel lines of females and males shuffling forward to a musical beat while using expressive hand gestures. No physical contact is made during the dance. Each dancer is a self-contained entity. The Hmong elders were pleased that by that point in our tour, Jonathan R., one or two of the other CIA officers, and I had become suitably proficient in the *lamvong* to be socially acceptable.

At around 9:00 P.M. the gathering thinned out, the Hmong ladies cleaned up the debris, and the hard-core drinking started. So did the war story exchanges. Vang Pao was particularly entertaining with his tales about life in the French Army fighting the Vietnamese. But as we all started to run down, I found myself talking to one of the Thai officers in close proximity to Vang Pao and R. The latter two had started a hot debate about something to do with what looked like Indian wrestling. The next thing I knew the six-foot-three R. was lined up with the five-foot-four Vang Pao in some sort of a wrestling face off. Before I could turn fully around—thud—Vang Pao and R. were on the floor, embraced in a catch-as-catch-can arm lock. Stunned by this unexpected development and not certain what the hell was going on, I noticed Vang Pao's bodyguards starting to move in from the other end of the hall. In a flash I hit the floor and like a wrestling referee tried to separate the two. Somehow I prevailed, and we all got up off the floor dusting off our clothes. The bodyguards were obviously pleased, R. was laughing, and Vang Pao was saying something that I understood as "Let's try again."

With that I closed down the evening by asking Vang Pao for a jeep to take me to where my bed was located. Vang Pao issued an order and two uniformed Hmong appeared and escorted me outside to a jeep. Vang Pao and I saluted each other; I entered the jeep and was driven to the king's house. One of the Hmong escorted me inside, showed me my room, told me how to handle the mosquito netting, showed me my bag, and departed. I fell into bed and was sleeping in a matter of seconds.

The next morning at dawn I awoke with the mother of all hangover headaches. I shaved, dressed, and got ready to leave. A jeep and new driver picked me up and took me to the Sky offices. Hot American coffee started my rehabilitation process.

R. entered looking like death warmed over. I asked him what that close encounter with Vang Pao was all about when we all ended up on the floor rooting like pigs in mud. R. smiled sheepishly and said he and Vang Pao were arguing about such dumb things as arm wrestling, Indian wrestling, and push-ups and that it had gotten comical. I said that kind of encounter should be avoided at all costs in the future. R. agreed.

Having heard our Volpar land, I knew it was time to move on. My stomach was not well, so a speedy retreat to Vientiane was high on my priority list. Looking around for Devlin, I realized I had not seen him since midway through the previous evening's fun. I asked where he was and was told he was flaked out on a bunk in the Sky area. I said we should move to Vang Pao's house and start our good-byes while someone got Devlin and brought him there.

Vang Pao greeted us graciously, but one could tell he, too, needed to recuperate. We kept the farewells appropriately short, and just as we prepared to head for the airplane, Devlin made his appearance. Vang Pao and I both noticed that he had a black eye, but neither said anything.

We were escorted to the airfield by Vang Pao and a few of his staff. At the foot of the stairs to the Volpar, Vang Pao and I shook hands, saluted each other, and said good-bye. With that, Larry and I were in the Volpar. In a few seconds we were taxiing down the runway headed for Vientiane. As we were flying home, I asked Larry above the roar of the engines what had happened to his eye. His response was that he had stumbled in the night, fallen, and gotten a shiner. This has remained just one more of the unresolved mysteries that one collects in the world of intelligence and its related paramilitary wars.

There were more *bacis* in the days that followed. Those in Vientiane were usually family affairs and appropriately staid. One in particular was noteworthy for the glimpse it provided into Lao customs and culture. General Ouan hosted a *baci* at his home. As the usual gifts of eggs and fruit were placed in the travelers' bowls set before Hazel, Suzanne, and me, Ouan presented me with a ceremonial Lao general's dress sword. As he did he said the sword was symbolic on two levels. One, it represented acknowledgment of the status I had acquired with FAR through my service in Laos. Equally important, it was supposed to enhance my ability to keep the evil spirits at bay. Ouan then said that according to Lao custom, when a blade is given as a gift, the receiver must give something of value in return to ensure that the blade would never be turned against its giver. A token transfer of a few Lao *kip*, Ouan said, would do the trick. I reached in my pocket and pulled out a wad of *kip*. Ouan daintily picked out one banknote—a total value perhaps five dollars—and said we had satisfied the requirements of Lao folklore.

Finally, the day came for us to leave Laos. We were booked on Royal Air Laos for the Vientiane–Bangkok journey. The usual airport farewell ceremony centering on the flow of champagne had been arranged. Clyde M., my deputy at the time, outdid himself on this occasion in showing his organizational skills, and the Lao turned out in droves, as did our friends in the diplomatic and business community. Hazel and Suzanne had lots of friends in Vientiane, so the traditional departure bash exceeded the norm.

When it came time to board the aircraft, General Oudone came to me and said, "We have arranged for the stewardess to escort Hazel and Suzanne on board. We would like you to lag behind by a few seconds."

With that, Hazel and Suzanne were taken to the airplane. Then, it became clear what was happening on this hot, sunny day in September 1968. Generals Ouan, Kouprasith, and Oudone, decked out in full dress uniforms and all medals on display, were going to escort me to the airplane. At the foot of the stairway to the aircraft, we stopped. Oudone shook my hand and saluted, then Kouprasith did the same, and finally Ouan, the senior man, shook my hand while slapping me gently on the back. He then saluted. I returned all salutes and scrambled up the gangway.

As I entered the cabin, the door banged shut. So did this chapter of my family's life in the gentle land of a million elephants. It was a sad occasion. We had enjoyed service in Laos and had made lasting friendships.

20

NEUTRALIZING THE VIETCONG

AS I once warned my staff in Berlin, "Vietnam is not a question of if, but of when." Now it was my turn. I would have much preferred an interim assignment of as much as a year in the United States so that I could provide a home for Hazel and schooling for Suzanne. I thought a tour as a student at the National War College would be a great way to prepare for an eventual assignment to Vietnam and give my family time to get settled in Washington. Unfortunately, every time I raised the War College idea with my superiors, they said that the demand for experienced station chiefs was too great to permit any of them to be sent to such schools.

I was not unfamiliar with Vietnam. During my tour in Laos, I had met Ambassador Ellsworth Bunker and General Abrams and had visited not only Saigon but some of the regional capitals. And I had read everything I could find about the military and political situation there. So, as I approached my briefings in Washington, I came with one burning question. Did the Vietcong Tet Offensive of January 31, 1968, represent an intelligence failure? Had we no penetration agents who might have given us advance warning?

Evidently, we had no such agents. Instead of a proactive attempt to reach out into the enemy's camp, read his intentions, and influence his conduct, we were mired in a reactive program of pacification, with a controversial operation called Phung Hoang at its heart. Phung Hoang was supposed to identify and neutralize Hanoi's fifth column within South Vietnam, that is, the political and administrative entities through which the Vietcong tried to control the populace of South Vietnam. The idea was that within each of South Vietnam's provinces and districts, there would be an intelligence and operations coordination center (PIOCC or DIOCC) where captured enemy documents would be read, prisoners interrogated, and dossiers maintained on all suspected members of the Vietcong infrastructure (VCI). Once a dossier became large or convincing enough, the individual would be targeted for arrest by the Vietnamese police, the military, or one of the provincial reconnnaissance units (PRU).

Phung Hoang had had its origin in November 1966 when the Vietnam Station, MACV J-2, and the Vietnamese national police cooperated to form a combined intelligence staff called CT-4. Its mission was the identification and neutralization of the Vietcong infrastructure in MR-4, which at that time corresponded roughly to Gia Dinh Province plus the Saigon–Cholon metropolitan area. Then, on December 20, 1967, Prime Minister Tran Van Khiem issued a letter of instruction calling for cooperation and coordination by all government of Vietnam (GVN) agencies in a program to neutralize the VCI. This letter gave the activity its legal designation of Phung Hoang, the name of a mythological animal that appears only during times of peace and prosperity. (Perhaps the prime minister believed that invoking such a potent symbol would bring about the desired consummation.) Finally, by July 1, 1968, with some nudging from Bill Colby, then chief of MACV / CORD, President Nguyen Van Thieu put his stamp of approval on the program. As I did not arrive in Saigon until December 1968, I was not the godfather of Phung Hoang (or Phoenix, to give it the name that the Americans hung on it), as some would have it.

I did not approve of it, either. Each of the DIOCCs, each of the PIOCCs, each of the PRUs, and each of the provincial interrogation centers (PICs) had its American advisor, a CIA case officer who, I thought, would be better employed in more traditional intelligence pursuits. According to figures I was given in Washington, the PICs were processing a total of twenty-five hundred Vietcong prisoners per month. If this was true, I thought, more operational leads and more intelligence should be coming out.

CIA officers who had worked on the program and who I was able to talk to in Washington said they found the activity repugnant. They felt that the dossiers were based on dubious information. And it was obvious that all too frequently, arrest efforts turned into firefights, and more so-called VCI were killed than detained for processing.

I raised these points in my farewell interview with Dick Helms and asked whether, if Phung Hoang must for some reason be allowed to continue, it could not at least be turned over to the U.S. Army for management.

Helms told me, "Ted, I agree we need to refocus CIA's role in Vietnam. Unfortunately, we can't do that on our own. We are not free agents. A shift in our Vietnam posture would require interdepartmental coordination."

Shortly after arriving in Vietnam in December 1968, I began a program that the Vietnamese eventually named *dai phong*. Its methodology was simple but effective. We would take a recently captured Vietcong agent whose cooperation we had obtained and put him at a police checkpoint on a major road leading into a population center like Saigon. Watching the crowd from a concealed spot, he would look for faces he might remember having seen, for example, at a training camp. Any suspects so identified would then be followed into town by a Vietnamese surveillance team. On several occasions, the *dai phong* program hit pay dirt, leading us to arms caches and clandestine meetings with other Vietcong agents.

In one case it led us to Huynh Van Trong, one of Thieu's assistants for political affairs. By the time we had developed a good counterintelligence case on him, it was still early in my stewardship of the Saigon Station, so I decided to brief Thieu on this personally. Thieu listened impassively to my presentation. When I finished, he said, "This is a serious matter. Your case is persuasive but it is not yet solid enough to stand up in court."

"That is true, sir," I agreed. "To make a case that will stand up in court, we will need further investigation by your Special Branch. I am here to ask for your concurrence."

Thieu nodded. "Proceed on this case in the manner you think best," he said. "I know you have Ambassador Bunker's confidence. If you decide Special Branch must arrest Trong, give me at least twenty-four hours advance notice."

After a moment's pause and picking his words carefully, Thieu continued. "If you and your people are right on this approach and it is handled well, it will benefit our friendship as well as our dialog. Should you prove to be wrong, we will both be embarrassed.

That, of course, can not be favorable to a continuing exchange of views."

I got the message. I was the new boy in town. This was a test case, and I was being given a free hand but was on notice that there would be a price to pay for failure. We didn't fail. By July 1969 the Special Branch, under the very able leadership of Colonel Nguyen Mau, had a solid case against Trong and his handler, Vu Ngoc Nha, who reported to the strategic intelligence unit of the Central Office for South Vietnam (COSVN), the command entity that ran Hanoi's war in the south. After giving Thieu his twenty-four hour alert, Special Branch rolled up a network of over a hundred people. Trong confessed, and the court convicted him.

When all the loose ends were tied up, Thieu sent me an oral message via General Tran Van Hai, the director general of national police: "My door is always open to you."

We never discussed the Trong case again, but Thieu was true to his word. Thereafter, whenever I needed to see him, there was no problem in gaining timely access.

In 1969 an alert South Vietnamese policeman in South Vietnam's Mekong Delta noticed that an individual passing through the checkpoint spoke with a Vietnamese accent that did not match the data on his identity document, which indicated he was born and lived in the delta. The policeman pulled his suspect out of the pedestrian flow.

The preliminary interrogation of the suspect by Vietnamese police and military personnel showed him to be intelligent, well educated, and self-assured. Suspecting that they had their hands on a high-level intelligence operative from the North Vietnamese *Cuc Nghien Cuu* (CNC), or Strategic Intelligence Service, the police quickly moved the man to Saigon where he was put into the National Interrogation Center (NIC). This installation was run by the South Vietnamese Central Intelligence Organization (CIO) with significant levels of advisory assistance from the CIA. It was the appropriate place to send the subject for further interrogation because the CIO was Saigon's agency for coordinating all activities dealing with the CNC.

Major Hong Gou Chung, the administrator of the NIC, contacted his senior American advisor and asked for assistance in establishing who the suspect was and what he represented. This request was brought to my attention, and I assigned an experienced intelligence operative with expertise in interrogation, counterintelligence, and the Soviet Union to the case.

Under this officer's direction and personal participation with the use of an interpreter, it was soon learned that the South Vietnamese had captured Tran Ngoc Hien, a CNC officer probably with the rank of colonel. We saw this as a potential gold mine of counterintelligence information and looked forward to filling the gaps in our knowledge of the CNC. We knew, for instance, that the CNC reported to the Armed Forces General Staff of the Ministry of National Defense in Hanoi and was responsible for strategic intelligence on South Vietnam, but we needed to know what independent networks it ran in South Vietnam, how it functioned through the CNC Strategic Intelligence Office (B-22) of COSVN, which ran the war for Hanoi, and how it clandestinely collected intelligence outside of Vietnam.

Hien was doing his best to deny us this information. Hoping that Hanoi would learn of his detention and take appropriate action to preserve other intelligence resources in South Vietnam that he might able to compromise, he stalled for time. He could, however, not clam up entirely if he wished to avoid being returned to the exclusive custody of the South Vietnamese, where despite heroic efforts he might have found himself obliged to be informative. Thus, as the psychological intensity of our interrogation stepped up, Hien would peel back levels of knowledge and tell us just enough to keep the game going.

At the same time, the wily Hien managed to shift the focus of the interrogation from intelligence to politics. It emerged that he was a brother of, and had had recent contact with, Tran Ngoc Chau, who at that time was representing Kien Hoa Province in the National Assembly, the South Vietnamese equivalent of the U.S. House of Representatives. These revelations caused a stir among the Vietnamese members of the interrogation team because, as Neil Sheehan pointed out in his book *A Bright Shining Lie: John Paul Vann and America in Vietnam* (New York: Random House, 1988), secret contacts between family members from opposing sides in the war, although common in South Vietnam, were also illegal.

General Nguyen Khac Binh, the head of CIO, was aware that Tran Ngoc Chau had incurred the displeasure of President Nguyen

Van Thieu by accusing his government of corruption, and he lost no time in getting this fragmentary and unconfirmed information to the presidential palace. There it was promptly brought to the president's attention by General Dang Van Quang, Thieu's national security advisor and overseer of South Vietnam's police, security, and intelligence agencies.

Realizing that Hien was stalling for time, we knew that the truth content in whatever he told us was unlikely to exceed 50 percent, and we did not want half-truths to reach President Thieu as facts rather than as what they actually were—halfway points in a complex interrogation. We told Binh and Quang, therefore, that clarifying Hien's story was not going to be an easy task and advised them to reserve judgment on Hien's reliability. I periodically briefed Ambassador Bunker on Hien's status and saw to it that a steady flow of cable traffic kept CIA Washington fully informed. One and all understood the effects the case could have on the South Vietnamese body politic. We also anticipated a heated reaction from the coterie of American admirers that had clustered around Chau ever since his days as province chief in Kien Hoa. Chief among these was the bombastic John Paul Vann, whose role in America's pacification programs had raised him to the status of Vietnam War folk hero.

The interrogating team eventually got a coherent, if not necessarily truthful, story from Hien about his contacts with Chau beginning in 1965, when the CNC allegedly dispatched him from Hanoi to see if Chau could be persuaded to serve as an agent of influence, as a channel to the Americans, and as a source of information on South Vietnamese political developments. This being their first encounter in many years, Hien said he devoted much of his time to assessing what changes time might have wrought in his brother's personality, ambition, and ego and to sizing up Chau's current status in the South Vietnamese power balance.

Hien's conclusion, he said, was that Chau was a Vietnamese nationalist. While still ambitious, Chau came across as pessimistic about his future, feeling his Army career to be at a dead end, and he destined to rise no higher in rank than colonel. According to Hien's story, he had offered to help advance Chau's career by putting him into a prestigious situation. Chau, he said, could be the key figure in setting up a meeting between Ambassador Lodge and Hien acting on behalf of Hanoi's puppet instrumentality, the National Liberation Front (NLF). Chau allegedly did not commit himself to do anything on this matter other than to think about it.

After the first meeting in 1965, Hien admitted to having met with Chau on several more occasions (three or four, as I recall). On one such occasion, Hien said he reverted to the question of Chau playing a role in setting up a channel between the Americans and the NLF but that Chau brushed the idea aside with the terse response that the Americans were not interested. Hien claimed Chau gave no explanation of how he had determined that this was the American position.

Just prior to South Vietnam's October 1967 elections, Hien and Chau supposedly met again. Chau, visibly concerned about his future, allegedly said he had decided to leave the military to run for the National Assembly from Kien Hoa province. In that delicate exchange of nuances for which the Vietnamese and their language are famous, Hien understood Chau to be asking for help, both in money and in votes from secret Vietcong cadres. There was not enough time, Hien said, to get Chau money, but he did report Chau's desire for help in getting out the vote. Hien claimed he did not know what, if anything, his superiors had done about it, but he added slyly it was interesting that Chau had won his National Assembly seat by a wide majority. His interrogators were left to draw whatever conclusions from this clever gambit that they wished.

A report on Hien's version of the Chau contacts was passed to Major Chung in accordance with NIC standard operating procedure for sharing data derived from interrogations conducted at the NIC. We know the report was quickly translated into Vietnamese and sent to Binh, Quang, and Thieu.

The Vietnamese questioned Chau. He admitted having met Hien once and having received Hien's probe about setting up a meeting with the Americans. He claimed to have reported this to the Americans with a view to helping them set up a dialog with the NLF and Hanoi but that nothing had come of it. Chau said he saw himself as having acted throughout this affair as a Vietnamese nationalist. He denied having violated any South Vietnamese laws.

Now the political nightmare started. Binh and Colonel Nguyen Mau, the head of the Special Branch of the national police, both asked me if it were true that Chau had worked under American direction to set up a dialog with the NLF or Hanoi. I said we would check our files. The result of this exercise was inconclusive. We found no evidence that Chau had ever acted under CIA control or direction to open a channel to the other side or that he had ever told us he had a brother who was a senior CNC cadre. Chau, however, had told several of his CIA contacts that members of his family were in North Vietnam.

The embassy did its own file check, and the results were the same. Ambassador Sam Berger, the deputy chief of mission, and Martin Herz, the head of the Political Section, told me they could find no information in their files to confirm Chau's claim of having worked with the Americans to open a channel to the other side.

With Ambassador Bunker's concurrence, we eventually gave Binh and Mau an oral report on our findings. We said that we had been unable to confirm Chau's claim of cooperation with the Americans on the Hien matter but that one CIA officer did recall a brief exchange of views with Chau on opening a link to the other side. Nothing had ever come of it, we said, and we denied knowing anything about any part Hien might have played in an attempt to set up a channel to the NLF or Hanoi.

By late 1969 it was becoming increasingly clear to all concerned that President Thieu intended to eliminate Chau as a dangerous political enemy. Both men were putting their own spins on the situation, Thieu maintaining he was merely upholding the rarely enforced law against holding secret communication with relatives on the other side and Chau telling his American friends that Thieu was out to destroy him because he had tried to help the Americans.

It was not long before Vann stopped me at a social event in Saigon and said that Chau was a great guy and that the embassy shouldn't let Thieu railroad him. I told Vann we couldn't find any support for Chau's claim he had been meeting with Hien under American guidance. Vann blustered and said he could vouch for Chau's statements.

"Great!" I said. "Pull your thoughts together on that matter, find any file data you have on it, and go and see Ambassadors Bunker and Berger or Colby so they can get a report on it to the GVN. Time is of the essence, and you should act sooner rather than later."

"I know it," he snapped, turning from me abruptly. I never heard anything further from Vann on this matter, which led me to conclude he could not back up his claim with a factual presentation capable of standing close scrutiny.

In January 1970, Ev Bumgartner, a pacification specialist who worked for Colby, moved Chau to a helicopter pad in Saigon. Vann picked him up there in his government-furnished chopper and moved him to the delta where, according to some accounts, he was billeted with an American official in Can Tho while preparing to flee the country. Later, Chau decided to face the music at home, and Vann flew him back to Saigon. In Saigon at one point, Chau was being given sanctuary by Keyes Beech, an Asian expert who had won numerous prestigious awards as a correspondent for the *Chicago Daily News.*

This latter development created an unexpected problem for me, for while Chau was in hiding at Beech's Saigon house at 10 Alexandre de Rhodes, I appeared there one day for a long-standing luncheon date. There was unusual activity and tension in the Beech household that day, and this bothered me. Beech seemed to want to badger me on a range of issues including the Chau case. In fact, at one point in the luncheon, Beech asked if I wanted to meet Chau.

I responded with an emphatic no, pointing out that the Chau case was exclusively a GVN affair and that its outcome depended entirely on how the Thieu government wanted to interpret existing South Vietnamese law. I stressed that my interest lay only in the counterintelligence side of the case and that I only wanted the CIA to get as much as it could out of Tran Ngoc Hien about the CNC. The CIA owed Chau nothing, I said. He had not been an agent, we had not guided his dialog with Hien, and as Chau had freewheeled on this matter, he had to be prepared to defend himself against President Thieu's interpretation of the law.

This did not please Beech, so I broke off the luncheon early and we parted company.

A few days later, Beech visited the embassy to talk separately with Ambassador Bunker and with me. In our session, Beech chided me for not doing more for Chau because, as he said, America "owed Chau something for his past services in the cause of American–Vietnamese cooperation." I told Beech I could not agree with his view. He then told me Chau had been at his house when we last met for lunch.

At that, I blew up and said I felt that Beech had betrayed my trust. By having Chau at his residence while I was there, it looked like Beech was setting me up for a problem with the GVN, the media, and Chau. I made no bones about the fact this was not what I expected from a friend. There was an exchange of incivilities, which I'm sure he eventually came to regret as much as I did, and we terminated our meeting. For years after that, our relationship was not what it had been.

On February 25, 1970, a military field court tried Chau in absentia, sentencing him to twenty years in prison. He was arrested the next day at the National Assembly building in Saigon in a dramatic show of force by GVN authorities. He served time in South Vietnamese jails, was released, and was then rearrested by the North Vietnamese after they occupied Saigon. Beech, in an acrimonious conversation with me some time after 1975, said he felt Chau should have been evacuated from Saigon by the CIA when we lost the war. My retort that other Vietnamese were more deserving of our assistance than Chau fell on deaf ears.

In time we did obtain more of what we wanted from Hien on the CNC. The value of this achievement was outweighed, however, by the political trauma that the case caused for President Thieu, Ambassador Bunker, and Chau himself. Thieu, because of the way he mishandled the political side of this case, was partly to blame for it. He was not alone, however, for several Americans, believing in their arrogance that only they knew what was right or wrong for Vietnam, tried to apply a political solution to this matter. This group acted capriciously and in violation of their public trust as U.S. government officials.

Chau and Hien both somehow survived their ordeals. Chau is now in the United States, and Hien, if he is still alive, is somewhere in Vietnam. Perhaps some day the brothers will collaborate on a book. It would make interesting reading.

21

A SUPERNATURAL AGENT
OF INFLUENCE

INTELLIGENCE services like to have agents of influence, individuals or organizations in a position to exert influence over government policy. General Tran Van Don would have been an ideal one, but he had a fatal flaw: He was believed to have been the man who gave the order to kill President Ngo Dinh Diem. So, the word was "hands off!" Tran Van Don was often to be found at journalists' parties, and in such neutral venues, I could chat with him to elicit information or cross-check facts. On occasion we would also have a quiet lunch at my residence in order to defuse a Saigon rumor or two. But farther than that I did not want to go.

Thanks in part to Tran Van Don, I was able one day to employ a supernatural agent of influence on behalf of MACV. The occasion was the launching (or more accurately, the nonlaunching) of Lam Son 719, an Army of the Republic of [South] Vietnam (ARVN) spoiling operation designed to tear up North Vietnamese infiltration routes in Laos west of the Demilitarized Zone. Its main axis of attack was to be along Route 9, its ultimate objective was Tchepone in Laos, and the period designated for its completion was January through May 1971. Lieutenant General Hoang Xuan Lam, the respected MR-1 commander who was to lead the operation, had at his disposal the First Infantry Division, the First Airborne Division, the First Ranger Group, and the First Armored Brigade. Intelligence and logistical support were to be provided by the Americans.

MACV hoped for good things from Operation Lam Son 719. Planners there felt that if ARVN could act within the designated time frame and stay in Tchepone long enough to do real damage to the NVA's infiltration facilities, it could buy Saigon about nine to twelve months of additional time to prepare in an orderly manner for a diminished American role in combat operations.

But doubts soon arose as to ARVN's willingness or ability to move promptly. One launch date after another was set, but to the exasperation of all concerned, each launch was aborted at the last minute. At one of our regular meetings in Ambassador Bunker's office, General Abrams vented his frustration.

"Damn these cancellations!" he exploded. "They're costing us the element of surprise. What's going on? We've asked ARVN. They've given us answers, but the answers don't make sense."

The general asked if I could discover the true reason for the delays. Drawing on a few well-placed sources, I was able to tell Ambassador Bunker and General Abrams within a matter of hours that the launch dates selected thus far for Operation Lam Son 719 had been declared by President Thieu to be "inauspicious."

"What the hell does that mean?" Abrams wanted to know.

"I think it means," I said, "that Thieu's astrologer told him the stars weren't properly aligned for such an undertaking."

A stunned silence was finally broken with a mild comment from Bunker to the effect that incidents like this underscored Vietnamese–American cultural differences and complicated the running of the war. Abrams then asked half-seriously, "Can't we influence the astrologer?"

"No guarantees," I told him, "but I'll look into it."

As luck would have it, MR-3 commander Lieutenant General Do Cao Tri was in Saigon that day to review operations with General Cao Van Vien, chairman of the South Vietnamese general staff, and had set aside a short block of time for a chat with me at my residence. Tri had originally been introduced to me by Robert Shaplen of the *New Yorker* magazine and again by retired U.S. Army major general Charles Timmes, and his opinion of my trustworthiness was further enhanced by the knowledge that Tran Van Don was willing to share confidences with me. As a result we had developed a mutually beneficial relationship. Tri valued our intelligence input into his operational planning, which was done primarily through our base in Bien Hoa, and we in turn could sometimes use him as a channel for messages to the top South Vietnamese military brass.

On this occasion, coincidentally, Tri wanted to talk about

Operation Lam Son 719. Knowing of my previous service in Laos, he was full of questions about terrain, weather, and the population in the Tchepone area. Finally, he asked the key question: "How is planning proceeding?"

"Planning is fine," I told him. "It's in the execution that we're having problems. Every time a date is set, something happens to postpone it."

"Lam is being his usual cautious self," Tri said. Tri was a swashbuckling combat leader who fancied himself the Vietnamese George Patton. Overcaution was a sin he would never be guilty of.

"Lam's in the clear on this one," I replied. "It's Thieu and his astrologer who are causing the problem."

Tri was already one jump ahead of me. "Have you met the astrologer?" he asked.

"No, and I'd like to have a professional talk with him. I think I could show him how to align his stars and dates with MACV'S plans."

"This could be done," Tri said, "for just a small consultation fee."

"If it doesn't break the bank," I told him, "I can call my office and a courier will be here in minutes with the money."

"Only a modest amount," Tri assured me, "and well within my own means. All I need from you are the launch dates that will make you happy."

I recited the dates that Abrams had given me, and Tri took his leave saying I would hear from him by the next day at the latest.

The same evening I had a call from one of Tri's staff, who said the general had accepted my invitation for lunch on February 8, 1971. The next morning a sensitive intelligence source in the presidential palace provided us with confirmatory information. I told Ambassador Bunker and General Abrams, therefore, that Thieu and his astrologer had selected February 8 as an appropriate date for launching Lam Son 719 into Laos. And so they had. ARVN made its move on February 8, reaching Tchepone with moderately satisfactory results.

Abrams said to me, "Remind me never to play poker with you. You can probably always fill an inside straight."

"How do you like the astrology business?" Bunker asked.

"Well enough," I replied, "as long as I have my crystal ball."

I lost my crystal ball just two weeks later. On February 23, 1971, General Do Cao Tri was killed in a helicopter crash in Tay Ninh Province while supervising a major operation in the so-called Fishhook area along the South Vietnamese–Cambodian border. Fortunately, I was never again required to dabble in the occult.

22

TERMINATION WITH
EXTREME PREJUDICE

SATURDAY, June 21, 1969, began like any normal Saigon workday. It was not to end that way.

The first task facing me that morning was to review what had been happening to the station during the past two days. There was nothing unusual about this. I often had to be away from my office for one reason or another: visits to other parts of Vietnam, briefings of congressional delegations, attendance at MACV meetings, and the like. On such occasions I could always be sure my deputy, Joe Lazarsky, the station executive officer, Vince Lockhart, and my secretary, Dana Meigs, would pick up the slack. I expected no surprises on this day.

The incoming and outgoing cable boards with their two-day accumulations had first claim on my attention. Here were the matters that the originators, at least, considered the most urgent: orders and demands from headquarters, inquiries from other stations, requests for guidance or support from my regional offices, and whatever replies the responsible station officers might already have sent. If any of these balls had been dropped, the cable boards would be quick to tell me so. All was well, they assured me, as I riffled through the back traffic; all was well, that is, until I came upon a series of cables from my old friend from Berlin and Miami days, "Juan."

Juan was cabling from his post in the Nha Trang regional office, and he was unhappy. The burden of his complaint, couched in increasingly anguished terms, was that he had received no reply to a request of his for a detailed name trace on a South Vietnamese national who was working for a military unit in some intelligence capacity.

What, I wondered, had gotten Juan so agitated? Running a name trace for a fraternal American intelligence service was no big deal. It was a routine event provided for by Director of Central Intelligence Directives (DCID) coordination procedures to safeguard against the security breaches that are likely to occur whenever an agent tries to work simultaneously for more than one American intelligence agency.

Looking again at this sheaf of papers, I noticed that a key message seemed to be missing. I got up from my desk and walked across the front-office suite to the room occupied by Navy captain Bruce Scrymgeour and Army lieutenant colonel Clement Enking. Both of these men were CIA employees, doing their reserve time and using their reserve rank as cover for their posting to Vietnam. They had among their duties the management of the DCID coordination process with the military. This put them in regular contact with the 525th Military Intelligence Group, which was running various clandestine operations requiring prior coordination with the station.

I asked Enking what was happening to the military in Nha Trang and why Juan was so steamed up about it.

"The Fifth Special Forces Group thinks one of its Vietnamese interpreters or legmen might be a Vietcong agent," Enking explained. "They came here on ten June and asked for an isolated holding area where they could put him. Bruce and I told them we couldn't help. CIA has no islands where you can hold people like that. After talking to us in Saigon, the Special Forces types in Nha Trang went to see Juan. He offered to help them evaluate the case."

"If we can help, we should," I said. "If Special Forces want our assistance in turning a VC suspect over to the South Vietnamese Military Security Service or Police Special Branch, they should have it. That's where a case like that would belong. But we don't coordinate on Special Forces' intelligence operations. The DCIDs don't cover them. If Special Forces are running agents, MACV J-2 is responsible. Not us."

"I guess we got Juan into this unnecessarily," Enking said. "I'll cut it off now."

"Good," I said.

As I left Enking's office, I found Vince Lockhart waiting for me. "Did Dean Almy talk to you about the Special Forces case?" he asked.

"No," I told him.

"Well, he was in here after the ROIC meeting late on the nineteenth and wanted to chat. You were tied up with one of the other ROICs, so Almy left."

It was the meeting of the five regional officers in charge (ROICs), in-country CIA chiefs based in Da Nang, Nha Trang, Bien Hoa, Can Tho, and Saigon, that had kept me away from the paper flow for two days. We held these get-togethers about once a month. On the first day, in the free-and-easy exchange that was characteristic of a ROIC meeting, many a collection problem was identified and many a solution hammered out. There was a sharing of experience gained and lessons learned as we gradually evolved a doctrine for recruitment of agents within the Vietcong infrastructure and maintaining them in place. Issues of common concern, such as liaison with the Vietnamese military and police forces, were examined, logistics support was discussed, and personnel trends were reviewed. The second day was spent in one-on-one sessions with each ROIC, mostly discussing personnel matters such as rotation and replacement. The price I had to pay for these benefits—a two-day sacrifice of hands-on management of the station—I regarded as well spent.

Lockhart continued. "At dinner at your house that evening, Almy told me that Juan hadn't yet learned how to say no to the odd requests they frequently get in Nha Trang from the military."

I had been back in my own office no more than a minute or two when Dana entered with a white envelope. "Dean Almy left this with me late on the nineteenth," she said. "I told him you would get it promptly on the twentieth, but it got attached to some other papers, and I forgot about it. When I heard you discussing Nha Trang with Enking and Vince, I started searching for it. Here it is."

I found in the envelope a high-precedence Nha Trang cable. It was the puzzle's missing piece. Set in the context of the preceding and following traffic, it told me that Special Forces seemed to be on the verge of trying to solve their problem with their real or imagined Vietcong agent by killing him.

To be sure, we were in a war zone, and soldiers do sometimes kill the enemy in situations where life or death judgments have to be made in split seconds. But Nha Trang was not the scene of a close-in firefight, and consequently no Special Forces team there had any excuse for arrogating to itself the multiple roles of judge, jury, prosecutor, and appellate body. This could not be allowed to happen, and there was no time to lose.

I quickly sent Nha Trang an immediate-precedence cable. I don't remember its exact wording but am satisfied to quote a version of it that has appeared in print[1] and faithfully reproduces the essence of my message:

> 1. ADVISE SPECIAL FORCES WE HAVE NO CI INTEREST IN THE REFERENCE CASE.
> 2. CONTACT MAJOR CREW AS SOON AS POSSIBLE AND TELL HIM THIS IS NO SOLUTION TO THE PROBLEM, THAT IT IS IM-MORAL AND HAS THE HIGHEST FLAP POTENTIAL.
> 3. UNLESS YOU CAN GET HIS ASSURANCE NOTHING WILL HAPPEN TO THIS AGENT AS OF MINE AND YOUR CABLE, THEN WE WILL HAVE NO ALTERNATIVE BUT TO BRING IT TO THE AT-TENTION OF THE COMMAND LEVELS IN MACV INCLUDING GENERAL ABRAMS AND AMBASSADOR BUNKER.

As soon as the cable was on its way, I put in a secure telephone call to Dean Almy in Nha Trang. I gave him the gist of the cable he was about to get and asked him as soon as we got off the line to have Special Forces stand by to receive my message. Dean said he understood and would act at once.

I knew I had no authority to order Special Forces to stop what military commanders called a tactical intelligence operation; however, some Special Forces officers and senior NCOs knew me or of me from Cuban operations, or more recently from activities in Laos or Vietnam. They regarded me, according to what feedback I had acquired over the years, as a no-nonsense senior officer who did what he said he would do. I believed they would interpret my message to Nha Trang as a shot across their bow. If they then refused to heave to, I had no choice but to spell out, first to Ambassador Bunker, and with his concurrence to General Abrams, my concerns that a tactical-level military-intelligence operation appeared to be headed for inevitable disaster.

To prepare for that eventuality, I needed a firmer grasp of the chronology of events. I called for Vince Lockhart and Joe Lazarsky. Vince appeared first, and I asked him to find Scrymgeour without delay. "Once Bruce is in the office," I said, "I want a quick but detailed oral briefing on the unfolding of the Nha Trang Special Forces case."

As Vince hurried out the door, Lazarsky came in. I showed Joe the bundle of cables from Nha Trang and the message I had just sent out.

"I've seen some of that," Joe said. "Not all. And what I did look at didn't seem to call for action on my part because it looked like Nha Trang and Scrymgeour and Enking had this item under control."

Joe recalled that a couple of days earlier, he had seen two Special Forces types coming in to see Scrymgeour and Enking. Joe had asked Enking later what the field soldiers wanted. A CIA-controlled island where they could park a suspected Vietcong agent for a year or two, Enking had said. Scrymgeour had then quickly followed up by saying they had told the Special Forces types that the CIA had no such island. Joe had chuckled and gone on to do something else.

"Joe, old buddy," I said, "what I smell now is a small brushfire. If we put it out, we'll save those guys from getting burned. If Special Forces won't listen or it's too late, we've got a barnburner."

Lockhart, Scrymgeour, and Enking now joined Lazarsky and me in my office. To put everyone in the picture, I reviewed the day's events thus far. Then, I asked for a rundown of our conversation with the Special Forces personnel.

Enking began. The soldiers had said they needed help in dealing with a possible security threat. They produced two photographs, one of them an ID photo of Thai Khac Chuyen, a Vietnamese national employed by Special Forces as an interpreter, and the other a captured photo of an unidentified Vietcong soldier. The similarities were striking and disturbing, they said. Enking and Scrymgeour compared the two photographs, agreed there were similarities, but were unable to say with certainty whether they were of one and the same man.

Special Forces were apparently equally undecided. What he wanted, Major Crew had said, was to interrogate the suspect, polygraph him, and put him into some isolated CIA facility.

Scrymgeour chimed in to say that the two Special Forces types had been told the CIA had no facilities for doing what Special Forces wanted. The Special Forces types then left.

Enking continued with his report. Lieutenant Colonel Weil had come to see him two days later, June 12, to say Special Forces were still having problems with Chuyen. Enking said he had told him,

"Why not turn the guy over to the MSS [South Vietnamese Military Security Service]? Or just free him? Because you aren't getting anywhere in terms of clarifying whether you have a double agent operation or a case of mistaken identity."

Enking had subsequently run traces on Chuyen and sent a cable to Nha Trang saying Chuyen had worked for various military units since 1960. He had also suggested that Nha Trang see if they could give Special Forces any tips on how to deal with possible double agent operations. This had resulted in some dialog in Nha Trang between Juan and Special Forces. It was now obvious, however, that Special Forces were marching to their own drumbeat and not paying any attention to anything else that was being said. Sensing this, Juan had asked for file checks on other aspects of Chuyen's life story that were not known when Enking had done his file searches.

"Okay," I said. "This is the first time we've had an operational exchange with Special Forces, at least since I've been here, so I don't intend to second-guess anyone. The DCIDs don't give us any responsibility for coordinating on Special Forces' operations. In fact, the agreement that McCone made with Secretary McNamara specified that Special Forces would receive no more guidance or logistical support from CIA. Still, it's hard to convince people the umbilical cord has been cut. Especially the media. So from now on let's keep Special Forces at arm's length."

Shortly after that, a cable came in from Nha Trang. According to Special Forces, Chuyen had been dispatched on a mission to Cambodia. I read that message to mean one of two things. Most probably, Special Forces had already done something stupid. Alternatively, they were going to do some dumb thing and would not be waved off by what they saw as CIA interference.

Time was of the essence. I sent Nha Trang an immediate cable, the gist of which was as follows:

TELL MAJOR CREW TO UTILIZE HIS EMERGENCY COMMUNICATIONS PLAN AND RECALL THE AGENT. LET US KNOW WHEN THAT IS DONE AND WHEN CHUYEN IS EXPECTED TO BE BACK IN SPECIAL FORCES CONTROL.

The response to that rocket was devastating. Chuyen, it said, was on a mission in which Special Forces couldn't contact him. This to me was a clear sign that Special Forces had done something un-ethical. No one was sending anyone into Cambodia those days without an emergency recall plan. High-risk situations could develop there overnight. Any of the border areas could be selected with little warning for B-52 carpet bombing. By telling us they had no recall plan, Special Forces were either lying to us or admitting to having concocted an incompetent operation. In either case, it was bad news.

I now had no choice but to unload the problem onto others. I picked up the telephone, called Eva Kim, Ambassador Bunker's secretary, and said, "I need to see the ambassador urgently."

These were words I seldom used, and Eva reacted accordingly. "The ambassador will see you as soon as you appear at his office," she said. With that, I was out my door and down the stairs to the third floor and Bunker's office. True to her word, as soon as I arrived, Eva ushered me into Bunker's office.

Bunker and I worked well together. I admired him for his professionalism and his courteous and dignified demeanor, and I was impressed by his seemingly inexhaustible store of off-color limericks. He was the glue that kept the country team together, working in a true spirit of cooperation.

I put the key points of my concerns to the ambassador quite bluntly. I said my responsibility for coordinating the clandestine intelligence operations of the American intelligence community in Vietnam did not cover the tactical intelligence operations of military units like Special Forces. Despite that, Special Forces had contacted my staff on June 10 for advice and assistance on a possible double agent case involving a South Vietnamese national. We had been unable to provide the asked-for assistance, which had been a holding facility for the agent in some remote location somewhere in the world. We had given Special Forces the results of our file traces on the Vietnamese national. CIA officers in Nha Trang had then continued to discuss the case with Special Forces beyond the point that I would consider appropriate. This exchange, when it came to my attention, suggested that Special Forces were moving in a direction that would result in the improper death of the agent. In my view this was both immoral and illegal. Owing to the pressure of time, I had then exceeded my writ and told Special Forces to stop the operation they had planned. I had made it clear that if they did not, my action would be to bring the matter to the ambassador's and General Abrams's attention. Special Forces gave me a response that was utter nonsense. They said the agent had been sent to Cambodia and could not be recalled. My view was that either they had killed the agent or were about to do so. I therefore felt it incumbent on me to report the situation to the ambassador and to recommend first that I brief General Abrams on these developments and then that we defer to Abrams's judgment on how to proceed with what could be a violation of the Uniform Code of Military Justice.

Ambassador Bunker listened patiently to my presentation. "Well, Ted," he said when I had finished, "this is clearly a problem for MACV. CIA has done all it could, given its limited room for maneuver. It's now a military command matter, and Abe is the man to sort it out. Please get in touch with him as soon as possible."

Returning to my office, I called Abrams on the secure telephone. In a matter of seconds he was on the line. I told him, "A politically sticky problem has come up. It has been reviewed with Bunker in the past few minutes, and I now need to fill you in on this development. When can I come by for a fifteen-minute review of the bidding?"

Abrams had a finely developed appreciation for both the intelligence process and the utility of the end product. Sensing my urgency, he said, "Ted, I need to clean up a few tactical combat loose ends. Can you come to my quarters a little later?"

A time was agreed upon, and our telephone conversation was over.

The next step was to send another cable to Nha Trang. I asked them to write up as soon as possible a detailed chronology of their talks with Special Forces on the Chuyen case and to have Juan bring it to Saigon. I then briefed Lazarsky and Lockhart on my talk with Bunker, the telephone call to Abrams, and my latest message to Nha Trang. With that done, I organized my notes for the Abrams meeting.

After dinner I went to MACV and General Abrams's quarters. One of his aides showed me in to where Abrams was sitting, smoking a cigar, and listening with pleasure to the sounds of some classical symphony that I did not recognize. Abrams motioned me to sit down. "Ted," he said, "experience tells me intelligence chiefs come to field commanders at odd hours with either a gold mine of new data or a turkey. From my reading of the tea leaves, the odds favor your carrying a turkey. Which is it?"

"Abe, this is the season for turkeys," I said, proceeding then to outline the Chuyen case in the same manner as I had a few hours earlier to Bunker. Abrams listened without interrupting.

"What is your best estimate?" he asked when I had finished. "Is the Vietnamese dead or alive?"

"My hope is he is alive," I answered, "and that with prompt action we can keep him that way. But, given the responses we have gotten from Special Forces, all the indicators suggest he is dead. I can't prove that, but it's my best hypothesis."

"Damn!" was the reply. "Ted, starting when we first met in Laos, and continuing with our work together here in Vietnam, I have developed a great deal of respect for your analytical skills. This is one time I hope you are wrong. With My Lai[2] on the record books, we have to make certain our conduct since then is above reproach."

Abrams paused for a few seconds of reflection. He then said, "Colonel Rheault is a first-rate officer. We'll get in touch with him and sort this out. I will let you and Ambassador Bunker know how this turns out."

Following the June 23 meeting of the Mission Council, Ambassador Bunker asked Abrams and me to join him in his office for a minute. Once there, Abrams said, "Mr. Ambassador, Ted and I have talked about this Green Beret matter. After that I had Colonel Rheault come down from Nha Trang to talk to General Potts, MACV J-2. He also met with me. Rheault is a good man. He is on track to be a general. In response to my question, Rheault assured me the Vietnamese is on a mission. I am not entirely comfortable with that, but his assurances have been accepted. Let's see if this agent returns."

As Abrams and I walked toward the elevators, he said, "Ted, this type of case is tough. I have to accept Colonel Rheault's word. He has a fine record."

For a whole week I was allowed to forget the Chuyen case and concentrate on other matters. Then, the Jack popped out of the box. On June 30, Sergeant Alvin Smith of the Fifth Special Forces Group walked into the CIA office in Nha Trang, saying he feared for his life, expecting to be killed by his superiors. On June 20 Captain Robert Marasco had killed a Vietnamese employee named Thai

Khac Chuyen whom the officers suspected of being a Vietcong agent. Smith, who had been Chuyen's handler, had opposed the killing, and Marasco and his associates, fearing that Smith would reveal the murder, were going to kill Smith before he could blow the whistle. Smith had come to the CIA seeking asylum, as he knew the agency had been opposed to the killing of Chuyen.

The CIA officers in Nha Trang who talked with Smith found him agitated but lucid. With the basic points of Smith's story in hand and convinced that the sergeant was rational, Nha Trang sent a high-precedence message to Saigon outlining the situation they had on their hands.

I picked up a secure telephone and called General Abrams. My message was brief and to the point. I needed to get the sergeant into a nonthreatening military environment as soon as possible. Was there a Criminal Investigation Division (CID) or military police (MP) unit that could take the sergeant off our hands? What did Abrams want done on this case?

Abrams said, "Please hold the sergeant at your offices until I can arrange to have him picked up and brought to Saigon. Bill Potts, MACV J-2, will be handling this matter for me, so work with him on this."

By July 1, Smith was back in military channels. Meanwhile, CIA headquarters had its own investigation to make. While in our offices in Nha Trang, Smith had said that he had once worked for the CIA in the Middle East. As he had offered no further details, I assumed he had been seconded to the CIA for some special task, but I suggested in a cable to Washington that the point merited a records check.

When General Potts asked if the two CID warrant officers who were handling the investigation into Thai Khac Chuyen's possible murder could obtain a statement in Nha Trang from Juan, I saw no reason to object, this being merely a preliminary investigation with no linkage to any possible subsequent court martial. CIA headquarters agreed that we should be cooperative. Juan was therefore interviewed in Nha Trang on July 8 by Warrant Officers Robert Bidwell and Frank Bourland, giving them an oral account of events as he recalled them.

Our next exposure to the CID investigation came when General Potts asked if I could come out to MACV headquarters with

Lieutenant Colonel Enking to discuss with him and General Townsend various aspects of the Chuyen case. Again, as this was the investigative phase of the case, we agreed to a July 13 meeting. The two generals asked a series of questions about why we had suspected Chuyen had been or would be killed, what we and Special Forces had said to each other, and how the case had come to our attention.

Whether by chance or otherwise, it was about then that Warrant Officers Bidwell and Bourland entered the room. The two warrant officers were introduced to us, and General Potts asked them how far they had gotten with their preliminary investigation. Two important points emerged. One was that Warrant Officer Edward Boyle had admitted Chuyen had been killed; while this was progress, said the investigators, Boyle did not actually see the murder so his account was circumstantial evidence. The other point was that Colonel Rheault was not being cooperative.

One of the warrant officers then turned and faced Enking and me directly. He said, "Based on the questioning thus far, an allegation has been made that CIA officers in Saigon and Nha Trang encouraged the killing of Chuyen. Could that be true? Do you have any comment on that?"

So, this was a trap after all, I thought. Before I could answer, Enking preempted me. "I can't answer all of your questions," he said. "What I can say is I talked to Major Crew in Saigon on ten June. The major outlined the problem that Special Forces were having with an agent. He wanted help of a type CIA could not provide, holding the agent for an undetermined period of time at an isolated location. I told Crew that was not in the cards. We then discussed other options: turning the agent over to the MSS, letting the agent go, and giving him make-work tasks. None of this met the Special Forces' needs as they saw them. As we continued to talk, Major Crew floated the idea of assassination. My associate Captain Scrymgeour and I said assassination was out. No one could approve that. Then, in a joking, offhand way, I did say such action might be the most efficient course to take. That was nothing other than a flip comment."

Before I could say that Colonel Enking had just broken some new ground, which I intended to explore with him, one of the warrant officers broke the silence instead. "When can we take a formal statement from you and Colonel Enking? Perhaps now."

My response was curt. "We did not come here to be interviewed. In addition, I am not within the scope of your jurisdiction. Excuse us, gentlemen, our visit is at an end."

The warrant officer hung tough. He said, "Perhaps I can't interview you, but the gentleman next to you is in uniform and is within my jurisdiction. We will certainly interview him."

Once back at the embassy, I convened a meeting with Lazarsky and Lockhart and asked Enking to outline his part of the MACV meeting. When we started to break up, Enking sheepishly reminded me he was scheduled to leave the country for family visitation that evening. I told him to go to his quarters, pack, and keep moving toward his normal departure.

The day after Enking left Vietnam, the two warrant officer investigators appeared at our office. When they were told Enking was no longer in country, it was clear they were disappointed. They saw this as some diabolical ploy by the CIA to hinder their investigation rather than what it was, a routine family visit.

A day or two after the MACV meeting, Bunker was hosting one of the usual Mission Council luncheons at his residence. Abrams and I arrived almost simultaneously. We exchanged greetings, ordered our drinks, and stepped off to the side to await the others. Abrams said, "I gather you had a minor dustup with the CID investigators at MACV the other day."

"No," I said, "it was no dustup. Essentially I don't like surprises, either in intelligence or investigations. In addition, when it comes to providing testimony, there are so many issues involved from CIA's point of view, starting with the protection of sources and methods, that on a matter like giving testimony, I am not a free agent. This is something I have to coordinate in advance with Washington to get both their authority and guidance. Because of that, the CID approach was a nonstarter, particularly since I don't fall under the jurisdiction of the UCMJ [Uniform Code of Military Justice]."

Abrams said, "I understand. Bill Potts does not want a misunderstanding to develop out of that session, for he tells me cooperation between his people and yours is first-rate. We want to keep it that way. Potts had no idea the CID people were going to act as they did."

During lunch, in the usual exchange of views, Abrams said CID was investigating the Green Beret case as a prelude to a command decision about whether an Article 32 hearing (the military equivalent of a grand jury) was in order. He ended by saying he was both puzzled and disappointed by Colonel Rheault's behavior. No one asked him to elaborate. I volunteered no comments, and no one expected any. As the luncheon ended, Bill Colby, who was then working for Abrams as deputy for civic operations and revolutionary development support (DEPCORDS) and had the rank of ambassador, said to me, "You have handled the Green Beret case just right."

During the next month, the CID completed its investigative report, seven defendants headed by Colonel Rheault were put into custody at Long Binh Jail in MR-3, civilian defense lawyers began to arrive, and MACV decided to proceed with an Article 32 hearing starting July 31 at Long Binh.

Contrary to MACV's desire to keep the case under security wraps, the defense team saw that its only hope of keeping the defendants out of prison was to arouse the sympathies of the American public. Information about the case therefore began to leak to the American press corps in Saigon, touching off a feeding frenzy as each print or television journalist looked for his special angle. A great deal of nonsense appeared in print along with a small leavening of truth and one significant revelation: The Green Beret defense was based in large part on a claim that the CIA had told Special Forces, "Terminate him with extreme prejudice." This, according to what was attributed to the Green Beret attorneys, meant, Kill him.

The expression "terminate with extreme prejudice" is not, and has never been, in the CIA phrase book. "Terminate" does appear there. It means to sever the employer–employee relationship. "Terminate with prejudice" also appears there. It means to deny to an unsatisfactory employee the benefits that he could have earned through honorable service. "Terminate with extreme prejudice" is the invention of a journalist or novelist. I could not be certain, however, that Juan had not used it. To ease my mind, I arranged for him to come to Saigon with his boss, Dean Almy.

While that was in motion, a second piece of garbage floated to the top of the disinformation stream being generated by leaks to the media, primarily from the team of defense lawyers. Its centerpiece was that Juan had told Major Crew that I would not object to Chuyen's disappearance as I had been responsible for 250 political killings in Laos.

I could not conceive that Juan had said such a thing. On the face of it, the charge was absurd. CIA officers in Laos were planners, co-ordinators, logisticians, trainers, and advisers, but not combat leaders. There was no frame of reference in which 250 political killings could have taken place on my orders. Furthermore, I could see no reason why Juan should have wished to wound me. But, even assuming that he had deliberately tried to blacken my name, why should he have chosen Laos as the venue of my alleged crime? Juan had not served in Laos and had no first-hand knowledge of the war there. If he had wanted to concoct something credible, one would think he would have set his fabrication in Berlin or Miami where we had served together.

When Almy, Juan,[3] and I met in my office in Saigon, my first order of business was to address the "terminate with extreme prejudice" canard. Both denied they had used the expression in their conversations with the Green Berets. In fact, they had never heard it before. It was clear that on this point we were being victimized by those who had their own axes to grind and who didn't care if a steel splinter or two flew into the CIA's eyes.

I then asked Juan directly, "Did you tell Major Crew I was responsible for 250 political deaths in Laos?"

"Ted, I never told Major Crew anything like that," he answered.

Juan and I had had encounters in the past under circumstances that must have been most unpleasant for him, if not actually embarrassing. He had always owned up to his transgressions, so I knew what truth under pressure sounded like. I wasn't hearing it in full-bodied tones now. I probed further on this matter, but all my inquiries elicited the same basic response: Juan held to his position that he had not said what Crew had attributed to him. Finally, I decided I had to accept Juan's word; like Abrams in his exchange with Rheault, lacking any hard evidence to the contrary, I had to put my trust in my subordinate's integrity.

Later that same day, when I talked with Almy further about what had happened and where this Chuyen incident was heading, I could see that Dean was less than pleased with Juan's performance on this case. He also appeared to have some reservation about Juan's candor in answering my questions on the alleged Laos remarks.

In my cables to headquarters over the next few days, I made it plain that Juan was going to have to make some sort of an appearance at the Article 32 hearings if the case was to move forward and that both he and the station needed legal assistance. The complexities of the case were exceeding the station's knowledge of military law, I wrote. It would be most helpful, I suggested, particularly to Juan, if the agency would retain an expert on the Uniform Code of Military Justice and fly him to Vietnam. My request was under consideration, I was told.

Juan was scheduled to appear before the Article 32 hearing at Long Binh on August 20. We went out there together, and I sat with him in an anteroom while he waited to be called. For the hundredth time I reviewed with him the need to give clear, short, truthful answers. If some of those civilian defense attorneys such as Henry Rothblatt became abusive, I told him, he should seek an intervention from the presiding officer. I stressed again and again that while this case had turned into an administrative nightmare for him and a public relations disaster for the CIA, the worst thing he could do was to not tell the truth. That part of the briefing Juan adhered to with great tenacity.

He was in the hearing room for hours, and came out exhausted. We quickly exited the Long Binh chapel area, drove to a chopper pad, and returned to Saigon. Back in my office I had Juan outline the points that had been covered in the day's questioning. It turned out to be quite a list. On the positive side, Juan had put the details of the Chuyen case, as far as they were known to the Saigon Station, accurately into the record. He had also testified that the CIA had neither command nor control over Special Forces operations, that the CIA had no coordination authority over Special Forces intelligence operations, that he had advised Special Forces not to engage in assassination and that it was better to let Chuyen go free, and that Almy had also advised the Special Forces to let Chuyen go by turning him over to the MSS.

On the other hand, the loquacious Juan had handed the defense team new lines of inquiry by talking about Hanoi's intelligence relationship with Moscow, discussing assassinations as practiced by the Soviets and others, revealing operational methodology of agent handling and communications procedures, and mentioning operations into Cambodia and the Phoenix program.

All these points were put in a cable to Washington. The next day we were advised that John Greaney, a CIA staff officer serving in the general counsel's office, was on his way to Saigon to help the station prepare for the expected general court martial of the arrested Green Beret defendants. While not ungrateful for the assistance, I couldn't help feeling that it might profitably have been sent a little earlier. The legal cavalry was on its way, but we had already been scalped.

The media, meanwhile, were having a field day with the story, and we had to consider whether the CIA should be getting its version out into the public ear. My opinion, and that of the embassy Public Affairs Office, was that trying the case in the media would violate the Green Berets' right to a fair trial. This kept us from trying to put on an aggressive campaign of spin control and left the defense lawyers free to run roughshod over the fragile issue of truth if they chose to do so.

However, when asked pointblank by various journalists what the essence of this case was, I did not dodge the question. Wendell Merrick of *U.S. News & World Report,* Bob Shaplen of the *New Yorker,* Keyes Beech of the *Chicago Daily News,* George McArthur of *Associated Press,* and syndicated columnist Joe Kraft were all given the facts as I knew them. Generally, they were willing to accept the logic of the CIA–Special Forces dialog and to credit the Special Forces' ruthless treatment of Chuyen. Perplexing to them was Rheault's involvement in the case and Abrams's decision to launch an investigation. Was this Abrams's way of destroying Special Forces, they wondered. No logical explanation could deflect them from the suspicion that there was more to the MACV side of the tale than had been revealed thus far.

Surprisingly, South Vietnamese interest in the Chuyen case was muted. General Quang asked me at one of our routine meetings what the case was all about. He said General Cao Van Vien, ARVN chief of staff, was curious about the matter but did not want to raise it with Abrams for fear of embarrassing his American counterpart. More likely, I thought, Quang was making this probe on President Thieu's behalf. In any event, I gave him a factual rundown on the case as we understood it at the time. Quang listened attentively to my presentation and asked few follow-up questions.

Later, the head of CIO, Nguyen Khac Binh, and the chief of the special police, Nguyen Mau, asked about Chuyen. Each time we were questioned on this matter, we gave straightforward replies to our GVN liaison contacts. One had the distinct feeling our Vietnamese friends were bemused by the quandary the Americans had created for themselves as a result of their non-Indochinese manner of handling a "rather insignificant incident."

Tormented by the media, Washington clearly did not view the Chuyen case as insignificant. Deputy Director for Operations Tom Karamessines, acting on his own or perhaps prodded by Helms, decided to send someone to Saigon to check on this Chuyen caper from beginning to end. William ("Bill") Wells, the deputy division chief for Far East Asia, was selected for the task. When Wells arrived in Saigon, I asked him bluntly, "What specifically have you been instructed to do and by whom?"

"I'm to look at the entire Chuyen case to see what happened and where it's going," said Wells. He added, "Tom K. wants to be able to tell Congress and the White House that he had a second opinion on the matter from an experienced officer not involved with Vietnam."

"Politically that's a sensible thing to do," I replied. "However, if that's a nice way of saying you're checking to see whether we've reported accurately on the murder, that's another matter. In that case, you can tell Tom K. when you return that I do not want to stay at any post where headquarters thinks it has to question the integrity of my reporting."

Bill assured me he was not being diplomatic. Tom K. simply wanted a second opinion. We arranged for Bill to visit Nha Trang for talks with Juan and Almy. I briefed him on how the case had unfolded from my perspective, and he talked to Vince Lockhart, Joe Lazarsky, and Dana Meigs.

In his spare time, Wells talked to station personnel about collection priorities, openly criticizing the massive commitment of the CIA's human and financial resources to the Vietnam War. He made no secret of his belief that Vietnam was an aberration that was distracting us from the strategic-intelligence challenge of China and the Soviet Union. There was something to be said for his point of view, but it did not go down well with everybody. Those of my staff who were serving voluntarily and at some personal sacrifice in a war zone resented suggestions that their efforts were not necessarily contributing much to the nation's highest interests. When reports of discontent with Bill's comments on national collection priorities reached me, I asked him to avoid this topic in his chats with station personnel. Bill quickly agreed.

Now, Greaney made an interesting discovery in the station files maintained by Scrymgeour and Enking. An operational plan for Cambodia called Project Blackbeard, originating with Special Forces and drafted by them, was laced with the words "terminate with extreme prejudice." Here was a classic case of life imitating art. The Green Berets had been reading too many spy novels and had adopted their terminology. It was also obvious now that elimination of a troublesome agent was not a course of action that had belatedly occurred to them in June 1969 but one that had been part of their contingency planning all along.

We now knew that Sergeant Smith had in fact been a CIA employee in 1957, had done a stint in Port Said, Egypt, under diplomatic cover, and had left the agency abruptly. Greaney expressed concern that conspiracy buffs would go into convulsions over this fact if it surfaced. For me, this was a low-ranking worry. What Smith did in 1957 had no relevance to his actions in 1969 as an Army sergeant.

When Wells finished his fact-finding, he sent a long wrap-up message to Washington incorporating our newly acquired knowledge about Project Blackbeard and Sergeant Smith, then returned to Washington. According to what he told me, he had found no inconsistencies with what the station had reported previously. That was that. I never heard anything more on this matter from Wells, Karamessines, or anyone else.

There was actually nothing more to be said because on September 29 the Army decided to drop the case. As the CIA, it said in its public announcement, was not directly involved in the incident, the Army had determined that in the interest of national security, it would not make available any of its personnel as witnesses in connection with the pending trial in Vietnam of Army personnel assigned to the Fifth Special Forces Group.

It was over. Why had it ended the way it did? Frankly, I don't know. I was not a party to the decision making on this point. In fact,

I first heard about the decision from George Neuman, the embassy public affairs officer, when he came to my office and told me and Lazarsky that the story was on the wire services. In the days that followed, I heard from Bunker and Abrams that the decision had been a political one made by the only person who could make it—President Nixon.

23

POLITICAL ACTION IN SANTIAGO

IT was probably inevitable that having tried and failed to overthrow the government of Cuba, I should now be suspected of having contrived the murder of the Chilean president.

In May 1972, as I entered on my new duties as chief of the Western Hemisphere (WH) Division, my "welcome home" interviews with Tom Karamessines and Richard Helms provided me with glimpses of what lay ahead. Tom K. told me that the division was facing a real challenge over Chile, had zero Soviet operations, and had been slow in seeing the need to combat the narcotics traffic. Dick said he wanted no surprises in the Western Hemisphere, particularly in Chile. Although nothing specific was said, it was clear that Chile was much on the minds of both the DDO and the DCI.

When not otherwise occupied, I spent time networking with my counterparts in other government agencies, particularly State and Defense, in an attempt to see whether we all had the same priorities in the hemisphere. This led to a free-flowing dialog with Charles Meyer, the assistant secretary of state for Latin America and a former senior executive in Sears Roebuck's Latin American operations. Meyer told me that I needed to understand that Salvador Allende's victory in the Chilean election of September 1970 was regarded by many in Washington as a major policy failure directly attributable to the CIA. Because of that, both the agency and its leadership were in bad odor at the White House. Meyer's advice to me, therefore, was to keep focused on Chile.

"If the military decides to take Allende out with a coup, don't let that be a surprise on the day it occurs," said Meyer. "Should

Allende consolidate power and start to turn Chile into a police state à la Cuba, Washington can't afford to be blind or deaf. We must have a continuous and timely flow of intelligence from Chile. Sorting out the options in Chile is vastly more important than chasing Soviets or finding out whether the Communist Party of Brazil is thinking about initiating a war of national liberation."

Meyer's candor was refreshing and surprising. This was the first hint I had heard that Allende's electoral victory was due to an intelligence failure. All my briefings and readings had led me to the conclusion that the election outcome was more attributable to the position advocated by Edward Korry, the American ambassador in Santiago. Korry had favored a negative anti-Allende campaign and refused to support Jorge Alessandri, the candidate preferred by the CIA station chief Henry Heckscher. Considering that Allende obtained 36.3 percent of the vote, Alessandri 34.9 percent, and the Christian Democratic standard bearer Radomiro Tomic 27.8 percent, my preliminary view had been that a combination of Korry's and Heckscher's strategies would have carried the day. I couldn't understand why Korry and Heckscher had been unable to meld their different approaches. Personalities, in my view, undoubtedly had something to do with it. I didn't know Korry, but he had a reputation among newspaper people and CIA staffers who knew him as an opinionated, eccentric, odd duck. Heckscher, in contrast, I knew very well indeed from the mid-1950s when we both served in Germany and later in the 1960s when we were both involved in Cuban operations. Heckscher had also been chief of station in Laos in 1958. By the time I arrived in Vientiane in 1966, old Asia hands were still speaking with awe of Heckscher's acrimonious battles with Ambassador Brown. Thus, I thought Allende's victory was another case of America having the wrong team on the playing field.

A day or two later, I went to see Tom K. and gingerly broached the subject of attitudes at the policy level about Allende's election. I was hearing around town, I said, that in some quarters one school of thought held that this had been an intelligence failure.

Tom K. picked his words carefully. "I've heard variations on that theme, and some of it is obviously directed at putting the monkey on my back. As time permits, review the entire record of the 1970 election, including Track II, for if we do get one or more postmortems, the division will obviously have to be our institutional memory."

Track II, I learned, had been the last in a series of failed attempts by the U.S. government to prevent Salvador Allende from taking power in Chile. On September 15, 1970, in the presence of National Security Adviser Henry Kissinger and Attorney General John Mitchell, President Nixon told Helms he should "leave no stone unturned" in an attempt to block Allende. Helms was later to tell a Senate Select Committee, "If I ever carried a marshal's baton in my knapsack out of the Oval Office, it was that day," a statement that may have taken liberties with the Napoleonic quotation, but certainly was an accurate depiction of the sweeping delegation of authority he had just been given.

The result was a highly compartmented operation conducted without the knowledge of the ambassador, the Department of State, or the Forty Committee. Track II combed the upper ranks of Chile's military forces in hopes of finding a band of plotters willing to seize power.[1]

A variant of Track II was a plan for the abduction of the commander of the Chilean armed forces, General René Schneider, an officer known to be opposed to the idea of the military interfering in the constitutional process. It was thought that his abduction would either provoke the military to take control or compel outgoing President Frei to assume emergency powers, put the military in charge, and then call for a new election, which he could win. The CIA accordingly opened channels to two groups of plotters headed by Generals Roberto Viaux and Camilo Valenzuela. Contacts were handled by officers traveling to Chile on false third-country passports and posing as businessmen. One of these officers, Tony Sforza, told me about this adventure in some detail in 1973.

The CIA sent two or three .45-caliber submachine guns to the Santiago Station by diplomatic pouch. Colonel Paul Wimert, the embassy defense attaché, delivered them to Valenzuela's associates early on the morning of October 22. At around 8:00 A.M. on the same day, an attempt was made to kidnap Schneider. Shots were fired, and the general subsequently died of his wounds. Contrary to expectations, there was no coup. Allende was sworn in on schedule.

Was Schneider killed with CIA weapons? My review of the case in 1972 convinced me that he was not. Forensic evidence introduced at the Chilean court martial indicated that Schneider had been killed with handguns. And the suspects convicted by the court were members of the Viaux group, not the Valenzuela group to whom the submachine guns had been delivered. Viaux himself got twenty years for being the intellectual author of Schneider's kidnapping.

The Church Committee also concluded that the CIA was not directly implicated in Schneider's death. As the word "directly" implies, there is not much comfort to be derived from this.

Against this backdrop, the covert-action requirements levied on WH Division in my time had become much more modest. My mission was to keep democratic forces alive in Chile and prevent the Marxist-oriented Allende from attaining dictatorial powers in order that he might be defeated at the next general election. I was also expected to be alert to any prospect that the military would act on its own to remove Allende from power.

The newspaper *El Mercurio* was one of the democratic forces most in need of sustaining because the Allende government was doing its best to close it down. The esteem in which the rest of Latin America's media held *El Mercurio* was shown by the Inter-American Press Association's (IAPA) decision to hold its October 1972 meeting in Santiago. The initiative for this came from influential journalists like Hal Hendrix and publishers outside of Chile, but once the idea was broached, *El Mercurio* and the rest of the free press in Chile heartily endorsed it. At the conclusion of its session, the IAPA declared that in Chile freedom of the press was threatened. This ringing challenge to Allende did not go unnoticed in the rest of the hemisphere.

El Mercurio's circulation of about three hundred thousand per day was important to our plans, and we were determined not to lose it through lack of trying. The Forty Committee had given us the necessary resources. Now I only had to see that we got our money's worth. To discuss plans and trends in the *El Mercurio* operation, I met two or three times in Washington with a Chilean attorney who was well grounded in Chilean business priorities and who was an astute political practitioner. He was no expert on newspaper publishing, but he had excellent connections with professionals whose cooperation he could count on. The net result was an effective propaganda operation. The man was clearly under a lot of pressure, a combination of the Allende government's attempts to put him out of business and his fiduciary responsibilities to the Edwards clan. From what I know of that period, he handled these multifaceted responsibilities in an exemplary way. He was a real hero in the anti-Allende struggle.

We subsidized radio stations supportive of the moderate, but conservative, National Party and the center-left Christian Democratic Party. We also made funds available to the parties so that they might increase their memberships, campaign in a 1972 by-election, and keep up their anti-Allende agitation.

In the March 1973 congressional election, the anti-Allende forces fell two votes short of the two-thirds majority in the Senate that would have permitted Allende's impeachment. Since the Chilean Supreme Court pointed out in May 1973 that Allende was violating the constitution, impeachment would have been assured. Instead, Allende was able to continue his attempts to manipulate bank credit, silence the opposition radio and press, and provoke strikes by the radical left. But opposition to him continued to grow. As reported in *El Mercurio* on August 23, 1973, the Chilean Chamber of Deputies passed a resolution by a vote of 81 to 47, saying, "It is a fact that the present government from the beginning has attempted to seize total power with the evident purpose of subjecting everyone to the most rigorous economic and political controls, and achieving by this means the installation of a totalitarian order absolutely opposed to the system of representative democracy that the constitution upholds."

Allende's desire to break up land holdings greater than eighty hectares and to nationalize all firms with a net worth greater than $500,000 was recognized by small businessmen as a deadly threat. For our part, we saw their mutual support groups, collectively called *sindicales,* as potential allies in facilitating voter registration, getting the vote out, and keeping up the tempo of the anti-Allende rhetoric. After getting the approval of the Forty Committee in October 1972, we began to work along these lines with the Confederation of Chilean Professionals, trade associations, and private economic think tanks such as the Institute of General Studies.

During the national truckers' strike of October 1972, the most strident of the right-wing Chilean paramilitary groups, *Patria y Libertad* (Fatherland and Liberty), helped bring Chile's trucking industry to a dead stop by putting five-pronged steel spikes on the highways. As this was a technique previously used by the CIA in Cuba in the 1960s, I foresaw the possibility that someone might conclude we were associated with these radicals, but fortunately we were never tarred with that brush.

As a matter of fact, before 1971 the CIA did arrange for funds to be channeled to *Patria y Libertad* through some third parties, and the question arose during my time with WH whether we should do it again. With the complete agreement of the Santiago Station and Ambassador Nathaniel Davis, it was agreed that this group was to be avoided like the plague.

The level of coordination implied by this episode was the rule rather than the exception during my watch. Gone was the compartmentation of Track II. Now all covert-action programs were fully discussed with the station, Ambassador Davis, the State Department, the Department of Defense, and the Forty Committee. In fact, I was once coordinated out of a trip that I had been looking forward to. Ambassador Davis, when told I was considering taking a first-hand look at the situation, told station chief Ray Warren that a visit by me would be unacceptable. His reasoning was that if Allende learned from the Cuban DGI that Shackley, a veteran of CIA activities in Cuba, Laos, and Vietnam, was visiting Chile, there could be unforeseen and unpleasant diplomatic fallout that would far exceed the benefit of any trip.

To keep Allende isolated, we began a hemispherewide propaganda campaign depicting the struggles of the democratic forces in Chile. We repeated constantly to this audience that Allende was a convinced Marxist, that he wanted to move Chile to Marxist socialism, and that the Soviet Union and Cuba were the models he was following in scrapping democracy.

This message would have been wasted on Chile's armed forces. With few exceptions, they were already totally opposed to communism and committed to the democratic process. Somewhere in this group, we were certain, were officers who, once convinced there was no democratic alternative, would take violent action to halt the communization of the country. I was determined to know who these officers were.

A program already under way to recruit classic collection agents in the Chilean military and the *Carabineros* (a kind of paramilitary police force) was intensified under my direction. Judging the tank and elite ground-force units as most likely to be involved in planning or implementing a coup, we contacted selected officers both inside Chile and while they were in training in the United States and Panama. Forces considered to be most likely to try to block a coup—the Air Force, the *Carabineros*, and the Navy—received the same attention.

As a result, our coverage of the Chilean military was significantly enhanced, and we knew who in the military was plotting. The coup that took place on September 11, 1973, came as no surprise. There is no better authority for that than the words of the Senate Select Committee: "It is clear the CIA received intelligence reports about the coup planning of the group which carried out the successful September 11 coup throughout the months of July, August, and September 1973."[2]

In addition, assistant secretary of state for Latin America J. B. Kubisch said on September 12, 1973, that Washington had received warning of a military coup beginning ten days before it unfolded. He also said the last coup alert came in on September 10 and was known at senior policy levels.

In retaliation for my year in Chilean operations, I have had to put up with suggestions that I was somehow involved in the assassination of Salvador Allende. There are three ways to refute such charges. One is to point out, as Dave Phillips (my successor as chief of WH Division) and others have done, that when Allende died I had already been out of WH Division for four months and that the life expectancy of the average Latin American coup plot is considerably shorter than that. A second way is to impugn the integrity of the source: Most of the slander on this topic seems to have been inspired by the Christic Institute, whose integrity has already been sufficiently impugned by the U.S. federal court system.

The third way, and the one I prefer, is to call my own witnesses. The first to come to the stand will be Fidel Castro. If anybody knows how Allende died, it ought to be Fidel. He had multiple sources reporting to him on this matter, including Allende's daughter Beatriz, who was married to an officer of the Cuban DGI. Castro's verdict, which he publicly unveiled on September 28, 1973, was that Allende died in battle.

Only one eyewitness to Allende's passing has come forward, his personal surgeon, Dr. Patricio Guijón Klein. Dr. Guijón has said he was in the presidential palace (*La Moneda*) at the time of the coup and saw Allende shoot himself. Three other witnesses have added credibility to the story:

- On the very day of the coup, September 11, 1973, France's François Mitterrand said he remembered a conversation held two years earlier in which Allende told him he would commit suicide if he were ousted in a coup.
- Four days after Mitterrand's statement, Allende's widow, Hortensia Bussi de Allende, said the same thing in a telephone interview with a Mexican TV station, conducted from the residence of the Mexican ambassador in Chile.
- In 1990 the Chilean magazine *Análisis,* which has left-wing views, said Allende committed suicide. This conclusion was based on an examination of Allende's remains after his body was exhumed. Evidently, a gunshot wound was where it should have been according to Dr. Guijón's statement.

Death in battle or suicide? The Havana version or the Santiago version? It will probably take historians years to sort this out. My own opinion is that suicide was not a sufficiently heroic end to satisfy the communist image makers and that Castro was merely putting out a little disinformation. One point on which both sides agree was expressed by Havana Radio in a broadcast on May 19, 1990: "Former Chilean President Salvador Allende [words indistinct] it cannot be said CIA's hand directly took his life."

24

A NEW STRUCTURE[1]

PUNCTUALLY at 7:00 A.M. on February 12, 1990, our corporate Gulfstream-3 cut through the clouds and started its final approach to Warsaw's Okecie Airport. Cleared for landing, we started down the runway, our eyes glued to the windows for a first glimpse of the country that was then setting the pace in Eastern Europe for a return to democracy.

As we rolled to a stop far from the terminal, I saw three jeep-like vehicles positioning themselves around us. Hard on the heels of this unpromising sight came a report from the flight engineer: "Stay where you are," the tower had radioed. Was this the warm welcome we had been led to expect?

Being the only Polish-speaker aboard, I lowered the aircraft stairs and descended to the ground where I found myself looking at a young officer wearing a captain's insignia and the uniform of what I recognized as the Border Guards. "Good morning," I said cheerily in Polish.

The captain responded with a salute. Then, I asked him bluntly whether there was a problem.

There was no problem, he assured me. His mission was merely to confirm that the aircraft that had just come in was the one that had been cleared for landing. Surprised by the primitive state of affairs that this implied, I asked, "What about your radar?" The radar, the captain said, was not working.

Could this situation, I asked myself, be typical of the air-defense system in the Warsaw Pact, a military grouping that we in NATO had been concerned about for decades? If so, a dramatic change had occurred, and our perception of the European power balance would have to change accordingly.

Easier said than done. Although, as philosophers tell us, there is nothing permanent except change, the thought that tomorrow's reality may be different from yesterday's makes us uneasy. We comfort ourselves by quoting *plus ça change, plus c'est la même chose* and close our eyes to the little shifts that go on about us all the time. When we finally open our eyes, the result is often shock. "Shocked" was the word that President Jimmy Carter used in 1979 to describe his reaction to the news that the Red Army had invaded Afghanistan. They had never done this before. What in the world would make them do it now?

Carter was not the only key decision maker to be caught unprepared by the Soviet invasion of Afghanistan, despite unambiguous indicators that such a thing might happen. Lacking then, and still lacking today, was the flexibility needed if intelligence collectors are to be able to shift their human and technical resources onto new targets as they develop.

Unfortunately, the intelligence community is generally only able to concentrate on the actual crisis of the day. This became quite apparent in 1979 when Senator Richard B. Stone of Florida revealed the presence of a Soviet brigade in Cuba and asked what, if anything, was known about the unit's military mission and the political significance of its deployment on the island. The answer, embarrassingly, was that nothing was known about these things. Although conditions in Cuba had obviously changed since 1962 when the Soviets withdrew their intermediate-range missiles, the change didn't yet amount to a crisis. So, not only did we have no answers to Senator Stone's questions, we had no agents in place on the island to task to provide the answers.

If policy makers could be surprised in 1979 by the volume of change that had taken place in the seventeen years since 1962, think how they must feel now. The pace of change is definitely accelerating, and we remain behind the power curve.

Fortunately, the imaginative use of intelligence can help policy makers catch up with change, particularly in the national security field, where "security" is defined in political, military, and economic terms. For example, in the defense sector, intelligence could facilitate the formulation of comparative assessments of the various world power centers that pose a threat to vital U.S. interests. This would help the Defense Department to develop realistic force structures and weapons systems, thereby saving taxpayers billions of dollars.

In the economic sector, it would be prudent to know what the Organization of Petroleum Exporting Countries (OPEC) plans to do about oil supply, not only in the next year but in the next decade. The departments of Energy, Commerce, and Treasury could benefit enormously from such information.

Early warning of the outbreak of hostilities would protect presidents from the kind of shock that President Carter experienced when the Red Army invaded Afghanistan. For intelligence agencies to be able to provide this service, as well as to point the finger at embryonic stress points, they must upgrade the skills of their risk analysts. Surveillance should not be limited to those few areas that the media seem to favor, whether they be the strategic nuclear capability of the Soviet Union or the germ-warfare potential of Iraq, but should include a multiplicity of other problems that endanger our future. Why not look at the fading wars of national liberation or drought and famine in Southern Africa and see events in Angola, Mozambique, Namibia, and South Africa in a regional perspective? The Department of State might well profit from a broader vision of such events, capable as they are of impacting simultaneously human dignity and freedom, American access to strategic minerals, and the safety of vital sea routes.

In my judgment, it is possible to identify the major elements of a missions-and-functions statement that is likely to remain valid for intelligence agencies over the next ten years, and I will set forth my ideas on this subject in the pages that follow. But of equal, perhaps greater, importance is the need to free the intelligence community from its present muscle-bound condition, enabling it to observe change in the very process of occurring so that it can respond more readily to changing requirements. My thoughts on how this may be done will form this book's final pages.

The first thing that we are entitled to expect of American intelligence agencies is that they contribute to the protection of the nation's military interests. This involves primarily the collection of intentions and capabilities intelligence about our perceived major adversaries and their ability to launch a surprise intercontinental attack. At the moment, there are only two such major adversaries—China and Russia.

It is too easy to say that the cold war is over, that Russia and the United States are now in the process of negotiating down their inventories of nuclear warheads, and that the nuclear clock has been set so comfortably far back that it would be a waste of resources to commit any American intelligence agencies to this mission (i.e., "protection of the nation's military interests . . ."). Maybe so. But even if the negotiators' most ambitious goal is realized, which is to say the reduction of the two sides' inventories to three thousand warheads each, it must be remembered that each of these warheads has ten times the destructive power of the weapon that devastated Hiroshima in 1945. No, Russia and China will remain capable of causing us major harm for at least the next decade, and two questions—How capable are they? and What do they intend to do with this capacity?—must continue to dominate our strategic thinking.

But not to the exclusion of attending to other countries that may reasonably be hoping to be able to cause us major harm. In this category the chief suspect is North Korea, which is known to have produced plutonium at its nuclear reactor and processing plant at Yongbyon, sixty miles north of Pyongyang. Despite reassurances to the contrary, authorities on nuclear proliferation believe that North Korea is secretly stockpiling nuclear fuel. CIA Director Robert Gates told Congress in May 1992 that North Korea is carrying out deception activities to throw International Atomic Energy Agency inspectors off the track and that it might be able to build a nuclear weapon within months.[2]

Here the CIA has obviously detected a power factor, one of vital importance to the United States, in the very act of changing. Let us hope that if the process of change is permitted to work itself out and North Korea obtains its nuclear weapon, the intelligence community will not be taken by surprise but will already have reallocated resources to provide for this new reality.

Certainly we should not allocate resources away from assets capable of covering this target, even though our interest in Russian strategic-missile forces is much diminished. Assets can be cut back but should not be phased out, for they can still alert us to the imminence of surprise ballistic-missile attacks from Russia or China, as well as keep us up-to-date on progress that North Korea may be making in this field.

We also need to be concerned about the proliferation of nuclear, chemical, or biological weapons in the hands of countries whose rivalries and antagonisms may appear to be purely regional. According to Gates, about twenty countries are building or already possess such weapons and the delivery systems for them.[3] They include Argentina, Brazil, India, Iran, Iraq, Israel, Pakistan, and South Africa. India, for instance, is believed by some analysts in Washington to be within a screwdriver's turn of arming itself with a nuclear weapon.

Our executive branch tries, with varying degrees of emphasis and relatively little success, to discourage and limit the spread of these weapons of mass destruction, which, according to Gates, may within ten years directly threaten U.S. territory.[4] An attempt in 1992 by the Russian space company Glavkosmos to sell India $250 million worth of cryogenic rocket engines and related technology was opposed by the U.S. government on the grounds that the sale would violate the Missile Technology Control Regime. India has said that it wants the equipment only so that it can launch its own weather and communications satellites, but since India has already exploded a nuclear device and developed a ballistic missile with a range of fifteen hundred miles, nobody really takes this disclaimer seriously. Even if we are looking here at a threat that could materialize only in ten years, as Gates has said, it is not too soon for a flexible intelligence agency to begin trying to anticipate India's next moves.

To move from the essential to the merely important, our intelligence agencies should also be given the mission of collecting data that will contribute to the survival of politically stable and representative governments in areas of vital concern to the United States. To be quite specific about what I mean, it would not be in our interest to see Germany dominate or destabilize what was Eastern Europe.

The potential for instability in this region was brought home to me in February 1990 when I was in Poland for talks about oil transactions. Pipelines, refineries, and gasoline stations were on the table. We asked about buying the land on which these installations would stand and were told instead, "We will give you a lease, a long-term lease." We asked again about buying the land, and again were fobbed off with talk about "leases in perpetuity." We pressed the point a third time, and finally our negotiating partner, a gentleman of ministerial rank, laid his cards on the table.

"Well," he said, "I guess we have to give you an explanation. We want to assure you of land usage, but we will not sell land to you or any other foreign group, and the reason for it is quite simple. If we sell land to anybody, then within a very short period of time the Germans will have bought all of our land, and we're not sure the Germans don't have aspirations for recouping Silesia."

It is all too easy for us to forget that two of the technical developments upon which our military preponderance rests, nuclear fission and rocketry, originated or were perfected in the laboratories of Central and Eastern Europe. With all due humility, we should keep in mind that other such world-shattering developments may be quietly germinating in little isolated pockets of research in what used to be the Eastern European satellite states. Now that the scientists in these countries are free once more to travel and communicate with one another, any one of their projects could suddenly achieve critical mass with unpredictable effects. This is not an area that we can afford to ignore. Not only our military security but our economic health may depend on developments in this area.

Military and economic matters are not as mutually exclusive as was implied by the young CIA officer who is supposed to have said to a newspaperman in 1992, "I am willing to die for my country, but not for Corporation X." Military security, which the young man seems to have approved of, and a prosperous economy, for which he seems to have shown contempt, are equally important elements of national security and, to a degree, mutually supportive. While concentrating on military and political matters, intelligence should not lose sight of the economic.

Probably no change in international relations since World War II has been more dramatic than that which has taken place in world trade and finance. It used to be said that when the United States sneezes, Latin America catches pneumonia. Now it might be said that sniffles anywhere in the world force the United States to reach for its handkerchief. To continue the analogy, what the United States requires is an economic Center for Disease Control to provide early warning of contagion and to help limit its spread. Intelligence must assume this role.

Proposals advanced and decisions reached at the supranational level on fiscal, monetary, and energy matters can impact heavily on our economy, sometimes only incidentally and sometimes quite deliberately. To cite only two examples, take the so-called Environmental Summit in Rio de Janeiro in June 1992 and OPEC's semiannual attempts to control the production and price of oil. Intelligence needs to be on top of these developments and to position itself to be able to provide our policy makers with accurate information on the plans, intentions, and capabilities of such forums.

Individual countries, not all of them our historical enemies, are waging what is in effect economic warfare against us by trying to steal our technology. The KGB, which once performed this service for the Soviet Union, is now doing it for Russia. India may try to do the same if it is frustrated in its attempt to buy missile technology from Russia. The large numbers of Indian nationals who have attended U.S. universities and taken advanced degrees in nuclear physics may present New Delhi with too great a temptation to resist. A forward-thinking intelligence service will remain alert to this possibility.

France is also playing in this arena, but with Gallic sophistication. A Washington-based financing company called the Carlyle Group has formed a joint venture with the French company Thomson CSF for the purpose of buying American companies. Having already bought the BDM Corporation and some others, in 1992 the joint venture bid on LTV, one of whose subsidiaries makes various kinds of missiles. Since the French government is part owner of Thomson CSF, one could postulate that it is trying in effect to tunnel into a repository of some of our more sensitive secrets.

Japan is known to be plundering U.S. technology by means both legal and illegal. In one case of illegal industrial espionage that has come to public notice, Hitachi and Mitsubishi recruited an IBM employee. The legal maneuvers were executed by the Japanese External Trade Organization (JETRO). Under the guidance of the Ministry of International Trade and Industry (MITI), JETRO seeks to improve Japanese industry's competitive position by analyzing American companies' proprietary data. Although not illegal, this practice certainly constitutes economic warfare, and it is damaging to our national interests.

The world being what it is and economic warfare being an undeniable fact of life, there is no reason the United States has to wage a purely defensive struggle. Policy makers must take a more active role in this sphere than they have in the past, defining which items of economic intelligence are of vital interest to the nation so that collectors can go out and look for them in a cost-effective manner. From public statements made by Director Gates throughout 1992, I feel confident that he agrees with this point of view, but I have yet to hear an answer to the question of what one does with economic intelligence once it has been obtained. This needs to be considered in advance, long and hard, and once again a solution to this thorny problem can be found only at the policy-making level.

For much of the economic intelligence that will be sought and acquired—information on bilateral trade negotiations, perhaps, or foreign currency exchange rates—the government itself will be the consumer, but some of the intelligence that will be obtained as a by-product of this effort will have commercial value, and herein lies the problem.

Suppose, for example, that country x has decided on a construction project of the scale of the Aswan Dam and has invited bids. Suppose only two U.S. companies are capable of handling a project of this size. This project, whatever it is, will cost a billion dollars, a sum that the government would like to see added to our gross national product. Suppose that our intelligence-collection efforts have revealed conditions that country x will want included in the contract but has not yet publicized. Some U.S. agency, Commerce perhaps, could call in the two companies simultaneously and make them both beneficiaries of this information in order that they may make more competitive bids. This solution does not appear to pose serious questions of propriety or legality.

The problem becomes more difficult, however, when economic intelligence has relevance to multiple companies, for instance, some new development in computer chip technology that in a number of years would wipe out Silicon Valley as we now know it. In solving such a problem, a formula would have to be found for disseminating this kind of information without at the same time risking a charge of favoritism. I don't know what the solution is, but I do hope that responsible government officials are now addressing the problem with greater urgency than they have in the past. This was an issue that was on the policy makers' plate when I retired in 1979. As no known solution has surfaced, I asked former Treasury Secretary Bill Simon, when I ran into him in October 1991 at a seminar in Washington's Embassy Row Hotel, if this problem could be resolved. His shorthand answer was yes.

Before leaving the subject of our intelligence agencies' missions and functions in the future, I don't want to overlook two other threats to our security, terrorism and narcotics trafficking, that were not even thought of back in 1947 when the concept of central intelligence was first written into law. There used to be one fundamental distinction between the two activities—that the terrorists' ends are political whereas the traffickers' ends are monetary—but this distinction eroded when Fidel Castro allowed Colombian drug cartels to use Cuban airspace and territorial sea because of the harm he knew they were inflicting on American society. Terrorism and drug trafficking are sometimes lumped together under the single heading of "narcoterrorism" for the simple reason that traffickers defend their business by whatever means they deem necessary, means that sometimes include terrorism, and that terrorists finance themselves by all available means, which sometimes include the cultivation and sale of poppy, coca, or hemp.

Nevertheless, clear thinking requires that the distinction between the two forms of activity be retained, for terrorism and drug trafficking attract two different sorts of people as recruits. While sociopaths can be found in both types of organization, religious or political zealots are found more often in the former, and would-be entrepreneurs in the latter. Penetration and neutralization of either kind of group calls for an understanding of the people involved.

Penetration of a terrorist cell or a drug cartel differs in one fundamental respect from penetration of any other kind of intelligence target and that is the great probability that the penetration agent will not be trusted by the malefactors until he has thoroughly compromised himself by committing a criminal act, which usually means killing somebody. Under the laws that govern U.S. intelligence, it is illegal for a case officer by word or deed, wink or nod, to sanction murder, and it is not likely that this will be changed, nor is it desirable that it should be.

So, as matters now stand, the only penetration agent we can realistically hope to get into a terrorist cell or a narcotics cartel is somebody who is already there, who has "made his bones" but now wants to earn his way back into society. In all honesty, that hope is not very realistic. Much ingenuity is called for in devising new ways to attack these targets. It is possible that terrorism and narcotics trafficking will yield more readily to attack by signals intelligence or photographic intelligence than by the third member of the SIGINT–PHOTINT–HUMINT triad.

Otherwise, HUMINT is coming back into its own after a long period of neglect that began under the directorship of Admiral Stansfield Turner, who seemed to understand systems better than he understood people. Recognition is now growing that technical collection systems are not necessarily infallible when it comes to detecting a foreign power's capabilities (recall, for example, Iraq's underground weapons plants that totally escaped observation by satellite photography) and are quite inadequate sources of information on a foreign power's intentions. Notice has also been taken of the fact that intelligence collected by the old-fashioned human agent costs far less than the product delivered by electronics.

Yes, we are looking at another decade of the human collector, but in no way does that mean that all the collectors will be covert operators. This fact was brought home to me in June 1991 while I was visiting Albania as a member of a four-man oil-company delegation. Here we were in a country that for forty-five years had been sealed off from the rest of the world. During that time, anything that the West might have wanted to know about Albania's petroleum resources had to be obtained, if at all, by aerial photography supplemented by the most painstaking clandestine activity. By contrast, in the week that our team spent in Albania, we were able to go everywhere we wanted to go and see everything we wanted to see, coming away with an appreciation and evaluation of the Albanian oil industry that I can guarantee existed nowhere in Washington's files. This again underscores the reality of change.

In short, the collapse of the communist system in Central Europe has created a new situation for intelligence collectors. I estimate, based in part on my commercial discussions since 1990 in East Germany, Poland, Albania, Czechoslovakia, and Hungary, that 80 percent of what is on any intelligence agency's wish list for this area as of 1991 is now available overtly. This means that now and in the future, the prime sources for much of our informational needs will be newspapers and magazines; scientific, academic, and trade journals; radio and television; international agencies such as the International Monetary Fund and the World Bank; international private bankers, businessmen, and academics; Central European trade delegations traveling to the United States, Germany, England, and Austria; and commercially available electronic databases. The collectors of this material will resemble college professors more than they will covert operators.

Unique and novel opportunities await these people. For instance, elite centers of knowledge exist at this time in Central Europe and the Commonwealth of Independent States (CIS), or whatever is left of the former Soviet Union, and I hope thought is being given to how to harness them. The subsidy to the Soviet nuclear scientists, which was put forth in 1992, was certainly a good first step, if a belated one. Using this as a precedent, one might think of the people Germany has acquired from its former neighbor and rival, the German Democratic Republic, who are trained experts on the CIS economy. They are Russian speakers educated in the former Soviet Union; many of them went to higher schools of learning in Moscow and went on to administer a command economy in which the prime customer was the Soviet Union. For a window onto the economies of Russia, Belarus, Ukraine, and the rest, one could do worse than turn to these people.

After crossing off the 80 percent of the wish list that can be satisfied by such means, the remainder becomes the province of the undercover intelligence officer, and in digging the intelligence out, he or she will employ all the tools of the clandestine trade. But it is important to stress that the work of covert collectors is made easier in at least two ways by their colleagues in the overt side of the house. Overt collection identifies those items that can only be collected covertly and thus tells the covert operator what to look for. And, with an accumulation of openly available material to work with, the covert operator can make a more informed guess about where to look for it.

The establishment of collection requirements and priorities will require greater precision and greater authority than in the past. Therefore, I would move this function straight to the White House, investing it in a Cabinet-level director of national intelligence (DNI) who would be a coequal of the national security advisor. This individual would also be tasked with the drafting of the intelligence-community budget, defending it before the Office of Management and Budget, selling it to the president, coordinating its movement through Congress, and managing the intelligence-community staff that would coordinate the entire American intelligence effort.

These are the political or quasi-political functions that directors of central intelligence have been expected to carry out but have rarely been able to manage well from their base in suburban Virginia. The purely professional functions of command and control over CIA operations and the writing of national intelligence estimates would remain with the professionals in my vision of a reorganized intelligence community. The DNI would have no part in them.

While these changes are in progress, it would be a good time to get rid of a set of initials that are carrying a heavy load of opprobrium and suspicion, however unjustified, and invent a new set. The CIA would in effect disappear and be replaced by a new agency, the Foreign Intelligence Service (FIS), that would inherit all of the CIA's functions that did not go to the DNI. The FIS would prepare coordinated national estimates and be the nation's primary center for analysis; it would provide policy makers with covert-action support; it would debrief, resettle, and protect defectors; and it would act abroad to conduct clandestine counterintelligence operations and collect intelligence.

Although this may sound like business as usual, it is not, for the changes that have taken place in Western and Central Europe, as well as in Asia, will result in at least two major changes in the way the clandestine service does its work.

The first of these changes is in the realm of cover. When the CIA first began sending intelligence officers abroad in the late 1940s, the vast majority of Americans who were then already living abroad were working for the government in one capacity or another, usually either diplomatic or military. If agency personnel were to blend naturally into this environment, they had to have either diplomatic or military cover.

With the reduction of our overseas military forces and the growth of our commercial representations abroad, this is no longer true, but the CIA has been slow to adapt to changed circumstances.

The majority of our personnel stationed abroad still use diplomatic or military cover. Perhaps we should remember and apply President Coolidge's dictum that "the business of America is business."

In the city of Düsseldorf, Germany, alone there are around forty thousand Japanese. Does anyone think that none of these worthy merchants are spies? I don't. I think we also need to do a lot more with commercial cover.

One benefit that would accrue immediately from an increased use of commercial cover is that our officers would no longer need to be domiciled in just those cities where there are embassies, consulates, or military bases. Living in commercial centers as they would, they would enjoy improved access to economic targets, and by being dispersed more widely, they would make host countries' counterintelligence jobs more difficult.

The clandestine service's operating environment has also changed, at least in Europe, in that travel has become simplified. A legal resident of any of the member countries of the European Community will be able to enter another without restriction, and movement between cities like Berlin and Warsaw is now no more difficult than flying from Washington to Miami. This will give the FIS much more flexibility than the CIA enjoyed in assigning agent-handling responsibilities, and this in turn is likely to minimize overstaffing and reduce costs.

One more change still needs to be made if the FIS is to function efficiently and that is in its relation with Congress. That Congress has the power of the purse is beyond dispute, and that it must be free to criticize performance and check abuse is also axiomatic. Problems have arisen, however, in the way that these powers and responsibilities have been divided between the two houses, there being no fewer than eight committees and subcommittees with a finger in the pie. It is this fact, in my opinion, that has led to the regrettable leaks of highly classified information, which have in turn caused some intelligence sources to dry up.

In *The Third Option* (1981), I advocated that congressional oversight be carried out by a single joint committee of the two houses and that a cabinet-level post of DNI be created. I am greatly encouraged by the fact that in February 1992 the chairmen of both the Senate and House intelligence committees introduced bills that would achieve the second of these two objectives. Once this battle is fought and won, will it be too much to hope that bills setting up a single joint oversight committee be dropped into the hopper? Even though passage would have the effect of eliminating one of the two committees, and hence the position and perquisites of one of the two chairmen, I remain optimistic that a spirit of statesmanship will prevail.

Abbreviations and Acronyms

ADC	*auto-defense de choc* (Laotian village-defense groups)
ADDO	associate deputy director for operations
ARVN	Army of Republic of [South] Vietnam
AWOL	absent without leave
B-22	CNC Strategic Intelligence Office
BfV	*Bundesamt für Verfassungsschutz;* West German internal security organization
BND	*Bundesnachrichtendienst;* West German intelligence service
BNDD	Bureau of Narcotics and Dangerous Drugs
BV	volunteer battalion
C/TFW	chief, Task Force W
CASI	Continental Air Services
CAT	Civil Air Transport
CI	counterintelligence
CIA	Central Intelligence Agency
CIC	Counterintelligence Corps
CID	Criminal Investigation Division
CINCPAC	commander in chief, Pacific
CIO	Central Intelligence Organization [of South Vietnam]
CIS	Commonwealth of Independent States
CNC	*Cuc Nghien Cuu;* North Vietnamese Strategic Intelligence Service
COMOR	Committee on Overhead Reconnaissance
COPS	chief of operations
COSVN	Central Office of South Vietnam [in North Vietnam]
CP	command post
CPSU	Communist Party of the Soviet Union

DCI	director of central intelligence
DCID	director of Central Intelligence Directive
DDCI	deputy director of the CIA
DDI	deputy director, intelligence
DDO	deputy director, operations
DDP	deputy director, plans
DDR	German Democratic Republic (communist East Germany)
DEPCORDS	deputy for civic operations and revolutionary development support
DGI	Cuban intelligence service
DIA	Defense Intelligence Agency
DIOCC	district intelligence and operations coordination center
DNI	director of national intelligence
FAC	forward air controller
FAG	forward air guide
FAN	neutralist armed forces cooperating with FAR
FAR	*Force Armée Royale* (Laotian Army)
FI	foreign intelligence
FIS	Foreign Intelligence Service
GMs	*groupements mobil*
GSFG	Group of Soviet Forces Germany
GVN	government of Vietnam
IAPA	Inter-American Press Association
ICC	International Control Commission
ISR	Interagency Source Register
IUS	International Union of Students
JCS	Joint Chiefs of Staff
JETRO	Japanese External Trade Organization
KGB	*Komitet Gosudarstvenoi Bezopasnosti* (Soviet intelligence service)
KMT	*Kuomintang* (ruling party of noncommunist China)
LZ	landing zone
MACV	Military Advisor Command Vietnam
MACVSOG	Military Advisor Command Vietnam, Studies and Operations Group
MfS	*Ministerium für Staatssicherheit* (East German Security Ministry)
MI6	British secret intelligence service
MIA	missing in action
MITI	Ministry of International Trade and Industry
MP	military police

MR	military region
MRBM	medium-range ballistic missile
MRP	Revolutionary Movement of the People
MRR	Movement for Revolutionary Recovery
MSS	South Vietnamese Military Security Service
NATO	North Atlantic Treaty Organization
NCO	noncommissioned officer
NIC	National Interrogation Center
NLF	Hanoi's puppet National Liberation Front
NSA	National Security Agency
NSC	National Security Council
NVA	North Vietnamese Army
OB	order of battle
OO	Office of Operations
OP	observation post
OPC	Office of Policy Coordination
OPEC	Organization of Petroleum Exporting Countries
OPIC	Overseas Private Investment Corporation
OSO	Office of Special Operations
OSS	Office of Strategic Services
OWVL	one-way voice-link radio
PFIAB	President's Foreign Intelligence Advisory Board
PICs	provincial interrogation centers
PIOCC	province intelligence and operations coordination center
PL	Pathet Lao
PLA	People's Liberation Army
PM	paramilitary
POW	prisoner of war
PRU	provincial reconnaissance unit
RFE	Radio Free Europe
RLAF	Royal Laotian Air Force
RLG	Royal Lao government
ROIC	regional officer in charge
SAM	surface-to-air missile
SAR	search and rescue
SAS	special affairs staff
SDECE	*Service de la Documentation Extérieure et du Contre-Espionnage* (the French intelligence service)
SEACORD	Southeast Asia Coordination
SGU	special guerrilla unit
SIGINT	signals intelligence

SOG	Studies and Operations Group
SOT	special operation team
SPD	Socialist Party of Germany
SSB	Single Sideband radio
StB	*Statni Bezpecnost* (Czechoslovak intelligence and security service)
STOL	short takeoff and landing
SW	secret writing
TACAN	Tactical Air Navigation system
TFW	Task Force W
TSD	Technical Services Division
U-2	high-altitude photoreconnaissance aircraft
UB	*Urzad Bezpieczenstwa* (Polish intelligence service)
UCMJ	Uniform Code of Military Justice
UDT	underwater demolitions
ULR	Union of Lao Races
UR	revolutionary unity
USAID	U.S. Agency for International Development
VC	Vietcong
VCI	Vietcong infrastructure
VoPo	East German *Volkspolizei* (People's Police)
WH	Western Hemisphere
WT	wireless telegraph

Notes

Preface

1. F— it, I've got my orders.

Chapter 2

1. Ladislav Bittman, *The Deception Game* (Syracuse, N.Y.: Syracuse University Research Corporation, 1972), pp. 11–12.

Chapter 3

1. Whittaker Chambers, *Witness* (New York: Random House, 1952), p. 475.
2. Eugene H. Methvin, *The Riot Makers* (New Rochelle, N.Y.: Arlington House, 1970), p. 27.

Chapter 4

1. Major General Edward G. Lansdale reached the high point of his career in 1950 as adviser to the Philippine intelligence services and liaison officer to Secretary of National Defense Ramón Magsaysay.
2. Richard Helms with William Hood, *A Look over My Shoulder* (New York: Random House, 2003), pp. 201–2.

Chapter 7

1. Years later a copy of Zbigniew Blazynski's *Mowi Jozef Swiatlo* published by the Polish Cultural Foundation in London in 1985 came into my possession. It was written in Polish and dealt with Swiatlo's revelations,

most of which RFE had already broadcast in Polish to Poland. I was pleased to see that the book covered all of the information I had developed in my initial debriefing of Swiatlo and nothing else. Evidently, the intervening years had produced no surprises.

2. This was the dismissal, by Turner, director of central intelligence under President Jimmy Carter, of about 800 experienced case officers from the agency's directorate of operations.

Chapter 8

1. In KGB parlance, an illegal was a case officer living in a target country under false identity and with no apparent connection to the USSR.

Chapter 11

1. A CIA intelligence memorandum titled "Buildup of Vietnamese Communist Forces Continues after Resumption of Air Attacks," dated February 21, 1966, with identifier SC No. 06810/66, available from the Lyndon Baines Johnson Library, says on page 14, "The actual amount of tonnage moving through the Laotian Panhandle since the latter part of December 1965 has probably averaged from 70 to 90 tons per day."

2. These 550-man battalions were the elite fighting units in the 40,000-man CIA-funded paramilitary force.

Chapter 12

1. Timothy N. Castle, *At War in the Shadow of Vietnam* (New York: Columbia University Press, 1993), p. 88.

Chapter 13

1. Different versions of what happened in 1966 at Nam Bac, based on secondary sources, can be found in Jane Hamilton-Merritt, *Tragic Mountains* (Bloomington: Indiana University Press, 1993), p. 147, and Kenneth Conboy with James Morrison, *Shadow War: The CIA's Secret War in Laos* (Boulder, Co.: Paladin Press, 1995), p. 157.

2. CIA intelligence information cable dated January 14, 1968, titled "Account of FAR Positions in the Nam Bac Area," obtained by means of Freedom of Information procedures. This report from the Vientiane Station made it clear that the tactical situation was deteriorating rapidly. A copy located in the Lyndon Baines Johnson Library bears the stamped imprint "Seen by Mr. [Walt] Rostow," head of President Johnson's National Security Council staff. Obviously, the Nam Bac operation was known to and followed closely by senior policy-level officials in Washington.

3. CIA intelligence information cable dated January 30, 1968, titled "Appraisal of the Lao Armed Forces' Defeat at Nam Bac and Repercussions from the Defeat as of 30 January 1968," obtained by means of Freedom of Information procedures.

Chapter 14

1. After retiring, I had a chance encounter with Burr ("Mr. Clean") Smith while the latter was doing some hang gliding in Northern Virginia. In that meeting Smith, who had served with me in Laos, said the ground fire that brought Ly Lu to an untimely end had come from a friendly Hmong who had decided to take a few random shots at anything that was flying in his area on that particular day. Smith said he saw the entire event as it unfolded, and it took him months to overcome his bitterness over this unjust turn of events.

2. CIA intelligence information cable dated January 13, 1968, titled "Aircraft Involved in the Attack on Phu Pha Ti (Site 85)," obtained by means of Freedom of Information procedures. This was an early report on events when it was thought Hanoi had used 250-pound bombs.

3. CIA intelligence information cable dated January 30, 1968, titled "Enemy Encirclement of Phu Pha Ti, Site 85, in Houa Phan Province and Indications That an Attack on Phu Pha Ti Is Imminent," obtained by means of Freedom of Information procedures. This report was typical of the alarm signals that CIA was sending to the policy makers indicating that Phu Pha Ti's days were numbered.

4. CIA intelligence information cable dated March 9, 1968, titled "Appraisal of the Security of the Guerrilla Base at Phu Pha Ti, Site 85, as of 9 March 1968," obtained through Freedom of Information procedures.

5. According to Kenneth Conboy with James Morrison, *Shadow War: The CIA's Secret War in Laos* (Boulder, Colorado: Paladin Press, 1995), p. 193, 20 North Vietnamese commandos, led by a Lieutenant Truong Moc, headed up the western face of the mountain and at 3:00 A.M. on March 11 arrived at the summit 100 meters northwest of the radar site. They then launched their attack.

6. See also James C. Linder, "The Fall of Lima Site 85," *Studies in Intelligence* 38, no. 5 (1995): p. 87. Linder says the "sappers" (i.e. commandos) scaled the northeast face of the mountain to launch the critical attack.

Chapter 15

1. Henry Kissinger, *Years of Upheaval* (Boston: Little, Brown, 1982), pp. 58–9.

Chapter 16

1. Quoted in U.S. Congress, Senate, Select Committee to Study Governmental Operations with Respect to Intelligence Activities, S. Rept No. 94-755, 94th Cong., 2nd sess., 1976, *Foreign and Military Intelligence,* Book 1, p. 228.

2. Quoted in S. Rept No. 94-755, 94th Cong., 2nd sess., Book 1, p. 230.

3. S. Rept No. 94-755, 94th Cong., 2nd sess., Book 1, p. 232.

4. S. Rept No. 94-755, 94th Cong., 2nd sess., Book 1, p. 227.

5. Veterans of the Nationalist Chinese (*Kuomintang*) military units that resettled in Burma in 1950 and engaged in the opium trade.

Chapter 17

1. On October 18, 1979, Roland A. Paul, a former counsel to the Senate Foreign Relations Subcommittee on Military Commitments, wrote to the *New York Times* to comment on a book review. The issue was the validity of John Le Carré's comments concerning Thomas Powers' work titled *The Man Who Kept the Secrets* (New York: Knopf, 1979). In this letter Paul said, "The CIA operation in Laos was brilliantly conducted and fostered significant American interests. It was done with a minimum of American involvement in terms of resources, personnel, and most important casualties."

2. See also Richard Helm's *A Look over My Shoulder* (New York: Random House, 2003) and James C. Olson's *Stuart Symington: A Life* (Columbia, Mo.: University of Missouri Press, 2003).

3. Other versions of this operation are in the public domain. One is by another first-hand participant whose perspective is different from mine. See Richard Secord with Jay Wurts, *Honored and Betrayed* (New York: John Wiley & Sons Inc., 1992), pp. 66–70. Another is based on a nonparticipant's research. See Kenneth Conboy with James Morrison, *Shadow War: The CIA's Secret War in Laos* (Boulder, Co.: Paladin Press, 1995), pp. 175–7. A complete account of this operation will be obtained only when the CIA releases its documents on this case and if Walter Floyd, Tom Fosmire, and Pat Landry write their memoirs or cooperate with a historian.

Chapter 18

1. The Hmong associated the CIA officers whom they knew personally with air-delivery systems. Everything these men handled seemed to come from the sky. Airplanes made rice and ammunition drops to remote mountain outposts. Two generations of Hmong children had never seen rice grown. These same machines evacuated the sick and wounded. Building materials were brought to Long Tieng by air. Thus, it didn't take

long for some Hmong to use the term *sky people* in their fractured English when discussing CIA contacts. In time this term became synonymous with CIA officers working in North Laos.

Chapter 22

1. Jeff Stein, *A Murder in Wartime: The Untold Spy Story that Changed the Course of the Vietnam War* (New York: St. Martin's Press, 1992), pp. 132–133.

2. The massacre of Vietnamese civilians at the village of My Lai was not yet widely known in the United States, but it was very much on the minds of the military in Vietnam.

3. Identified by David Corn in *Blond Ghost: Ted Shackley and the CIA's Crusades* (New York: Simon and Schuster, 1994) as Harold Chipman. See Corn's description of events on pp. 195–201.

Chapter 23

1. U.S. Congress, Senate, Select Committee to Study Governmental Operations with Respect to Intelligence Activities, *Alleged Assassination Plots Involving Foreign Leaders.* Committee Print, 94th Cong., 1st sess., 1975, pp. 227–8.

2. U.S. Congress, Senate, Committee to Study Governmental Operations with Respect to Intelligence Activities. *Covert Action in Chile 1963—1973.* Washington, D.C.: U.S. Government Printing Office, 1975.

Chapter 24

1. Editor's note: Although this chapter was written in 1992, much of the author's thinking is still timely.

2. Warren Strobel, "N. Korea Vows Access to Suspected Nuke Sites," *The Washington Times,* May 12, 1992, p. A7.

3. Bill Gertz, "CIA Says Rogues Get High-Tech via Third Nations," *The Washington Times,* May 9, 1992, p. A3.

4. Gertz, "CIA Says Rogues," p. A3.

INDEX

About the Authors

Theodore G. "Ted" Shackley was born in Springfield, Massachusetts, in 1927, grew up in West Palm Beach, Florida, and attended the University of Maryland. He served in Army counterintelligence during World War II and in postwar Germany. After joining the Central Intelligence Agency (CIA) in 1951, he held consequential posts in Berlin, Miami, Laos, Vietnam, and Washington, where he was intimately involved in some of the key intelligence operations of the cold war. Ted Shackley's final CIA position was associate deputy director for operations. He died in December 2002.

Richard A. Finney served for twenty-seven years in the Operations Directorate of the CIA, working as a case officer and a training officer. He was stationed in Austria, Germany, Miami, Mexico, Vietnam, and Spain, with temporary duty assignments in Argentina and Liberia. He died in July 2004.